Aggregate Supply and Demand Analysis

PAUL DAVIDSON University of Pennsylvania

and

EUGENE SMOLENSKY Haverford College

with a section on

Social Accounts: Theory and Measurement

by CHARLES L. LEVEN, University of Pittsburgh

HARPER & ROW, PUBLISHERS

New York, Evanston, and London

To SIDNEY WEINTRAUB, of course

56/-

AGGREGATE SUPPLY AND DEMAND

ANALYSIS

Contents

v

III. AN EQUILIBRIUM MODEL OF EMPLOYMENT, OUTPUT, AND PRICES

Preface

. . . the true law relating the aggregate demand and supply functions. . . is a vitally important chapter of economic theory . . . without which all discussions concerning the volume of aggregate employment are futile.

—J. M. KEYNES, *The General Theory of Employment, Interest, and Money*

What can be the justification for writing a text on macroeconomic theory when, by necessity, a large part of it must be given over to topics adequately covered in existing texts? What this book offers, which other texts do not, is a treatment of Keynesian theory into which price theory has been directly incorporated. We think it is now appropriate to place such an analytical treatment before the well-trained undergraduate and beginning graduate student.

The issues are by no means resolved, but policy makers throughout the free world are acting on the conviction that the price level is related to the money-wage rate. There is ample theoretical support for this belief. Keynes himself, the Cambridge economists close to Keynes, Hicks, and Weintraub, have erected the appropriate theoretical framework, albeit not in terms or places that make it readily comprehensible or available to the beginning student. Thus we have taken it as a fundamental task to promote an interest in and generate an understanding of this body of macroeconomic theory. All of Part III in this book is devoted to this task. The section will appear novel to some readers, since a portion of the analysis is just now appearing in the professional journals, while some ideas appear for the first time in this text.

In Part III, value and distribution theory is linked to Keynesian macroeconomics. Once a bridge between micro- and macroeconomics is established, it becomes possible to call upon all the theoretical concepts and generalizations of microtheory to increase our understanding of price level and employment phenomena. (After all, it is at the firm level that prices are determined and hiring decisions are made.) The ability to use the "homely but intelligible concepts" [1] of microeconomics in the analysis of macroeconomic phenomena represents an external economy in the development of macroeconomic analysis. The pedagogical advantage of a textbook which forces the student to use his microtheory in developing macroconcepts and solving macroproblems is obvious.

Of course, not everyone will agree with all the implications of this analysis. Our concept of a good textbook, however, is one that brings to the student the excitement of being at the frontier. We think a good text must challenge the student's critical acumen.

Much of this book (all of Part II) is devoted to a careful exposition of that orthodox body of post-Keynesian theory which is formulated in real terms and which normally ignores price level changes before full employment. From both a pedagogical and theoretical point of view, there is much to be gained by laying down the "real" Keynesian functions without the distraction of price level phenomena at the beginning. Even in this section some novel points are made; but, in general, it covers the familar ground treated in many macroeconomic texts. An instructor who has neither the time nor the inclination to get involved in price level problems may consider Parts I, II, and IV adequate for his purposes.

We have asked Charles L. Leven to write the chapter on social accounting in Part IV. Our feeling is that, too often, the discussion of

---

[1] In comparing neoclassical price theory with neoclassical macroeconomic theory, Keynes noted: "So long as economists are concerned with what is called the Theory of Value, they have been accustomed to teach that prices are governed by the conditions of supply and demand; and, in particular, changes in marginal cost and the elasticity of short-period supply have played a prominent part. But when they pass in volume II, or more often in a separate treatise, to the Theory of Money and Prices, we hear no more of these homely but intelligible concepts and move into a world where prices are governed by the quantity of money, by its income-velocity . . . and little or no attempt is made to relate these vaguer phrases to our former notions of the elasticities of supply and demand." From J. M. Keynes, *The General Theory of Employment, Interest, and Money*, Harcourt, Brace, 1936, p. 292.

the national accounts is presented as an expendable prologue by theorists who have little interest in the sophistry of sectoring and double-entry notation. Professor Leven, however, is an innovator in the theory and practice of social accounting and has a keen appreciation of the dependence of accounting practices on economic theory. We think his treatment of social accounting will be the most rewarding brief statement available to undergraduate or graduate students. Moreover, his rationale for presenting the accounting framework after the theory has been developed, and not before, should prove convincing to all teachers.

The last chapter contains a brief discussion of the empirical and econometric implications of Keynesian theory. The discussion is designed to give the student the flavor of an econometric investigation and raises the many problems which must be overcome in any attempt to test econometrically a macroeconomic model. The emphasis is on econometrics as an art rather than a science.

Since we believe that public policy is an integral part of economic analysis, policy discussions are found throughout the book. Normally they follow immediately after the development of the relevant analysis. The theoretical approach taken here permits a fruitful discussion of wage-, price-, and income-distribution policy, as well as monetary and fiscal policy. The relationships between the balance of payments, international wage and price behavior, and domestic full employment policy are also discussed after the appropriate theory has been developed.

In conclusion, we should like to acknowledge our indebtedness to a few of the many people who have helped us in this undertaking. Our interest in this area began when we were graduate students of Professor Sidney Weintraub. His always provocative and oftimes controversial approach was a continual challenge; and even when we disagreed with him, the result was to generate many ideas which appear in this volume.

Several economists read all or part of the manuscript at various stages and offered constructive suggestions. For their efforts we wish to thank F. Gerard Adams of the University of Pennsylvania, Barbara R. Berman of Brandeis, Kenneth K. Kurihara of Rutgers, and Sidney Weintraub of the University of Pennsylvania. Most especially we owe thanks for their extraordinary efforts to Miles Fleming of the University of Bristol and Thomas Mayer of the University of California.

No preface would be complete without indicating our families' contributions to this work. Our indebtedness due to the high marginal and average propensities to consume of our wives, Louise and Natalie, was an important motivator in this venture. The natural, rambunctious personalities of our children, Robert, Diane, and Greg Davidson, and Paul and Beth Smolensky drove us back to the peaceful solitude of the manuscript day after day. On the other hand, the ability of our wives and children to tolerate the ebbs and flows of our frustrations as the manuscript progressed was superhuman. Their contribution to this volume can go neither unacknowledged nor unpaid.

PAUL DAVIDSON
EUGENE SMOLENSKY

Philadelphia
June, 1963.

PART I

THE SYSTEM IN BRIEF

CHAPTER I

A simplified equilibrium model

Sometimes, market economies use every available resource to the fullest in a drive to get maximum output. More often, however, market economies use only a part of their available labor and other resources. There were periods in the 1930s, for example, when the United States employed less than 80 percent of the individuals able and willing to work. Why is it that at certain times market economies fail to employ all those who desperately want work, while at other times, grandmothers must be lured into the labor force to meet the demands of industry? It is this fundamental question which we seek to answer in this book.

The basic theory of that which determines the degree to which a market-oriented economy employs its available resources was laid down in 1936 by J. M. Keynes in *The General Theory of Employment, Interest and Money*. In the years since, that theory has been elaborated upon by many others and has become highly sophisticated. In this book only the bare Keynesian essentials, and just those additions which represent fundamental improvements in the model, will be presented in a unified, meaningful form.

THE MODEL

The entrepreneur plays the key causal role in the system. The formidable task facing the entrepreneur is to determine simultaneously what will be produced, the quantities he will produce, the techniques he will employ, and the input mix that will be least costly. These decisions must, in a market economy, be made in advance of actual

3

sales. Consequently, entrepreneurs must incur considerable costs in anticipation of future sales in making rational production decisions.

There will be some quantity of workers that each entrepreneur will seek to hire for each level of expected sales. In the aggregate, therefore, there will be a systematic relationship between the number of workers (N) that employers will want to hire and the total sales (Z) which entrepreneurs expect. This relationship is called the *aggregate supply function*, and is drawn as the Z-curve in Fig. 1.1. The exact

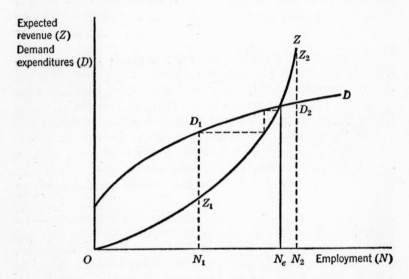

FIG. 1.1. Aggregate Supply and Aggregate Demand.

form of this function will depend upon a number of strategic variables (discussed in Chapter 9). In general, the more entrepreneurs expect to sell, the larger the number of workers entrepreneurs will want to hire, so that the aggregate supply function (in Fig. 1.1) is upward sloping.

Entrepreneurial expectations of sales revenue determine hiring decisions, which, in turn, give direction to the production of goods and services, and set off a flow of money payments to the owners of productive inputs. There will, for example, be a flow of money-wage payments to workers to compensate them for their efforts. Rentiers, who have previously contracted with business firms to receive a fixed sum of money will be paid, whatever the level of economic activity. Furthermore, managers of enterprises will distribute some of the profits of the firms to the owners. These money income flows to workers, rentiers, and profit recipients provide the funds with which consumers can purchase the goods and services that are produced by industry. Based on a variety of considerations (discussed in Chapters 3 and 10), the recipients of these money income flows will determine how much of their receipts they will spend on consumption goods. In general, the greater the level of employment, the greater the flow of money income payments, and therefore the greater the total spending on consumption goods by the community.

Consumers represent only one (although quantitatively the most important) class of buyers of the output of industry. Governments, foreigners, and businessmen themselves are also purchasers of the products of industry. The decisions as to how much will be spent by these buyers in any period will be based on factors that differ from group to group. Businessmen buy the products of industry mainly to obtain additional production facilities. Government spending is based on a host of considerations including the desire of the community for public services, threats of war, etc. Foreigners will buy domestically produced goods when they cannot purchase the same goods elsewhere at a lower delivered price. At any level of employment, the sum of expenditures by consumers, businessmen, governments, and foreigners *on domestically produced* goods is called aggregate demand. As employment varies, this sum of expenditures will vary. The relationship between the total sum of spending by the four groups and the level of employment is called the *aggregate demand function*. Since as employment increases, the money flow to consumers grows, we may assume that, in general, total spending increases as employment rises. Thus the aggregate demand function will slope upward as indicated by the *D*-curve in Fig. 1.1.

Given the aggregate supply function which shows how much entrepreneurs would expect to sell at any level of employment,[1] and the

[1] Some economists prefer to say that the aggregate supply function is the amount of actual receipts which would induce the hiring of every specified level of employment. Our formulation, however, is intended to emphasize the fact that, as a rule, hiring decisions precede sales and, therefore, it is the *expectations* of sales revenue which determines the level of employment.

aggregate demand function which indicates how much buyers would want to buy at any level of employment, it is now possible, with the help of Fig. 1.1, to explain what determines the level of employment and sales. For example, suppose entrepreneurs expected sales of Z_1 (in Fig. 1.1). They would hire N_1 workers. When N_1 workers were hired, however, the total sum that all buyers would want to spend would be D_1, which would exceed entrepreneurial expectations. If entrepreneurs hire N_1 workers, they will be pleasantly surprised to find that when they offer the output produced by N_1 workers on the market, demand will exceed supply at the going price. Thus, as Keynes noted,

> there will be an incentive to entrepreneurs to increase employment . . . and if necessary, to raise costs by competing with one another for the factors of production, up to the value of N for which Z has become equal to D. Thus the volume of employment is given by the point of intersection between the aggregate demand function and the aggregate supply function . . . . *this is the substance of the General Theory of Employment. . . .*[2]

If we started from a level of employment to the right of the intersection of the aggregate demand and supply functions (such as N_2 in Fig. 1.1), then, at that level of employment, entrepreneurs would be disappointed as they found that buyers wanted to spend only D_2 which is less than entrepreneurial sales expectations which are Z_2. This disappointment would induce entrepreneurs to reduce employment. As long as entrepreneurs hired more than N_e workers, however, buyers' spending would continue to be less than sales expectations. At the employment level N_e, desired purchases will just equal expected sales.

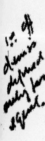

The value of total spending as given by the aggregate demand function where it is intersected by the aggregate supply function, will be called *effective demand*. It represents an equilibrium level of spending, where entrepreneurial expectations are just being realized, so that there is no inducement to change hiring policy. Obviously, the shape and position of the aggregate demand function and the aggregate supply function are essential to the determination of effective demand

[2] J. M. Keynes, *The General Theory of Employment, Interest and Money*, Harcourt, Brace, 1936, p. 25. Italics added.

and, therefore, employment. The various factors upon which these two functions depend are examined in detail in the remainder of this book.

ORGANIZATION OF THIS BOOK

This book is divided into four parts. Part I is devoted to a general statement of goals and procedures and to the development of the specialized vocabulary which is necessary for the precise exposition of the theory. Part II presents the orthodox body of Keynesian theory as it has been developed since 1936. In Part II only demand aspects of the system are emphasized in explaining variations in the total output of the economy. In Part III, on the other hand, aggregate supply and demand receive equal attention in explaining variations in employment and prices. In Part IV, empirical implementation of the theory is discussed. The social accounting framework is presented in such a way as to show how the theory has guided the formulation of generally used social accounting conventions. In the last chapter of the book, a discussion of some econometric applications, which provide a measure of the quantitative implications of the theory, is presented.

A DIGRESSION ON EXPECTATIONS IN A WORLD OF UNCERTAINTY

Economists often construct models that assume away uncertainty. These models are usually justified on the grounds that (1) they eliminate subjective factors, and (2) they ease the mathematical analysis and verbal exposition. Uncertainty, it is implied, merely "muddies the water" without changing the results.

In the real world, however, uncertainty is important and affects all economic activity. Many of the institutions of our modern economy would have no function in a world of certainty. There would be no need for stock market speculation, forward commodity and foreign exchange markets, or pecuniary contracts in a certain world; there would be less reason for holding money and there would be no profits.[3] These factors, however, play a vital role in the determination of employment only in a world—our world—where the future is uncertain.

The importance of uncertainty has been explicitly introduced into the expectational aspects of the aggregate supply function, as well as in many other relationships in the Keynesian system. Some investigators, however, in attempting to provide an objective, empirically testable formulation of the subjective Keynesian relationships, have given uncertainty elements little or no consideration. In fact, even in the following chapters, there is a tendency to slur the difference between the uncertainties of the real world and the surety of the economic model. We would not be playing fair with the student, however, if we failed to alert him to our own negligence and to the carelessness of others.

Since production decisions depend on future sales, the hiring of workers is clearly based on expectations. These anticipations have been categorized into short- and long-term expectations. Short-term expectations are concerned with the cost of output from existing facilities and anticipations as to the sales revenue obtainable from this output, while long-term expectations are concerned with what the entrepreneur can hope to earn in the future if he makes an addition to his capital equipment. /The aggregate supply function is usually thought to be based on short-term expectations, while the demand for investment goods is based on long-term expectations. /These two categories are not completely independent. (Entrepreneurs in the capital goods industries, for example, base their short-term expectations on their estimates of the long-term expectations of other entrepreneurs.) Both long- and short-term expectations are relevant for the hiring decision. Actual sales are irrelevant except to the extent that they modify present or future expectations. Similarly, past expectations which may have lead to the accumulation of the present stock of capital goods are not pertinent. Each decision that is made will take into account the present stock of capital, but will reflect current expectations of prospective costs and sales revenue and not prior expectations.

[3] See S. Weintraub, *An Approach to the Theory of Income Distribution*, Chilton, 1958, Chap. 10. See also J. F. Weston, "The Profit Concept and Theory: A Restatement," *Journal of Political Economy*, 62, 1954.

Any change in short-term expectations will alter the employment level desired by entrepreneurs. Time must elapse, however, before changes in hiring decisions can take effect and, therefore, the path of employment from, say, N_1 (in Fig. 1.1) to equilibrium is likely to be more complex than outlined above. Nevertheless, since there is a "large overlap between the . . . realised sale-proceeds of recent output and . . . the sale-proceeds expected from current input,"[4] normally it will be assumed that the economy takes a smooth, direct path to equilibrium.

CONCLUSION

At any point in time the level of effective demand may, or may not, be one which guarantees full employment or any of the other goals usually set for a market system. After just one more preliminary chapter we can turn to the determinants of the level of effective demand and start on the direct but long path towards an understanding of just why it is that the level of effective demand may not be the one which society would choose in the happiest of circumstances.

[4] J. M. Keynes, *op. cit.*, p. 51. Those readers who wish to explore possible subtleties involved in the adjustment path are referred to Keynes' classic treatment of expectations in *op. cit.*, pp. 47–51, 147–164.

CHAPTER 2

The rationale of a forecasting model

DISTINGUISHING BETWEEN FORECASTING AND EQUILIBRIUM MODELS

Those analytical systems which view the economy as being driven by two innately countervailing motives—maximization of profits by entrepreneurs and maximization of utility by consumers—and which examine the circumstances under which these motives result in a situation where neither entrepreneurs nor consumers act to change their economic environment, are termed *equilibrium models*. A model which fails to take into account one or the other of these driving forces will be called, for lack of a more appropriate name, a *forecasting model*, for it attempts to predict the actions of one group without analyzing the actions of the other group.

Typically, the conclusion that can be drawn from an equilibrium model is a statement about those effects which will follow from the eventual equilibrating of the profit maximizing and utility maximizing motives. The conclusion that market price equates supply and demand, for example, is the best known result of an equilibrium model. The components of this model are (1) a demand equation based on utility maximizing assumptions, (2) a supply equation based on profit maximizing suppositions, and (3) the equilibrium condition that the quantity supplied will eventually come to equal the quantity demanded. For example, if the demand and supply curves are linear, this model can be expressed algebraically as:

$$Q_d = a_1 - b_1 P \qquad (2.1)$$
$$Q_s = a_2 + b_2 P \qquad (2.2)$$
$$Q_d = Q_s, \qquad (2.3)$$

where Q_d is the quantity demanded of a commodity, say rum, P is the market price of rum, Q_s is the quantity of rum supplied, and the a's and b's are constants. Since the quantity of rum demanded depends upon the market price as shown by (2.1), while the quantity supplied depends upon the market price as shown in (2.2), the value of the market price which is obtained by simultaneously solving (2.1), (2.2), and (2.3) is

$$P = (a_1 - a_2)/(b_1 + b_2). \qquad (2.4)$$

This system can also be presented graphically, as in Fig. 2.1. The demand relationship (2.1) is drawn as the line D, while the supply relation (2.2) is the line S. The equilibrium price where the quantity

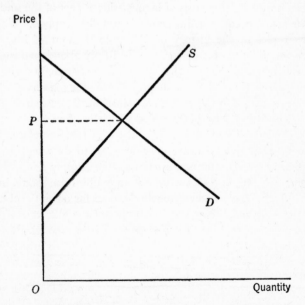

FIG. 2.1. Demand and Supply of Rum.

supplied equals the quantity demanded is given by the intersection of the two curves and is equivalent to (2.4). The price obtained in (2.4) would always be the price for rum if the demand and supply relations never changed, and if the rum market was one in which no transactions occurred until the price arrived at was such that the quantity demanded at that price equaled the quantity supplied at that price. Most markets, of course, are not such auction markets and therefore transactions occur at different prices through time, even when the underlying supply and demand determinants do not change. Consequently, not all prices observed in a market are expected to be equilibrium prices; rather, it is expected that the demand and supply equations represent basic determinants which are stable and which will persist long enough for the price of rum, as it fluctuates through time, to eventually approach the value $(a_1 - a_2)/(b_1 + b_2)$.

Not all economic models are equilibrium models. For some problems, either supply or demand relations may be assumed to have little direct relevance. When this is the case, analysis will be made easier by dropping the equilibrium framework. When the gains from such a simplification exceed the costs of laying aside a part of the underlying determinants, the equilibrium frame is usually dropped. There are many examples in the history of economic thought of instances in which the equilibrium framework was fruitfully abandoned for a forecasting approach. The Ricardian system, for example, in its treatment of the long-run growth problem, tended to skirt the question of demand and concentrated on supply phenomena instead. The Ricardian system was based on Say's Law of Markets, which is often paraphrased as "Supply creates its own demand." Ricardo felt, therefore, that he did not have to give separate consideration to demand conditions, and concentrated his attention solely upon the supply side.

Keynes, rejecting Say's Law, set out an equilibrium model in which both aggregate supply and aggregate demand for output and employment were analyzed.[1] Nevertheless, many of the followers of Keynes have treated his system as if it were a forecasting model. Two basic changes in Keynes' original model were required to effect the conversion. First, it was necessary to orient the analysis towards fluctuations in real income rather than fluctuations in employment. Second,

---

[1] J. M. Keynes, "The General Theory," S. E. Harris, ed., *The New Economics*, Dobson Ltd., 1949, pp. 190–193.

it was necessary to separate the wage rate from the price level. Once these two adjustments had been made, it became possible to invert Say's Law and to say that demand creates its own supply. Consequently, it was feasible to ignore the supply side.

The forecasting version of the Keynesian system assumes that prices are constant while employment varies directly with real income. This system is able to ignore supply phenomena by relying upon the concept of the *full-employment ceiling*. This concept allows economies to be categorized as either (1) underemployed economies in which changes in output and employment occur without any changes in prices or money wages, or (2) fully-employed economies in which prices and money wages change while output and employment remains fixed. Until the economy reaches some very high level of economic activity which is called full employment, the economy operates under the principles governing underemployed economies. At full employment, a ceiling on output is reached, so that any further increases in demand can affect wages and prices but can not influence employment or output. Making use of the concept of a full-employment ceiling is tantamount to assuming that until full employment is reached, aggregate supply merely accommodates changes in aggregate demand without any changes in prices, while, at the ceiling, output will not expand when demand increases. Thus, investigators believed that they could ignore supply phenomena and merely try to forecast demand in order to understand economies that were not at full employment. The weakness of this view will become apparent in Part III of this book; but in Part II, we shall hold to this simple view since it remains the dominant one among economists and because this model does have considerable value.

FUNCTIONS OF A FORECASTING MODEL

The Keynesian forecasting model concerns itself with the level and composition of aggregate demand in attempting to explain changes in real output. The real output (which is of the same magnitude as real income) of an economy consists of a bewildering array of goods and services which vary from nuclear reactors to tongue depressors. Some classification scheme must be imposed upon output, if the analysis is not to be swamped by a mass of detail. Many schemes are possible. Experience has shown that the classification scheme which views the economy in terms of the motives of those who choose to acquire the output produced by the economy is the most fruitful. This approach permits aggregate demand to be subdivided neatly into only four relatively homogeneous components: consumption, investment, government, and foreign purchases.

In what sense are these components homogeneous? They are homogeneous in that all buyers in any one of these categories are activated to acquire goods by a common set of motives, but motives vary drastically from category to category. Consumption goods are bought because the buyers want the goods for the utility they expect to obtain from using them. Investment goods, on the other hand, are purchased not because the buyers will derive direct satisfaction from them, but because the buyers want them to facilitate further production and sales. Thus, whether a good is classified as investment or consumption depends not on the physical attributes of the good, but on the motive of the purchaser. A can of peas, for example, that is bought by a grocer for his shelves is an investment good. A can of peas bought by the grocer's wife for her kitchen is a consumption good. The conceptual distinction is clear enough, though the national income accountant may often find measurement difficult.

Government and foreign purchases could each be decomposed, depending upon the motives of the buyer, into either consumption or investment. For many purposes it would be useful to do just that. For the purpose of understanding changes in the total level of economic activity, however, it is expedient to give government and foreign purchases special treatment. It is also consistent to treat these purchases as belonging to separate categories since the conditions which induce purchases in these cases differ greatly from those which dominate domestic consumption and investment spending. Government spending will depend on a number of considerations including the desire of the community for public services, threats of war, the ability of governments to tax or obtain credit, and the willingness of legislators to increase government activity. Foreigners, on the other hand, will purchase domestically-produced goods when they cannot purchase the same goods elsewhere at a lower delivered price.

In conclusion, a Keynesian forecasting model attempts to predict the magnitude of the four components of aggregate demand (consumption, investment, government and foreign purchases). The sum of these four components, in this model, is the level of real effective demand and national output.

EXOGENOUS AND ENDOGENOUS VARIABLES

All theoretical systems or models consist of sets of relationships among variables. These relationships or functions attempt to explain how one variable will change when another one varies. For example, the statement that, as price rises, the quantity demanded decreases, is a simple qualitative relationship between the variables, price and quantity demanded. As stated here, price is the *independent variable* while quantity demanded is the *dependent variable*. Quantity is the dependent variable since it changes only in response to changes in the independent variable, price.

If this single relationship constituted the complete model, then price would also be called an *exogenous variable* since the model would *not* explain why price changes. The model would explain why the quantity demanded changes, and, therefore, the quantity demanded would be the *endogenous variable*. Dependent variables are always endogenous. A variable which is independent in a single relationship may be a dependent variable in another function which is part of the same model. In that case, the variable would be an endogenous variable in the system. Exogenous variables are any variables in a model which are independent in every relationship in which they appear. For example, in most models of consumer behavior, consumer tastes are assumed to be exogenous, that is, no attempt is made to explain changes in consumer tastes.

An analytical model, therefore, consists of a set of endogenous variables expressed in terms of exogenous variables, and model building consists of making an increasingly larger number of relevant variables endogenous. That is how we will proceed in Part II. Real national output is taken as endogenous from the outset. We will always want to explain changes in this strategic variable. As Part II progresses, consumption, investment, and the rate of interest are added as endogenous variables, while government and foreign purchases, and the quantity of money are introduced as exogenous variables. The ultimate outcome is a set of simultaneous equations in which the number of endogenous variables is equal to the number of equations. Presumably, then, this system can be solved for the values of the endogenous variables, if the numerical values of the remaining exogenous variables and a set of statistically determined constants are known. The set of equations obtained in Part II form the basis of orthodox macroeconomic theory. More sophisticated macroanalytic models can and have been built, and these will be discussed in Parts III and IV.

A DIGRESSION: THE CONCEPT OF A SCHEDULE

All economic decisions involve making a choice among alternatives. Economic relationships typically are statements about alternative situations, and are usually expressed as functions. A function is a generalized expression in which all possible values of the dependent variable are related to all possible values of the independent variable. For example, the demand function, $Q = 10 - 2P$, is a simple statement about all possible alternative relationships between the price of a good, P, and the quantity demanded, Q. It is essential to realize that this function describes a schedule of alternative prices and demand quantities. If, for example, the price is \$1.00, then eight units will be demanded. Alternatively, if the price is \$4.00, then two units will be demanded. The number of possible alternative combinations of price and quantity is literally infinite. In the market, however, only one price and one quantity demanded can exist at a point of time, that is, only one alternative of all the possible combinations will occur under a given set of circumstances.

The ability of the reader to distinguish between a movement along the schedule and a change in the entire schedule is basic to an understanding of all economic models. If the price were to change from \$1.00 to \$4.00, then, according to our demand schedule we would expect the quantity demanded to change from eight units to two units. This change in the quantity demanded is induced by a change in the price. *It is not a change in demand.* A change in demand implies that the underlying determinants of the demand function have changed so that the whole schedule of alternatives has been altered, i.e., at any given price, the quantity demanded will be different than before. For example, a change in demand would imply that the demand function might now be $Q = 25 - 4P$.

Once the reader is able to distinguish between movements from one alternative situation to another on the schedule from a shift in the entire schedule, he will have made considerable progress toward understanding economics.

To distinguish movements along a schedule from shifts in a schedule, i.e., from changes in the entire schedule, phrases such as "at any given level of . . . ," "at each . . . ," or "in the schedule sense . . . ," will be used to indicate changes in the entire schedule. If, for example, there is an upward shift in the demand function for rum, we will state, "*at any given price*, the quantity of rum demanded increases"; or an increase in the aggregate supply function will be indicated by "*at any given level of employment*, entrepreneurial expectations of sales have risen."[2]

On the other hand, if we are discussing a movement from one equilibrium position on the demand schedule for rum to another (induced by an outward shift of the supply function for rum), we will say "as the price declined, the quantity demanded increased." Similarly, a movement along the aggregate supply function from one equilibrium position to another (due to an upward shift in the aggregate demand function) will be indicated by "as total spending increases, employment rises."

[2] The "Swedish School" of economists have distinguished between the concept of the entire schedule and the equilibrium point by using the term *ex ante* for the former and *ex post* for the latter. (See B. Ohlin, "Alternative Theories of the Rate of Interest," *Economic Journal*, 47, 1937, p. 423.) Unfortunately, this terminology has created further confusion. For this reason we prefer our longer but more precise phrases "at any level of . . . ," or "in the schedule sense . . . ," to fix in the readers mind the concept of a schedule change.

PART II

A FORECASTING MODEL OF REAL INCOME: SUPPRESSING THE SUPPLY SIDE

CHAPTER 3

Real consumption expenditures

During the second quarter of 1955, consumers in the United States were spending at the then record rate of $253.7 billion a year.[1] Just six months earlier, real consumption was a full $15 billion less, and six years before that, consumers spent 80 percent of what they were spending in that remarkable second quarter of 1955. Yet, as high as the level of real consumption expenditures was in 1955, by 1961 consumption expenditures were nearly $51 billion per year greater. It is obvious that real consumption expenditures vary considerably from year to year and, indeed, from quarter to quarter. It is the purpose of this chapter to seek out the causes and to elaborate upon some of the consequences of these variations in consumption expenditures.

CONSUMPTION AND OUTPUT

Explaining variations in consumer spending may seem a hopelessly difficult task. After all, consumption goods are characterized as those goods purchased for the satisfactions they will yield to the buyer, and the sources of an individual's satisfactions are rarely fully comprehended by others. Economists, however, have made considerable progress toward delineating those objective and subjective

---

[1] In 1954 dollars. *U. S. Income and Output*, Government Printing Office, 1958, pp. 118–119, and *Survey of Current Business*, July, 1962, are the sources for the data in these paragraphs.

factors which structure the consumption decision. Many of these factors will be discussed towards the end of this chapter. For now, it will suffice to point out that for individuals, families, households, and nations alike, there is one factor that stands as the key determinant of the volume of consumption spending. By and large, the greater the amount of income that families and nations have, the greater will be the amount spent on consumption goods.

That the level of real output is closely related to the level of real consumption for a nation can be seen by referring to Fig. 3.1. In that chart, the annual values of real consumption and real output in the United States are plotted for the years 1909–1957 (excluding the war

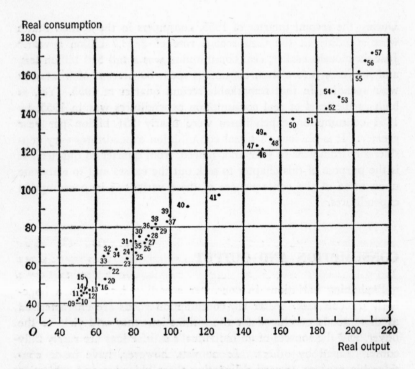

FIG. 3.1. Consumption and Output in the United States, 1909–1957 (Constant Prices). SOURCE: R. J. Ball and E. Smolensky, "The Structure of Multiplier-Accelerator Models of the United States Economy, 1909–1957," *International Economic Review*, 2 (*3*), September 1961, p. 325.

years). As the twentieth century progressed and output rose, so did consumption, so that the later years lie to the right and above the earlier years in the chart.

A SIMPLE FORECASTING MODEL

Algebraically, the relationship between consumption as the dependent variable and gross income as the independent variable is most generally expressed as:

$$C = f(Y), \tag{3.1}$$

where C is real aggregate consumption expenditures, Y is real gross income, and f is to be read as "a function of" or "depends upon." It is possible to say considerably more about the dependence of consumption upon income than simply that real consumption expenditures are some unspecified function of real output. It is possible also to make common sense judgments about the slope, shape, and intercept of the consumption function which can then be compared with the facts as suggested in Fig. 3.1.

The slope of the consumption function

It is self-evident that as output rises consumption increases. However, as income rises, does consumption spending rise as rapidly, more rapidly, or less rapidly than income? If both the consumption and income axes of Fig. 3.2 are calibrated in the same units, which of the functions in Fig. 3.2 makes the strongest appeal to common sense? Put still another way: Is the slope of the consumption function equal to, less than, or greater than one? There can be little doubt as to the answer: ultimately the slope will be less than one. As income rises, surely the urgency for current consumption must diminish, so that each family tends to spend something less than the increment in income. Furthermore, it would be physically impossible for a closed economy (i.e., an economy which does not engage in any foreign trade) to have continuous increases in its real consumption which exceed increments in its real income (or production). Finally, the data in Fig. 3.1 suggests that increments in consumption are less than in-

crements in income. Consequently, we may conclude that the slope
of the consumption function is less than one. The change in consumption that is associated with a change in income (i.e., the slope of
the consumption function) is an important concept. The change in
consumption associated with a change in income is called *the marginal
propensity to consume.*

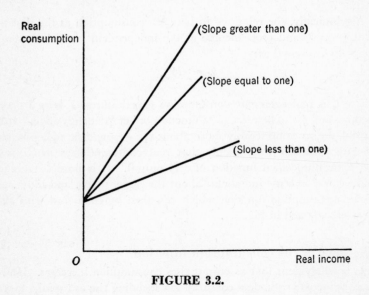

FIGURE 3.2.

Accepting that the marginal propensity to consume is less than one,
is it constant over every range of income, as Fig. 3.2 depicts, or does
it vary as in the two alternative pictures in Fig. 3.3 (C_a and C_b)?
Most investigators do not believe that as income rises, the marginal
propensity to consume also rises, as depicted by the curve C_a in
Fig. 3.3. There agreement ends. There is some empirical evidence
which supports those who argue that the marginal propensity to consume tends to be a constant. It is also possible to cite evidence which
supports the argument that the marginal propensity to consume falls
over the range of observed income changes. For example, a common
consumption relationship of the latter variety which is used in econometric studies posits a linear relationship between the logarithms of

the variables. This functional relationship implies that the percentage increase in consumption is always proportional to the percentage increase in income. Whether or not the magnitude of the marginal propensity to consume varies with income is an important question for econometric studies and for certain policy issues, but for most theoretical discussions of the simple forecasting model, it is a less

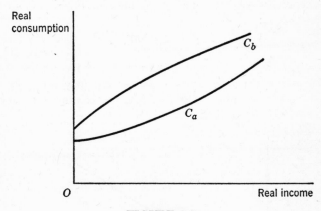

FIGURE 3.3.

significant matter. The important conclusion for this model is simply that the marginal propensity to consume should be less than unity. The simplest form of the consumption function, a linear one (i.e., a function with a constant marginal propensity to consume that is less than one) will be assumed here.

The intercept of the consumption function

Given that the consumption function is linear, what is its intercept? That is, what would consumption be if gross income were zero? This has provoked a controversy which cannot be resolved here,[2] but which is not terribly important in the theoretical development which fol-

---

[2] Although some economists claim that a positive intercept is merely a statistical artifact, a theoretical rationale for such an intercept will be presented in Chapter 10, when the effects of the distribution of income on *aggregate* consumption are fully discussed. At this point in the analysis, the question as to whether or not a positive intercept results merely from "curve-fitting" has no significance.

lows. Let us assume that at zero income, consumption will take a value, *a*, where *a* is equal to, or greater than zero. An *a* value greater than zero implies that households will draw upon prior savings and goods produced in prior years when gross income is zero. For a closed economy, *a* can be greater than zero only so long as consumable goods are carried over in inventory from prior production.

In a general way, the aggregate consumption function can now be fully specified as:

$$C = a + bY, \tag{3.2}$$

where *a* is the value of consumption when gross income is zero, and *b* is the marginal propensity to consume and may have any value between zero and unity. On Fig. 3.4, the consumption function, $C = 100 + .5Y$ is plotted.

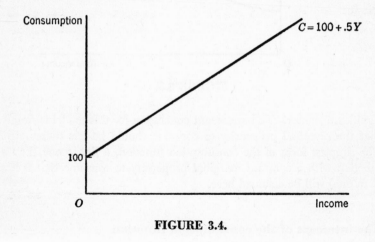

FIGURE 3.4.

THE SIMPLE MULTIPLIER

Our ultimate aim is to understand the causes of fluctuations in the level of real income and employment. One component of aggregate real income is aggregate real consumption. The burden of the argument in this chapter has been that the level of consumption expenditures depends to a large extent upon the level of aggregate income.

Aggregate income depends upon consumption, but consumption depends upon income. Are we caught in a circular trap? Not really; what is true is that the level of consumption and the level of income must be determined simultaneously. A little algebra will be instructive at this point. The analysis thus far can be restated algebraically:

$$Y \equiv C + I + G + X, \tag{3.4}$$

$$C = a + bY, \tag{3.5}$$

where I is the level of gross private real investment, G is real government expenditures, X is exports less imports,[3] and the triple identity sign ($\equiv$) signifies that (3.4) is true by definition. Substituting (3.5) into (3.4) yields

$$Y = a + bY + I + G + X. \tag{3.6}$$

This function which relates total real spending in the economy to the level of output is called the *aggregate demand function*.[4] Rearranging terms

$$Y - bY = a + I + G + X,$$

or

$$Y = \left(\frac{1}{1-b}\right)(a + I + G + X). \tag{3.7}$$

If the level of private domestic investment, government expenditures, exports minus imports, and the intercept and slope of the consumption function are given and assumed constant, then real income can be solved for via (3.7), and the real consumption level can be found via (3.5).

[3] Although it is true that gross output is equal to total sales to consumers, businessmen, governments, and foreigners, total purchases by any of these groups may exceed their purchases from domestic firms since, in an open economy, buyers may make purchases from foreign producers. If (3.4) is to be true, either C, I, G, and X must exclude purchases from abroad, or as is more usual, C, I, and G include foreign purchases, but X is defined to be sales to foreigners less purchases from foreigners.

[4] In the equilibrium model of Chapter 1 and Part III, the aggregate demand function relates the level of money spending by all buyers to the level of employment. In the forecasting model of this section, the analysis is oriented towards fluctuations in real output rather than in employment, so that the aggregate demand function defined here relates the real spending of all buyers to real output.

The right-hand member of (3.7) is composed of two terms: a constant, $\dfrac{1}{1-b}$, and a linear function in the variables, I, G, and X. At this stage of the analysis, I, G, and X are "exogenous" variables. An exogenous variable, as was noted in Chapter 2, is one which takes on numerical values which the theory does not aim to predict. Income, on the other hand, is endogenous; that is, it is to be explained by the model. The point to be noted here is that the endogenous variable, gross real income, would change if any exogenous variable, say government expenditures, was to change by some amount, but that changes in the exogenous and endogenous variables would not be of equal magnitude. This can be illustrated by considering a change in the exogenous variable, G. The new level of government spending can be expressed as $G + \Delta G$, while the new level of real income is $Y + \Delta Y$, where Δ is a shorthand symbol meaning "the change in." Thus, (3.7) may be rewritten as

$$Y + \Delta Y = \left(\frac{1}{1-b}\right)(a + I + G + \Delta G + X). \qquad (3.8)$$

Since we are interested in the change in income (ΔY), we subtract (3.7) from (3.8), which yields

$$\Delta Y = \left(\frac{1}{1-b}\right)\Delta G. \qquad (3.9)$$

Since b (the marginal propensity to consume) is less than unity, $\dfrac{1}{1-b}$ is a number greater than one. Accordingly, the change in income resulting from a change in government expenditures is larger than the exogenous change in government spending. This effect, which will be the same for a change in any of the exogenous variables, is obviously quite important in explaining much of the fluctuations in real income. The term $\dfrac{1}{1-b}$ is called the *simple multiplier*.

If, for example, the marginal propensity to consume is one-half, then an increase in government expenditures of \$1 billion would raise income by $2 billion. If the extra expenditure was made in 1963 and the multiplier effect worked itself out during the year, then income for that year would rise by $2 billion.

That the simple multiplier is greater than one can be readily explained. A rise in government purchases does, of course, initially create an equal increase in income for some members of the community. This increase in income then generates a smaller increase in consumption spending. The magnitude of the increase in spending depends on the marginal propensity to consume of the initial income recipients. An increase in their consumption implies an increase in income to others; this second increase in income leads to yet another increase in consumption, and so on. This income generation process continues *ad infinitum*. Since the marginal propensity to consume is less than one, each new increment in income is less than the one before, so that eventually the increments become small enough to be insignificant. This income generation process will take some time to work itself out and, given a large initial change in the exogenous variable, it may well be that effects of reasonable magnitudes may ripple into the next period.

It is important to realize that if income has risen because of an increase in an exogenous variable, then the higher level of that variable must be maintained if the new level of income is to be sustained. In the prior hypothetical example, an increase in government purchases of $1 billion increased income by $2 billion because the simple multiplier was two. If in the next period, government expenditures fell back to its original level, then income would fall by $2 billion. To raise income permanently by $2 billion, government expenditures must rise by $1 billion permanently (all other things remaining constant).

A GRAPHICAL RESTATEMENT

There is a graphical trick which has helped a generation of students to understand the two-way relationship between income and consumption. For simplicity, let us ignore the government and foreign sectors and assume that gross income consists only of consumption and investment expenditures, so that

$$Y \equiv C + I,$$

and

$$C = a + bY.$$

If I is assumed to be exogenous, we have an income model in which there are two equations and two unknowns (Y and C). Figure 3.5 is a graphical device for solving these two equations simultaneously.

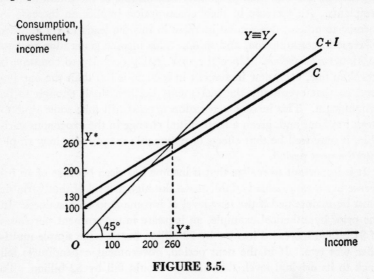

FIGURE 3.5.

Both axes are equally calibrated in units of constant purchasing power, and aggregate real income is measured along each. Since income is measured along each axis, a straight line which intersects the origin at an angle of 45 degrees has a unit slope and traces out the trivial identity $Y \equiv Y$. This 45-degree line has an important property: whatever the values of a, b, and I, the value of Y which satisfies the two simultaneous equations must lie on this 45-degree line. To find that value, it is necessary only to plot the consumption function and add I to it. The value of Y which solves these equations (Y^*) is found where the aggregate demand function, $a + bY + I$, crosses the $Y \equiv Y$ line.

In Fig. 3.5, for example, the functions $Y \equiv C + I$ and $C = 100 + .5Y$, (when $I = 30$) have been plotted. The level of income which satisfies these equations can be read off either axis as $Y^* = \$260$.

Figure 3.5 dramatically illustrates an extremely important fact about any economy: as an economy moves to higher and higher levels of real income, the gap between the consumption function and the $Y \equiv Y$ line grows. If real income is to rise over time, therefore, investment must increase to fill the gap. Since the population and the labor

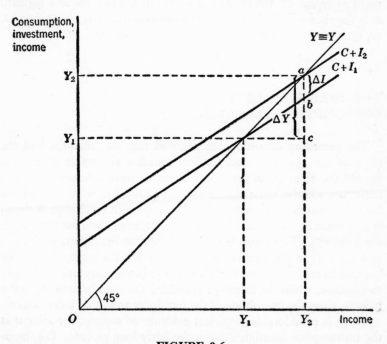

FIGURE 3.6.

force of a nation increases, real income must expand if unemployment is not to increase and if per capita income is not to fall. We shall see that there is nothing automatic about the growth of investment, and certainly there is no reason to believe that investment will grow at that rate just sufficient to absorb increases in the labor force. Consequently if per capita income is to increase and unemployment is to be avoided, it may be necessary for government to play an important role in determining the income and employment level.

Figure 3.6 is also an effective device for showing that the multiplier is greater than unity. Suppose, as before, that $C = 100 + .5Y$ and I is initially \$30. The resulting aggregate demand function is $C + I_1$ and the level of real income is Y_1. If investment were to increase by \$10 billion, then the new aggregate demand function would be $C + I_2$ and the new level of real income would be Y_2. The line segment ab represents the change in investment, while the line segment ac is the change in real income. It is obvious that ac is larger than ab, or, in other words, the multiplier is greater than one.

THE STABILITY OF THE CONSUMPTION FUNCTION

The preceding discussion has assumed that the intercept and the slope of the aggregate consumption function are stable over time. Should this assumption prove unwarranted, then, of course, the consequences will be quite significant. A parallel upward shift of the function (that is, an increase in the intercept with no change in slope) would result in an increase in real income greater than the increase in the intercept. This result is due to the simple multiplier, so that an upward shift in the consumption function has the same effect as an increase in any exogenous variable. A rise in the marginal propensity to consume, while the intercept remained the same, would also raise income, since the magnitude of the multiplier would be increased.

There is considerable empirical evidence to support the view that the consumption function is stable for fairly long periods. Consumption expenditures do, of course, vary greatly over time, but in a predictable way—largely in response to changes in real income. Sometimes, however, consumption departs from its expected (predicted) value. This occurs because while aggregate output is the major factor affecting the volume of consumption, many other factors also affect the level of consumption spending.

OTHER DETERMINANTS OF THE LEVEL OF CONSUMPTION

The level of consumer spending is not decided by consumers acting in concert, but is rather the outcome of deliberations by all the households in the economy, each of which makes its decisions more or less independently of the decisions being made, at the same time, by other families. In each household, the spending decision will be most influenced by total family income, but many other factors will also be affecting that decision, so that families with identical incomes may spend considerably different amounts. Among the many factors that lead different families with the same total income to spend different amounts, the eight that follow are probably the most important.

1. Tastes

Some individuals are frugal, while others have a strong preference for those good things in life that only money can buy. There can be no question that taste patterns vary from family to family, but tastes as between goods and savings are relatively constant over time for the nation as a whole, and are usually taken as exogenous and unchanging in economic analysis.

2. Socio-economic characteristics

The number of persons in the family unit, whether the family owns or rents its domicile, the age composition of its members, race, education, and occupation of the head of the household will also affect family spending decisions. As with tastes, these socio-economic characteristics do not change enough over short periods of time to affect the level of aggregate consumption in the short-run.

3. The rate of interest

A rise in the rate of interest will normally induce households to reduce their consumption out of each income level. If households refrain from consumption in the present and lend the funds so accumulated at the going rate of interest, they will be able to purchase a larger bundle of consumption goods in the future than they can at present. Moreover, if the rate of interest rises, then giving up the same amount of consumption goods in the present, will, if the consumer lends the funds not spent, enable the household to obtain even a larger quantity of goods in the future. That is to say, a rise in the rate of interest will reduce the cost of future goods relative to present goods. Since future goods have utility, it may be presumed that a rise in the rate of interest will encourage consumers to reduce consumption out of any given level of income.

There are, however, other motives which may lead households to increase their consumption out of each income level as the rate of interest rises. Suppose, for example, that a household is preparing for the day when the breadwinner retires. The belief that retirement living could be comfortable at some minimum income, coupled with the uncertainty as to whether or not one will live to enjoy the future goods, may encourage some households to desire a fixed money annuity on retirement. If the objective is some fixed future income, a rise in the rate of interest implies that the household may consume a larger amount of present income and still achieve their annuity objective.

Other motives which will affect the way in which a household will respond to a change in the rate of interest include: the desire to accumulate a contingency reserve; the desire for a sense of independence and power; the desire to bequeath a fortune; and pure miserliness. These and other motives for refraining from consumption, Keynes labelled "Precaution, Foresight, Calculation, Improvement, Independence, Enterprise, Pride and Avarice."[5] The effect of changes in the rate of interest upon the actual consumption out of each level of income for any household, will depend upon the relative importance of each of these motives to the household, since each of these motives implies a different relationship between consumption out of a given level of income and the rate of interest. A rise in the rate of interest will discourage present consumption for those who calculate the possible improvement in future consumption or for those who desire to bequeath a fortune; but it may encourage present consumption for those who desire a fixed annuity, or those who desire a specific sum for contingencies; while it may not affect the behavior of the miser at all.

Although normally it might be expected that on balance there is

[5] J. M. Keynes, *The General Theory of Employment, Interest and Money*, Harcourt, Brace, 1936, p. 108.

still a negative relationship between changes in consumption out of a given level of income and changes in the rate of interest, it is clear that, because of the variety of motives affecting consumption behavior, the usual range of short-run fluctuations in the rate of interest is not likely to have a *significant* effect on the consumption expenditures of individuals. As Keynes so cogently pointed out, "There are not many people who will alter their way of living because the rate of interest has fallen from 5 to 4 percent, if their aggregate income is the same as before."[6]

Changes in the rate of interest may affect the level of consumption indirectly through its effect on investment and income levels. This indirect mechanism, however, would suggest that a rise in the rate of interest will lead to a fall in consumption expenditures since the increase in the rate of interest is likely to reduce investment and income. These matters will be discussed in greater detail in the next chapter. For simplicity, however, we will assume that at each income level, aggregate consumption is unaffected by changes in the rate of interest.

4. Wealth

The assets that households have accumulated will also influence the spending decision. Normally, the more real wealth a family has accumulated, the greater their propensity to consume out of any level of real income. The real net worth of families will only occasionally change sufficiently to affect the community's propensity to consume. A rapid rise in commodity prices, for example, will reduce the real value of bonds and money holdings and may therefore adversely affect consumption. In the forecasting model, however, prices are assumed constant, and consequently this wealth effect on consumption is excluded by assumption. This wealth effect will be reconsidered in Chapter 11.

During a prolonged period of war, a nation's accumulated wealth may change sufficiently to affect the level of aggregate consumption. In the United States, for example, the rapid rise in incomes during

[6] J. M. Keynes, *op. cit.*, p. 94. See D. V. T. Bear, "The Relationship of Savings to the Rate of Interest, Real Income, and Expected Future Prices," *Review of Economics and Statistics*, XLIII, 1961. Bear has shown that a marginal propensity to consume of less than one must imply that, for households, there is a negative relationship between consumption out of any given level of income and the rate of interest.

the Second World War, together with the shortage of consumer goods, rationing, and governmental price-fixing led to a large and rapid accumulation of assets readily convertible to cash. After the war, a large portion of these assets were converted into cash in order to acquire consumption goods which were unavailable during the war. Conversely, high levels of taxation in the United Kingdom during the Second World War forced a reduction in the wealth of Britons which may have retarded consumption expenditures in the United Kingdom in the immediate post-war period.

Normally, however, the wealth position of families has little effect on short-run changes in consumption spending.

5. Consumer credit

The availability of consumer credit may affect the propensity to consume. It is undoubtedly true that the ease or difficulty with which consumers can obtain credit will affect the distribution of their expenditures between durables and nondurable goods. It also may be that a change in credit terms will affect the timing of consumption expenditures. The existence of consumer credit may lead consumers to spend a larger portion of their income in prosperous times while forcing them to restrain their consumption during recession, as they find themselves repaying the debts incurred during the previous prosperity.

Consequently, changes in credit terms will alter the composition of consumer purchases. The effect on the level of consumption expenditures, however, is not unambiguous. A sudden easing of consumer credit terms is likely to induce an expansion in consumption today, but this sudden expansion may only be borrowing demand from tomorrow. Except for temporary effects, therefore, consumption levels will not be significantly affected by changes in the availability consumer credit.

6. Taxes

Clearly, the consumption spending of households will be related to their disposable income, i.e., their personal incomes net of personal taxes, and not their gross income. As long as there is a predictable relationship between disposable and gross income, a consumption function can be derived in which consumption is related to gross income. If, however, there is a change in tax policy which alters the relationship between disposable and gross income, then the relationship between consumption and disposable will not change, but the relationship between consumption and gross income will be altered. Normally, a stable relationship between disposable and gross income will be assumed.

There are two important variables which influence consumption in the aggregate but which are not relevant at the household level. These are total population and the distribution of income.

7. Total population

Although average family size does not vary significantly over short periods of time, as the population of a country increases the number of families grows and the larger the number of family units the greater will be consumption out of any income level.[7] Analytical models which attempt to explain changes in the level of output in short periods of time can assume that the change in population during the period will be unimportant. Models which attempt to explain changes in consumption over long periods of time must deal explicitly with population changes.

8. Income distribution

With the same aggregate income, aggregate consumption will vary if income is distributed in different ways among the households. For example, taking income from small families and giving it to large ones will raise aggregate consumption. Other examples of changes in the distribution of income which will affect consumption are: transfers of income (a) from the rich to the poor, (b) from the old to the young, (c) from one race to another, (d) from workers to capitalists and (e) from individuals to corporations.[8] Speaking in terms of aggregates,

---

[7] Of course, changes in total population are usually accompanied by changes in socio-economic characteristics of the population. The impact of these socio-economic factors on the consumption function have been discussed above.

[8] Business firms also must make decisions on what to do with their income (profits). Should profits be paid out as dividends to the stockholders, or should they be retained by the firm? Motives affecting retention include (1) the desire to provide for contingencies, (2) the desire to be "financially prudent," i.e., to write off the costs of assets ahead of their actual wastage, and (3) the expected profitability of new investment (discussed in detail in Chapter 4). Since only dividends are directly available for consumption spending by households, changes in the distribution of the same aggregate income between households and corporations will alter consumer income and therefore aggregate consumption.

therefore, suggests that the distribution of income is an additional explanatory variable. The effects of changes in the distribution of income are a pivotal part of the analysis of Part III. In the forecasting model of Part II, it will be assumed that the income distribution does not change.

CONCLUSION ON THE EFFECTS OF FACTORS OTHER THAN INCOME ON CONSUMPTION

All of the factors that have been mentioned will affect household consumption expenditures and, therefore, aggregate consumption expenditures. Except for distributional effects (especially shifts from individuals to corporations) all these factors are relatively unchanging in the short run and therefore cannot explain short-run changes in total consumption. Income is the only variable which will change sufficiently in the short run to affect consumption, so that as a first approximation it may be assumed that consumption varies only with the level of income.

The analyst must bear in mind, however, that some factors do occasionally change and thereby affect the stability of the consumption function. From time to time consumers have increased their consumption spending at each income level, that is, the consumption function has shifted upwards. This shift may be due to the introduction of new consumer products and/or a change in tastes.[9] Sometimes, consumption departs sharply from its expected value for short periods because of a change in consumer expectations. Consumers may react to expected price increases by attempting to buy in advance of the increase, thereby pushing up prices and justifying their expectations. At other times, however, consumers may react to an expected price increase with a "buyers strike," precipitating a fall in the consumption function. Expectations of war and possible shortages (even if prices are controlled so that they cannot rise) may lead to temporary shifts in the consumption function.

[9] Consumers may change their preferences between present and future consumption. They may decide that they prefer to consume more today even if it means that they will have made less financial provision for their old age. For example, if many adopt the philosophy of "wine, women, and song, for tomorrow we die," we may expect the consumption function to shift upwards rather significantly.

Despite the many problems which face the analyst of consumption behavior, consumption has proved to be the most predictable component of gross output. Table 3.1 presents one example of the kind of results which have been achieved in the forecasting of consumption expenditures. To obtain the values in column (3) of Table 3.1, the

Table 3.1. Predicted and Actual Values of Aggregate Consumption

Year (1)	Actual Value (2)	Predicted Value (3)	Percentage Difference Between Predicted and Actual Values (4)
1952	141.4	145.8	3
1953	147.5	150.9	2
1954	150.3	150.4	0
1955	160.9	160.2	0
1956	166.3	163.7	−2
1957	170.4	167.1	−2

Estimating equation: Aggregate consumption = −30.30 + 0.569 output + 0.454 total population.
Source: R. J. Ball and E. Smolensky, "The Structure of Multiplier-Accelerator Models of the United States Economy, 1909–1951." *International Economic Review*, 2, 1961, p. 305.

historical relationship between real aggregate consumption spending on the one hand, and real national output and total population on the other, for the years 1929–1951, was statistically determined, and then this relationship was projected forward for the years 1952–1957. A comparison of the predicted values of consumption, as shown in column (3), with the actual values which occurred in those years, column (2), indicates that the predicted value never differed by more than 3 percent from the actual value, column (4).

Unfortunately, such good predictive results have not always been obtained in other studies,[10] since, in some years, variations in factors other than gross output and population have had a noticeable impact on aggregate consumption.

In short, while consumption is the most predictable element of the components of gross output, it is not as predictable as economists once believed. Its unpredictability has often raised some difficult problems

[10] R. Ferber, *A Study of the Aggregate Consumption Function*, National Bureau of Economic Research, Technical Paper #8, 1953.

for the economic forecaster. In general, forecasting difficulties are attributable to periodic upward shifts of the consumption function. These upward shifts have, however, had a stimulating effect and have reduced the burden on investment and government for maintaining full employment spending.

UNRESOLVED ISSUES

There are many unresolved issues which beset students of the consumption function. In the main, these issues are puzzles for those involved in statistical estimation of the consumption function, but they are not of great importance for a theoretical model. On the whole, the most difficult issue has been the appropriate measure of income to be used in fitting consumption functions to the data. Is the relevant income concept for the economy gross income or per capita income? Which of a number of different accounting measures (discussed in Chapter 15) is the relevant one for aggregate consumption analysis? Is income earned during the calendar year relevant, or should the income concept be something representing permanent income or expected average lifetime income?[11] If permanent income is the proper concept, how should inflationary price expectations be included in the function? Is it the absolute income a family earns which determines its consumption behavior, or is it its income level relative to the income of other families which is important?[12] Considerable effort is being expended at the present time to resolve these issues.

[11] Ohlin, in an early criticism of the Keynesian system, argued that Keynes' treatment of income as the primary determinant of consumption behavior is "a little superficial." Ohlin noted: "On what does this sum total of planned consumption depend? First of all on the consumer's income expectations. Not his expected income during the first coming period only, but on what he expects to earn over a long period in the future . . . . This fact every American would willingly testify to-day; most of them expect growing incomes and base their consumption plans thereon . . . they actually correlate consumption plans and income expectations for many future periods." (B. Ohlin, "Some Notes on the Stockholm Theory of Savings and Investment I," *Economic Journal*, 47, pp. 62–63.) Recently, Friedman has revived Ohlin's notion that consumption behavior is determined primarily by permanent income (i.e., the expected future income stream) rather than merely present income. See M. Friedman, *A Theory of the Consumption Function*, Princeton University Press, 1957.

[12] See J. Duesenberry, *Income, Savings and the Theory of Consumer Behavior*, Harvard University Press, 1949.

There is, however, one question which does have important theoretical implications and which will be discussed at length in Part III. That question is: Can income and consumption behavior be meaningfully analyzed (as we have attempted in this chapter) without taking account of all of the implications of concurrent fluctuations in income and the price level? There is pedagogical value in ignoring price phenomena initially; but, as it will be perfectly clear after Chapter 10 has been studied, that a thorough understanding of aggregate consumption expenditures requires an analysis of concommitant price changes.

CHAPTER 4

Real investment expenditures

Consumption is largely a passive factor in the determination of the level of national output. That is, in general (although by no means always), a rise in consumption spending follows a prior rise in output. In other words, if investment (or any other exogenous variable) were to rise, then this rise would initiate an increase in consumption and an even larger rise in output through the simple multiplier; but normally it is not expected that consumption will change autonomously and thereby trigger off an expansion or contraction. As an initiator of change, investment merits very careful and detailed consideration. Since each investment good is purchased with the expectation that it will generate the largest attainable stream of money-income payments over time, the discussion of investment must begin by considering just how an investor decides to make his purchases.

THE INVESTMENT DECISION

Investment purchases by individuals fall into two broad categories. These are purchases of:

1. *Financial assets or placements* which are stocks, bonds, and other debt instruments. These securities may be newly issued or may be purchased secondhand.
2. *Real assets or capital goods* which are commodities which can be used in future production or sales of goods and services. These real assets may also be either newly produced or purchased secondhand.

The purchase of a placement is considered an investment by the individual since he expects his future income stream to be increased by the transaction. There has been no new investment for the economy, however, since the sale of the placement represents a disinvestment of an equal amount by the seller. For the economy as a whole, investment and disinvestment in financial assets cancel out. Similarly, the purchase of a secondhand capital good represents an investment to the purchaser, but an equal disinvestment to the seller.

Only when there are newly created capital goods have some individuals invested without there being an offsetting disinvestment by others. The creation of new capital goods represents gross investment for the economy. To distinguish purchases of financial assets and secondhand real assets from purchases of newly created capital goods, the *term investment is used, in the Keynesian system, to denote only purchases of new capital goods*. Transactions in financial and secondhand assets are called *asset-transfers*. This distinction is made because the purchase of a new plant and equipment, inventories, and housing creates additional jobs and new output, while the purchase of placements and secondhand assets has no direct effect on these key aggregate variables.

The total value of newly created capital goods produced in the economy in a year is called *gross investment*. Since some capital goods will be used up during the year to produce the annual output of the economy, some of these newly created capital goods are replacement goods. The rest represents a net addition to the economy's stock of real capital and is called *net investment*. Net investment will be negative when the total volume of newly produced capital goods is less than the amount required to replace the real assets used up either in production or depleted inventories during the year. Gross real investment, however, can never be less than zero, since the output of industries producing capital goods cannot be negative. Negative net investment is called disinvestment and, for example, occurs at the firm level when individual businesses adjust inventories to expectations of falling sales.

If the economy as a whole is to invest during any time period, entrepreneurs must expect to earn a higher rate of return from newly created capital goods than from any other of the wide range of available assets.[1] Whether the investor is self-financed or whether he borrows to consummate the transaction this must be true. If the investor is

---

[1] The rates of return must be suitably adjusted for risks.

self-financed, then there are alternative assets which he could have bought. If he borrows, then he must promise a return to his creditors at least as large as the return his creditors could have earned from some other kind of promissory paper, or, indeed, from a real asset.

The expected future income stream versus the cost of investment

The key question facing each potential investor is simply, "How should I use my own or borrowed funds to maximize the rate of return I will receive?" Output and employment will rise only if the answer to this question is, "I will earn a higher rate of return if I purchase a newly produced capital good than if I buy some other kind of asset."

The comparison of rates of return on different assets is complicated since earnings generated by any asset are not usually received in a lump sum, but as a stream of payments through time. Any comparison of alternative returns must take account of the passage of time. Moreover, there is great uncertainty about what the future return will be. To paraphrase Keynes, the entrepreneur who has to make a practical decision as to his scale of investment, does not entertain a single undoubting expectation of what the future earning stream will be. Several hypothetical expectations are held, each with varying degrees of confidence. By expected future earnings stream, therefore, is meant that expectation of profits which, if held with certainty, would lead the individual to undertake the same actions as does the bundle of vague possibilities which actually makes up the state of his expectations when he reaches his decision. [2]

To illustrate the complications introduced by the time dimension, the following example may prove helpful. Suppose the price of charred oaken finishing vats to a Kentucky bourbon distiller to be $1,000 per vat. Suppose further, that if the distiller buys a vat, he can use it for five years, at the end of which time he can expect to sell the whiskey that emerges for $1,150 over and above all the variable costs associated with the whiskey making (including the excise tax on liquor). At the end of the five years, he also knows he can sell the vat to a moonshiner for $50.00. Should the distiller buy the vat?

[2] J. M. Keynes, *The General Theory of Employment, Interest and Money*, Harcourt, Brace, 1936. p. 24, note 2.

What alternatives are open to the distiller? Suppose one alternative to be the purchase of a five-year U.S. Treasury Certificate paying 4 percent per year. Should the distiller invest in the new vat, or buy the certificate? The answer to this question is easily arrived at once the return on the Treasury Certificate is set down, year by year, as in Table 4.1.

Table 4.1.   Return on U.S. Treasury Certificate vs. Bourbon Vat

Item	One	Two	Three	Four	Five
			(years)		
U.S. Treasury Certificate	$40.00 $+$	$\left\{\begin{array}{l}\text{\$40.00} \\ +\text{\$ 1.60}\end{array}\right. +$	$\left\{\begin{array}{l}\text{\$40.00} \\ +\text{\$ 1.60} \\ +\text{\$ 0.064}\end{array}\right. +$	$\left\{\begin{array}{l}\text{\$40.00} \\ +\text{\$ 1.60} \\ +\text{\$ 0.064} \\ +\text{\$ 0.0027}\end{array}\right. +$	$\left\{\begin{array}{l}\text{\$ 40.00} \\ +\text{\$ 1.60} \\ +\text{\$ 0.064} \\ +\text{\$ 0.0027} \\ +\text{\$ 0.0001} \\ +\text{\$1000.00}\end{array}\right.$
Bourbon Vat	$0.00 $+$	$ 0.00 $+$	$ 0.00 $+$	$ 0.00 $+$	$\left\{\begin{array}{l}\text{\$1150.00} \\ +\text{\$ 50.00}\end{array}\right.$

In each year, holding the bond entitles the owner to forty dollars in interest payments. As each forty dollar interest payment is received, that amount can be used to purchase additional securities. In year two, therefore, the bondholder receives another forty dollars on his bond purchase, plus a return of 4 percent on the forty dollars added to his principal the year before.[3] In the fifth year, the bondholder gets a stream of interest payments, plus his original one thousand dollars. All of this is a long way of saying that since we live in a world in which compound interest can be earned with a large number of assets, all assets must pay a comparable *compound* rate (adjusted for risk differences) in order to attract funds. In this case, even if the bourbon business is as riskless as a Treasury Note (which it may well be), the certificate is the better purchase. The vat pays a simple rate of return of 4 percent, while the certificate pays a rate of 4 percent compounded annually.

[3] The assumption that the investor can use the interest income paid to him in years one through four to earn the same rate as he receives on his original purchase is an unreal assumption which, however, simplifies the exposition considerably.

The present value of a future income stream

If the present cost and the earnings stream which an asset will pay over its life could be estimated, then the compound rate of return on the asset could be computed. The formula required for this calculation is:

$$P = \frac{A_1}{(1 + r)} + \frac{A_2}{(1 + r)^2} + \frac{A_3}{(1 + r)^3}$$

$$+ \cdots \frac{A_n}{(1 + r)^n} + \frac{J}{(1 + r)^n}, \qquad (4.1)$$

where P is the present value (or supply price) of the asset, $A_1 \ldots A_n$ is the expected money income above expenses in the years 1, 2, to the last year of the assets life, J is the scrap value of the asset, and r is the rate of return.

This formula may be solved for the compound rate of return (r) when the A's, J, and P are known, or it may be solved for P when the A's, J, and r's are known. In the latter case, the computation is straightforward. In the former case, however, a trial and error approximate solution offers the best approach. In the case of the bourbon vat:

$$\$1,000 = \frac{\$1,150}{(1 + r)^5} + \frac{\$50}{(1 + r)^5} = \frac{\$1,200}{(1 + r)^5},$$

where in this example, $A_1 = A_2 = A_3 = A_4 = 0$, $A_5 = \$1,150$, and $J = \$50$. Therefore:

$$(1 + r)^5 = 1.20,$$
$$r \approx 3.7 \text{ percent.}$$

Thus, once all expected rates of return are expressed as compound rates, the choice among assets of the same risk becomes obvious. In terms of the vat vs. U.S. Treasury Certificate example, it requires no special wisdom to say that a compound rate of return of 4 percent on a Treasury Certificate is more desireable than a 3.7 percent return on a bourbon vat.

That rate of discount which makes the expected future net income stream of an *additional* unit of newly produced capital just equal to the present cost of producing an *additional* unit of the asset is called the *marginal efficiency of capital*. As the comparison between the Treasury Certificate and the oaken vat clearly illustrates, for a real asset to be newly created, the marginal efficiency of the new real asset must at least be equal to or exceed the rate of interest or the rate of return on placements (or secondhand real assets) since the investor always has the option of acquiring either an interest paying security or existing facilities.

THE MARGINAL EFFICIENCY OF CAPITAL SCHEDULE

At any point in time, entrepreneurs are aware of a large number of possible uses for new capital goods. The expected rate of return on any one of these new investment projects depends upon factors which influence (1) expectations about the size of the future net income stream, and (2) the present cost of the capital good.

Expectations of future profits, as we have already suggested, depend primarily on the relationship between anticipated product prices and input costs. The number of new investments in which the present value of the expected future income stream is two or three times larger than the initial investment are quite small, but opportunities to lose money are legion. Why? First, it is inherently difficult to think of new ways of making large profits, since this is an activity in which many are engaged, so that most of the extremely profitable ventures have already been undertaken. There is the additional complication that if gross investment is increasing, the capital goods industries will normally find the costs of additional output rising. This rise in capital costs, given the same absolute amount of expected income, implies a decline in the rate of return.

If all the various opportunities for utilizing *new* capital goods are arrayed by their expected rate of return, they can be plotted as in Fig. 4.1. The curve in Fig. 4.1 is arrived at by adding the dollar volume of new investment at each particular rate of return to the dollar value of investment at all higher rates of return. The resulting curve is called the *marginal efficiency of capital schedule*. The slope of this function is clearly negative, but its shape cannot be readily discovered by *a priori* reasoning. For simplicity only, therefore, the function in Fig.

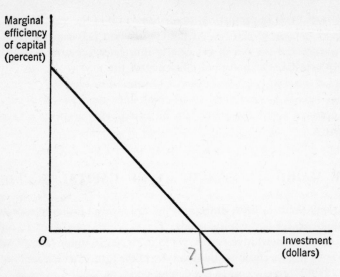

FIG. 4.1. The Marginal Efficiency of Capital Schedule.

4.1 is assumed to be linear. *The marginal efficiency of capital schedule relates the demand for new capital goods to the expected rate of return.* At any level of expected return it indicates the volume of investment demand for the economy as a whole.

THE LEVEL OF GROSS INVESTMENT

What part of potential investment represented by the marginal efficiency of capital schedule will actually be carried out? The guiding principle has already been indicated. New investment will be carried to the point where the expected rate of return on the marginal new investment just equals that which can be earned by buying existing facilities or placements.[4]

[4] The ability of an entrepreneur to borrow funds may be an important constraint limiting aggregate real investment. For example, if an individual expects a 30 percent return on investment project *A*, while the going rate on loans is 6 percent, if he could borrow the funds he would make the investment. If, however, he is such a poor credit risk that no one will lend him the money at the going rate (or at any other rate up to 30 percent), then he will not be able to finance the project and the new investment will not be made.

To talk of a single rate of return on placements and secondhand assets is obviously a simplification. Debt placements, for example, pay widely different rates of return. This scattering of rates is due to the diverse degree of risk associated with the various assets. These risks are manifold. There is, of course, the risk of default by the borrower. There is the risk that the lender will suddenly need cash and will have to sell the asset at an unfavorable price. There is the risk that at the time the principal is repaid, opportunities to reinvest will be poor. There is the possibility of a general rise in commodity prices in the interim between the time of purchase and redemption, and consequently a fall in the real value of the financial asset. These factors combine to spin an elaborate structure of rates of return which need not be discussed at length here. Underlying this structure of rates it can be hypothesized that there is a rate of return, the rate of interest, on a riskless, perpetual placement. The determinants of this riskless rate of interest will be indicated in Chapter 6.

With this in mind the discussion thus far can be summarized in the following way. Gross investment will be carried to the point where the marginal efficiency of capital is equal to the opportunity cost of capital i.e., to the cost of alternative foregone opportunities. The opportunity cost of capital, in turn, will depend on the going rate of interest on a riskless perpetual security adjusted by the degree of risk inherent in the investment project under consideration.

For example, if the rate of interest on a riskless perpetuity is equivalent to a rate of return of r_1 (in Fig. 4.2), then all investment projects whose expected yield is equal to or exceeds r_1 will be undertaken, and the dollar volume of investment spending will be I_1. If the riskless rate were to fall to the equivalent of r_2, the level of investment would expand to I_2. The extent to which the level of investment will change when the rate of interest changes will depend upon the elasticity of the marginal efficiency of capital schedule[5] (if that schedule is stable).

---

[5] The elasticity of the marginal efficiency of capital schedule measures the proportional change in the level of new investment for a proportional change in the marginal expected rate of return, i.e.,

$$\eta = \frac{\dfrac{\Delta I}{I}}{\dfrac{\Delta r}{r}},$$

where η is elasticity.

Aggregate supply and demand analysis

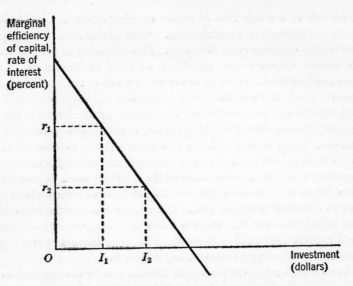

FIG. 4.2. Determining the Level of Investment.

If the schedule is elastic, a small percentage change in the rate of interest will induce a larger percentage change in the level of investment. However, most economists believe (and this belief is supported by empirical evidence) that the marginal efficiency of capital schedule is interest inelastic, so that large percentage changes in the rate of interest produce smaller percentage changes in the level of investment. For this reason, and for others soon to be discussed, shifts in the marginal efficiency of capital schedule tend to be more significant than movements along any such schedule.

REAL INVESTMENT AND PRODUCTIVITY

The preceding discussion has emphasized that new real investment generates income for the investor and the economy. It is appropriate at this point to probe more deeply into the relationship between increments in investment and increments in real income. There are two ways by which increases in real gross investment generate increases in real income. To begin with, real gross investment is, by definition, newly produced capital goods and as such constitutes an increment in the gross output of the economy. The production of these capital goods generates incomes for the owners of those factors of production engaged in the capital goods industries. The additional consumption spending induced by this increment in income will further expand gross output via the simple multiplier process.

In addition, an increase in investment which increases the stock of capital in the economy results, *ceteris paribus*, in an increase in output per worker. At any level of employment, therefore, the larger the stock of capital the larger the volume of goods that the economy can turn out. In other words, net investment, which is an increase in the capital stock, creates an increase in the capacity of the economy to produce goods and services, while an increase in gross investment increases the ability of consumers to purchase more goods. (As the next chapter will demonstrate, there is no necessity for consumers to in fact absorb all the potential output of the economy. It is possible, therefore, in a market economy, for capacity to outrun sales. When this occurs the marginal efficiency of capital schedule will shift downwards.)

EXPECTATIONS AND THE STABILITY OF THE INVESTMENT DEMAND FUNCTION

Real investment goods fall into three basic categories: plant and equipment, residential construction, and inventories. Uncertainty as to future yields surrounds investment of each kind.

Plant, much equipment, and residential construction are long-lived capital goods of considerable initial cost. The investor may have to wait ten, fifteen, perhaps even twenty-five years before the profitability of an investment is proved. Belief that the purchase of so long-lived a good will be profitable, therefore, involves a bold plunge into an unforeseeable future.

What factors, for example, must enter into calculating the rate of return over cost of a newly proposed oil refinery in Puerto Rico? First there is the question of future demand for oil and its derivative products. How fast will energy consumption increase in the next twenty-five to fifty years? How much of that increase will be met with oil? How much of that oil increase will be met by this firm? How much of that can be economically supplied from Puerto Rico?

The location of the refinery raises a host of other questions. For how long will Puerto Rico's cheap labor and low rate of taxation continue? Will the east coast of the United States remain a satisfactory market? How long will Venezuela be a cheap source of crude oil to the United States?

Then there are technological uncertainties in the type of plant to be built. Are technological changes imminent in the refinery process? There are also timing problems. Will it be cheaper to borrow in the international capital market six months or a year from now? And on and on endlessly. (It might be instructive for the student to set down the host of questions entering into the purchase of a house by a family. Even for this good, one for which a well-developed secondhand market exists, the questions which arise about the next twenty-five years—the likely life of the mortgage—are overwhelming.)

Many of the questions posed cannot be answered with any great degree of confidence. But investment decisions must be made, and they are made. They are made with one-third fact and two-third animal spirits.[6] These animal spirits largely depend on the mood of the business community. Often, transient factors such as the current stage of the business cycle set the mood of the investing community. Although the level of business activity tends to go through a cycle averaging some three years in duration (therefore having little or no relevance for a project with an expected life of twenty-five years), still, in the absence of reliable foresight, present optimism or pessimism inherent in each stage of the cycle often gets projected indefinitely into the future.[7]

The existence of the business cycle means that even such short-term investments as inventory purchases are clouded by uncertainty. For small merchants, for brokers, for wholesalers, even for department stores, the costs of carrying inventories are a substantial part of the costs of doing business. Inventories are carried because of the uncertainty surrounding the actual level of future sales. Inadequate in-

---

[6] J. M. Keynes, *op. cit.*, p. 162.

[7] Changes in the phase of the business cycle may feed back into the system by altering expectations and inducing a shift in the marginal efficiency of capital schedule.

ventory levels will result in lost sales and foregone income. Too large
an inventory implies excessive carrying costs.[8] Since the appropriate
level of inventories is related to the level of sales, failure to guess when
the boom will end (or start) may cost sellers dearly. Predicting turning
points in the cycle has proved an uncertain art, and inventory management remains uncertain and ulcerous business.

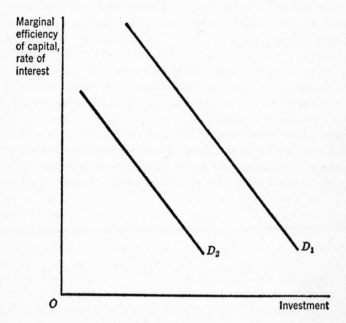

FIG. 4.3. Shifts in the Marginal Efficiency of Capital Schedule.

With the investment decision based upon expectations, which in
turn are based on today's optimism or pessimism, which in turn are
based on an uncertain appraisal of the state of the economy, it may
well be that movements along any marginal efficiency of capital
schedule are considerably less important than shifts in that function.
In Fig. 4.3, for example, D_1 represents the marginal efficiency of
capital schedule as perceived by American businessmen the day be-

[8] T. M. Whiten, *The Theory of Inventory Management*, 2nd ed., Princeton University
Press, 1957.

fore a presidential election, while D_2 represents the business community's perception of this schedule the day after the election of the Democratic candidate. Because of uncertainty, this abnormal occurrence is likely to shift radically the marginal efficiency schedule as expectations fluctuate in response to external factors which are only dimly related to the long-term profitability of investment. The instability of the marginal efficiency of capital schedule is a major source of instability in the level of economic activity. As long as expectations about an uncertain future remain ephemeral, they will remain unpredictable, and will impose a permanent and drastic limitation on the ability of economists to forecast the course of business.

The instability of the marginal efficiency of capital schedule prevents the econometrician from empirically determining its shape as it shifts erratically through time. Nevertheless, it is a useful economic concept which dramatically highlights the uncertainties which surround the investment decision. These uncertainties are often lost sight of in more formalistic and determinate economic models, yet it is precisely these uncertainties which are at the root of economic instability in market economies.

CHAPTER 5

Keynesian dynamics: a digression

ONE APPROACH TO ENTREPRENEURIAL
EXPECTATIONS AND THE INVESTMENT DECISION

The concept of a marginal efficiency of capital schedule is an extremely useful expository device. The volatility of this schedule is the cornerstone of contemporary economic theory and the touchstone of contemporary economic policy. It would be desirable, however, to know more about the investment decision than that it rests on expectations which are grounded on uncertainty. It would be a significant improvement if the marginal efficiency of capital schedule could be empirically approximated, and shifts in its position could be predicted. Economists have not advanced very far in this direction up to now, and one suspects that when the body of Keynesian theory is significantly modified, the basic alteration in the theory will be a better way of looking at the investment process.

There is one line of reasoning that does take a different tack, and which, if not altogether satisfactory, does contain some elements of truth and has significant implications. This line of reasoning has developed about what is called *the acceleration principle*, or merely the *accelerator*. The acceleration principle rests on the assumption that profit-maximizing entrepreneurs desire to maintain a fixed ratio between the stock of capital and the level of output. In itself, this principle is not a complete explanation of the level of investment, although it could be made part of a more complete theory. Because of weaknesses inherent in a naive accelerator model, a full explanation of investment which made use of the accelerator would have to be quite complex and no attempt will be made to present such a model here. Rather, the elementary theory, its significance and its limitations will be developed in the rest of this chapter.

INVESTMENT, THE STOCK OF CAPITAL, THE ACCELERATOR, AND FUTURE EFFECTIVE DEMAND

Gross investment creates jobs. It creates jobs directly in the capital goods industries, and, as a consequence of the multiplier relation, indirectly in the consumption goods industries. Investment spending is volatile and because of the multiplier it induces even greater fluctuations in total spending. This is a fundamental lesson of macroeconomics. *Net* investment, on the other hand, constitutes an addition to the nation's stock of capital; so that net investment in one year means a greater capacity to produce in subsequent years. Additions to the stock of capital in any one year, therefore, reflects a collective judgment on the part of entrepreneurs that aggregate effective demand will be sufficiently greater in the future to absorb the additional future production made possible by current net investment. In a world marked by uncertainty, this judgment about future effective demand may or may not turn out to be correct.

Investment therefore has a dual role. Gross investment creates jobs in the present, while net investment creates productive capacity which will be used in combination with labor in future periods, only if effective demand increases sufficiently in the future. The dependence of present gross output (or income) on present gross investment was discussed in Chapter 3. The next section explores the implications of the relationship between net investment and the capacity to produce.

The capital-output ratio

The acceleration principle assumes that there tends to be a simple relationship between the economy's stock of capital and the level of output. In particular, it assumes the capital stock to be some constant multiple of output, i.e.,

$$K \equiv \sigma Y, \tag{5.1}$$

where $\sigma(\equiv K/Y)$ is the capital-output ratio, since K is the stock of capital and Y is the level of output. If the capital-output ratio is a constant, then any expected change in output ($\Delta \hat{Y}$) will lead business-men to want to change their capital stock ($\Delta \hat{K}$) so that they will have the proper capacity for the expected new level of output. Thus,

$$\Delta \hat{K} = \sigma \Delta \hat{Y}, \tag{5.2}$$

where the circumflex is meant to convey the idea that these values rest on expectations about the future. Since the actual change in the capital stock is equal to net investment (I_n) during the period:

$$I_n \equiv \Delta K, \tag{5.3}$$

and since entrepreneurs want the actual change in the stock of capital to equal the desired changes ($\Delta K = \Delta \hat{K}$), then it follows that

$$I_n = \sigma \Delta \hat{Y}. \tag{5.4}$$

Equation (5.4) indicates that entrepreneurs want their net investment in every period to be a constant multiple of their expectations of changes in output.

How entrepreneurs decide on what future income levels will be and how they decide upon the appropriate time path along which to adjust their capital stock to these income expectations is not clearly under-stood. Since entrepreneurs can perceive the future and adjust to it in several ways, the accelerator model is compatible with different time paths over which the economy may proceed. In certain cir-cumstances, which have been labeled "a golden age," entrepreneurial behavior can lead to a smooth, steady, and continuous advance in output.

A golden age[1]

Assume that net investment in some initial period reflects business-mens' anticipations about the actual level of output in the next period. If, in the second period, effective demand increases just enough to absorb the extra output made possible by the net investment of the first period, then businessmen will feel that their investments were

[1] This highly suggestive term owes its popularity to Mrs. Robinson. See J. Robinson, *The Accumulation of Capital*, Irwin, 1956, pp. 99ff.

Table 5.1. A Golden Age in a Mythical Economy

Period (t)	(1) C	+ (2) I_n	= (3) Y	(4) $\frac{1}{\sigma} \times$	(5) $I_n =$	(6) $\Delta\hat{Y} =$	(7) $\Delta Y =$	(8) $k \times$	(9) ΔI_n	(10) K
1	80.00	20.00	100.00	.25	20.00	5.00	5.00	5.00	1.00	400
2	84.00	21.00	105.00	.25	21.00	5.25	5.25	5.00	1.05	420
3	88.20	22.05	110.25	.25	22.05	5.51	5.51	5.00	1.10	441
4	92.60	23.15	115.75	.25	23.15	5.79	5.79	5.00	1.16	463
5	97.24	24.31	121.55	.25	24.31	6.08	6.08	5.00	1.22	486
6	102.12	25.53	127.65	.25	25.53	6.38	6.38	5.00	1.28	511

justified. Output in the second period, however, depends on investment and the multiplier in that period. Period two's net investment, nevertheless, will be set in accordance with anticipated effective demand in period three. Consequently, actual output in period two need not be at that level which just justifies the previous period's net investment. If, however, gross investment in period two does lead to a level of effective demand which just justifies the net investment of the previous period and, at the same time, the net investment in the second period correctly anticipates the effective demand in the third period, then the economy will be in a golden age. In a golden age, entrepreneurs will find that events always just justify their expectations.

Table 5.1 illustrates the economic conditions of a golden age. This table was constructed on the following assumptions. First, it was assumed that the consumption function of this mythical economy is

$$C = .8Y,$$

so that the simple multiplier (k) is 5. It was further assumed that the capital-output ratio (σ) is equal to 4, that is, it takes $4.00's worth of capital equipment to produce $1.00's worth of output in a period. Thus the reciprocal of σ, the output-capital ratio, is equal to .25, that is, for every $1.00's worth of capital added to the capital stock, output in the next period can expand by $.25. Finally, for simplicity in this first model, it is assumed that *all* investment expenditures increase capacity. In other words, it is assumed that, at least during the period encompassed by the table, the economy's stock of capital does not wear out, and therefore no replacement investment occurs (i.e., net investment and gross investment are equal).

Table 5.1 indicates that in period one, the output of the economy (Y) is $100.00, and this output consists of $80.00 in consumption goods and $20.00 of investment goods. These figures are recorded in columns (1) through (3) in row (1) of the table. Since net investment in the first period is $20.00, the output-capital ratio of .25 implies that businessmen expect the output in period two to increase by $5.00 to $105.00. These figures are recorded in columns (4) through (6) in row (1) of the table. Under what conditions will income actually rise by $5.00 in period two? Given a multiplier of 5, if investment is $1.00 higher in period two than it was in period one, then output would increase by $5.00. These figures are recorded in columns (7) through (9) in row (1) of the table. Finally, column (10) indicates the stock of capital available to the economy at the beginning of each period. If the stock of capital as recorded in column (10) is what entrepreneurs want it to be, it will be four times the level of income in the same period, as recorded in column (3).

If investment does rise by $1.00 (to $21.00) in period two, then, as shown in columns (1) through (3) of row (2), output will rise to $105.00, as consumption increases to $84.00. Comparing columns (10) and (3) in row (2), indicates that the actual stock of capital is four times as large as the level of output in period two and since $\frac{K}{Y}$ is equal to 4, effective demand has increased sufficiently to allow complete utilization of the larger capital stock. Businessmen will feel that their investments of period one were wisely made.

Since net investment in period two was $21.00, then businessmen must have anticipated that the output in period three would increase by $5.25 (.25 × $21.00). A rise in output of $5.25 in period three will occur only if investment in period three is $22.05, since with a multiplier of 5, investment will have to increase by $1.05 over the level of investment in period two for output to increase by $5.25.

If entrepreneurs are to find each successively higher level of net investment justified by events in the subsequent period, then the output of the economy must continue to grow. Examination of column (3) indicates that if businessmen's expectations of future output levels are to be continuously met (assuming that the multiplier remains at 5 and the capital-output ratio remains at 4) then the level of output must grow by 5 percent in each period. Of course, if output is to grow at a rate of 5 percent per period, and if there is to be a constant relationship between the stock of capital and the level of output, then investment must also grow at a rate of 5 percent per period as the figures in column two indicate.

The numerical results that have been culled from Table 5.1 can be obtained algebraically. Since net investment in any period is undertaken in anticipation of a rise in output in the subsequent period which is just sufficient to keep the capital-output ratio constant, then as has been noted before in (5.4)

$$I_n = \sigma \Delta \hat{Y}, \tag{5.4}$$

where, once again, the circumflex signifies that these are desired levels and that in a world of uncertainty, of course, the desired levels may not actually be realized. (Table 5.1 depicts a situation in which desired levels are actually obtained—and that is why it is a representation of a golden age.)

Given the income identity

$$Y \equiv C + I_n, \tag{5.5}$$

and the consumption function

$$C = bY, \tag{5.6}$$

then, by substituting (5.6) into (5.5), the level of output (Y) is

$$Y = \left(\frac{1}{1-b}\right) I_n = kI_n, \tag{5.7}$$

where k is the simple multiplier. The change in output resulting from a change in investment is[2]

$$\Delta Y = k \, \Delta I_n. \tag{5.8}$$

Thus, actual changes in output in any period will be equal to the change in investment in that period multiplied by k. In a golden age economy, the desired change in output in any period equals the actual change in output, i.e.,

$$\Delta \hat{Y} = \Delta Y. \tag{5.9}$$

Substituting (5.4) and (5.8) into (5.9), we obtain

$$\frac{I_n}{\sigma} = k \, \Delta I_n,$$

or

$$\frac{\Delta I_n}{I_n} = \frac{1}{\sigma k}. \tag{5.10}$$

Equation (5.10) indicates that in a golden age, the rate of change in net investment is a constant. This constant is equal to the reciprocal

---

[2] If investment increases by ΔI_n, then the new level of output is

$$Y + \Delta Y = k(I_n + \Delta I_n). \tag{5.7a}$$

Subtracting (5.7) from (5.7a), yields equation (5.8).

of the capital-output ratio times the reciprocal of the simple multiplier. In the hypothetical example of Table 5.1, where σ was equal to 4, and k was equal to 5, the rate of change in investment is $1/20$, or 5 percent per period. Moreover, from equations (5.8) and (5.7), it follows that output must grow at the same rate as net investment in each period.

The accelerator, the multiplier, and replacement investment[3]

In the preceding model of the golden age, it was assumed that all investment spending added to capacity. In reality, however, the production of goods and services during the period will involve some wearing out of capital. Thus, some of the investment in each period will merely replace those capital goods that have been used in the production process, and therefore not all investment will add to capacity.

Under certain circumstances, the addition of replacement investment expenditures to the golden age model does not substantially alter the conclusions. Specifically, assume that replacement investment is a simple proportional function of the stock of capital, i.e.,

$$I_\rho = \beta K, \tag{5.11}$$

where I_ρ is replacement investment, while β is some constant which has a value between zero and unity. Since the capital stock is related to output via the capital-output ratio ($K = \sigma Y$), equation (5.11) can be rewritten as

$$I_\rho = \beta \sigma Y = \gamma Y \tag{5.12}$$

where $\gamma = \beta \sigma$.[4]

Given the output identity

$$Y \equiv C + I_n + I_\rho, \tag{5.13}$$

and the consumption function

$$C = bY, \tag{5.14}$$

---

[3] The importance of replacement investment is treated by R. Frisch, "The Interrelation between Capital Production and Consumer Taking," *Journal of Political Economy*, vol. 39, 1931.

[4] Since capital is long-lived and only a small part wears out each period, we may normally expect that γ is very small and typically will be less than .2.

then substituting (5.14) and (5.12) into (5.13), and solving for Y yields

$$Y = \left(\frac{1}{1 - b - \gamma}\right) I_n.$$

Letting k^* equal $\left(\frac{1}{1 - b - \gamma}\right)$, then the change in output as a result of a change in net investment is given by

$$\Delta Y = k^* \Delta I_n. \tag{5.15}$$

The term k^* is called the *super-multiplier*[5] for it indicates the effects on total output of an increase in expenditures on consumption *and replacement investment* induced by an initial increase in net investment. The suffix *super* is used for this multiplier formulation since the introduction of an additional kind of induced spending (on replacement investment) will obviously result in a larger increase in income for any initial increment in expenditures. If, for example, γ is equal to .05 while b is equal to .80, then k^* will be equal to 6.67, while the simple multiplier had a value of 5.

As before, a golden age assumes that the desired change in output is equal to the actual change in output, so that

$$\Delta \hat{Y} = \Delta Y, \tag{5.16}$$

while the actual level of net investment is related to the expected change in output

$$I_n = \sigma \Delta \hat{Y}. \tag{5.17}$$

Substituting (5.15) and (5.17) into (5.16) and rearranging terms, we obtain

$$\frac{\Delta I_n}{I_n} = \frac{1}{\sigma k^*}. \tag{5.18}$$

As in the previous example of a golden age, net investment and therefore output grow at a constant rate. In the present case, however, the

---

[5] The term *super-multiplier* was coined by J. R. Hicks. See his, *A Contribution to the Theory of the Trade Cycle*, Clarendon Press, 1950, p. 62.

Table 5.2.   A Golden Age in a Mythical Economy with Replacement Investment

Period	C	$+\ I_n$	$+\ I_\rho$	$=\ Y$	$\frac{1}{\sigma}$	$\times\ I_n$	$=\ \Delta\hat{Y}$	$=\ \Delta Y$	$=\ k^* \times \Delta I_n$		K
1	80.00	15.00	5.0	100.00	.25	15.00	3.75	3.75	6.67	.56	400
2	82.99	15.56	5.2	103.75	.25	15.56	3.89	3.89	6.67	.58	415
3	86.10	16.14	5.4	107.64	.25	16.14	4.04	4.04	6.67	.61	431
4	89.33	16.75	5.6	111.68	.25	16.75	4.19	4.19	6.67	.63	447
5	92.69	17.38	5.8	115.87	.25	17.38	4.34	4.34	6.67	.65	464
6	96.18	18.03	6.0	120.21	.25	18.03	4.51	4.51	6.67	.68	481

rate of growth depends on the reciprocal of the product of the capital-output ratio times the super-multiplier, while in the previous case, the growth rate was equal to the reciprocal of the capital-output ratio times the reciprocal of the simple multiplier. The economic rationale of this difference is that the second model allows for the realistic situation in which an increase in output induces an increase in replacement investment, whereas in the first model, investment depends only upon expected demand in the next period.

In Table 5.2 a hypothetical example of a golden age economy which allows for replacement investment is given. Table 5.2 assumes the same values for the marginal propensity to consume and the capital-output ratio as was assumed in Table 5.1. Furthermore, it is assumed that 1.25 percent of the stock of capital at the beginning of each period is replaced during the period, i.e., β is equal to .0125. Both models start with an output level of $100 in the first period. A comparison of the output and net investment columns of the two tables indicates that the rate of growth in output and net investment necessary for a golden age is less in Table 5.2 than in Table 5.1. Introducing replacement investment spending as a function of the current stock of capital (and therefore of the current level of output) reduces the rate of growth of output and net investment that will be exhibited by an economy in a golden age with a given marginal propensity to consume and a given capital-output ratio. The economic rationale of the lower growth rate of the second model is that replacement investment generates employment and output, but does *not* increase capacity. Since capacity grows more slowly, effective demand need not grow as rapidly.

Significance of golden age models

There are two significant implications which can be drawn from these models of a golden age. First, these models drive home the fact that the causal flow between output and investment runs two ways. The level of investment is a key determinant of the level of output, but expected changes in the level of output are strategic determinants of the level of investment. Secondly, these models illustrate the dynamic nature of investment. Net investment itself is a rate of change—the rate of change in the stock of capital during the period. In addition, the change in the capital stock induces changes in the level of output in the period, and as it increases capacity, a further change in the level of output will be desired in the subsequent periods. Consequently, for an economy to achieve a smooth, continuous, and constant rate of growth in output requires a delicate balance between increases in productive capacity and increases in effective demand for the products that can be turned out by this additional capacity.

Departures from the golden age

Unfortunately, the golden age does not describe economic reality. A model which accurately describes the time path of a market economy must encompass not only an upward trend, but also a cyclical path. In other words, a market economy does not normally exhibit a constant rate of growth in output. Typically, the economy will experience fluctuations in production along with a general upward secular trend in output. These fluctuations are called "business cycles."

Two methods of introducing cycles into accelerator models have often been suggested. One common practice is to bound the range over which the simple growth model can expand by postulating a *ceiling*. At the ceiling, there is a physical limitation to further expansion in output. As a result, the relationship between desired and actual output increases, as expressed in the golden age model, can no longer hold. A substitute relationship must be introduced. The other procedure is to relate current values of the dependent variables to prior values of the independent variables. Such a relationship is called a lagged function. For example, the consumption function $C_t = a + bY_{t-1}$ states that consumption in the t-th period depends on the level of output in the $t - 1$ period. In the following sections of this chapter, both procedures are illustrated.

The Ceiling. Cyclical instability can be built into an accelerator model when entrepreneurs expect a rate of growth in output which, given the resource base of the economy and the technical knowledge of the community, exceeds the rate at which output can grow. For example, suppose that in the hypothetical economy of Table 5.2 that in the early periods the existing stock of capital is being efficiently utilized. Suppose that by period four, however, the economy has grown so rapidly that resource utilization has been pushed by overtime work and postponement of maintenance, to the point where further increases in the rate of output are physically limited to slower rates than have occurred in the previous periods. In other words, the ceiling is reached in period four, and the desired 3.75 percent rate of growth is physically impossible for the economy to achieve. Under these circumstances, what will be the path of the economy?

Because of the physical limitation to increases in output at the ceiling, let us assume that, in period five, net investment does not reach the $17.38 level required if the economy is to stay in the golden age. Instead, only $17.00 worth of net investment goods can be produced in the period. Gross output in the period will increase by less than 3.75 percent to $113.48. As a result, businessmen will find that their capital stock of $464.00 in period five has a productive capacity of $116.00 and therefore exceeds the stock of capital that is necessary to produce the actual output of $113.48. We have the paradoxical result, that the decrease in the rate of growth of the stock of capital induces excess capacity in the existing capital stock. In other words, if the economy could continue to add to the stock of capital at a higher rate than it actually did in period five, then it could have had a larger stock of capital which it would have used more intensively than it used the smaller stock it actually obtained at the ceiling. A slowdown in the rate of growth of capital induces a redundancy in the stock of capital which would not occur if the capital stock could grow more rapidly.

How will businessmen react to having excess productive capacity? If businessmen interpret the percentage increase in output from period four to period five as being the maximum rate of growth that can be obtained at the ceiling, then they will project this lower rate forward. Consequently, they would expect output in period six to be $115.00, so that with a capital-output ratio of 4:1, entrepreneurs would desire a stock of capital of $460.00 and therefore they will replace only $2.00 worth of capital out of the $6.00 that will wear out. Net investment in period six would be −$4.00, and the net change in gross investment between periods five and six would be approximately −$20.00. With a decline in gross investment, output in period six would fall. If businessmen then project this rate of decline in output into period seven, they would not desire any increase in the capital stock and might even refuse to replace investment goods as they wear out in period seven. Net investment therefore would be negative while gross investment falls to zero.

Of course, the real world is not as unstable as our economic model; this model is clearly too simple. It does illustrate a point, however, which is significant. *The downturn was initiated by a rise in effective demand which was insufficient to occupy additional productive capacity as it was installed.* As long as final demand was expected to rise at a constant rate, net investment increased at a constant rate. When the rate of increase in effective demand decreased, then the level of net investment declined. This decline in net investment, which was not offset by an expansion of replacement investment, lead to a decline in the level of output and the economy turned down. A slowdown in the rate of growth, therefore, does not lead to stability, rather, it induces a downturn.

The swiftness of the decline once the hypothetical model turned down was so pronounced because of the large magnitudes assumed for k^* and σ. Moreover, the consumption function was assumed to have a zero intercept, i.e., to emanate from the origin. Furthermore, no allowance has been made for investments which are made independent of expectations of next year's output, and the role and behavior of the interest rate has been ignored. A model which introduced these other factors, and had smaller magnitudes for k^* and σ, would exhibit a much slower descent, and would have a floor below which output could not fall. This floor would set the stage for the subsequent upturn since gross investment could not fall below zero, and, therefore, if these factors held output at some positive level, there would be a continuous depletion of the capital stock until businessmen found it was necessary to initiate investment just to maintain the current level of output. This increase in gross investment, $\Delta I_n + \Delta I_\rho$ magnified by the multiplier, would induce an upturn in the economy.

Lagged Relationships. Lagged relationships may also be introduced into the model. The introduction of such lags leads to fundamental change in the characteristics exhibited by the model. In this section, both consumption and investment spending will be related to the magnitudes of the variables in prior periods. Specifically, it will be assumed that both aggregate consumption and aggregate investment in any period depend upon the output of prior periods, i.e.,

$$C_t = a + bY_{t-1}, \tag{5.19}$$

and

$$I_t = \sigma(Y_{t-1} - Y_{t-2}). \tag{5.20}$$

Where C_t is consumption in period t, I_t is investment in period t, Y_{t-1} is output in the period $t - 1$, Y_{t-2} is output in period $t - 2$, b is the marginal propensity to consume, σ is the capital-output ratio, and a is the intercept of the consumption function.

The rationale of these functions is as follows:

The consumption function (5.19) indicates that it takes time for consumers to adjust their consumption to their income level. Specifically, this function states that consumption in any period is related to consumers' income a period earlier.

The rationale of the investment function (5.20) is more complex. It is based on two primary assumptions:

1. *In each period, entrepreneurs will adjust the stock of capital*, so that the capital-output ratio (σ) is a constant. Accordingly, in the $t - 1$ period, the stock of capital (K_{t-1}) will be adjusted to the level of output in that period (Y_{t-1}), i.e.,

$$K_{t-1} = \sigma Y_{t-1}. \tag{5.21}$$

It is also true that entrepreneurs will desire the stock of capital in period $t, (\hat{K}_t)$, to bear the same relationship to the expected level of output in period $t, (\hat{Y}_t)$, i.e.,

$$\hat{K}_t = \sigma \hat{Y}_t. \tag{5.22}$$

Thus, entrepreneurs in period t will undertake a level of investment in period t which will be sufficient to adjust the stock of capital to the desired level, i.e.,

$$I_t = \hat{K}_t - K_{t-1}. \tag{5.23}$$

Substituting (5.21) and (5.22) into (5.23), and rearranging terms,

$$I_t = \sigma(\hat{Y}_t - Y_{t-1}). \tag{5.24}$$

2. *Entrepreneurs expect that gross output in the t-th period ($\hat{Y}_t$) will exceed gross output in the $t - 1$ period (Y_{t-1}) by the same absolute amount as output in period $t - 1$ exceeded output in period $t - 2$, (Y_{t-2}),* i.e.,

$$\hat{Y}_t - Y_{t-1} = Y_{t-1} - Y_{t-2}. \tag{5.25}$$

Substituting (5.25) into (5.24), yields the investment function

$$I_t = \sigma(Y_{t-1} - Y_{t-2}). \tag{5.26}$$

All that is needed to complete the system is the output identity

$$Y_t \equiv C_t + I_t. \tag{5.27}$$

Substituting equation (5.19) and (5.26) into (5.27) yields

$$Y_t = a + bY_{t-1} + \sigma(Y_{t-1} - Y_{t-2}). \tag{5.28}$$

Equation (5.28) states that output in period t is functionally related to output in the two prior periods via the marginal propensity to consume (b) and the capital-output ratio (σ). This equation in which income is a lagged endogenous variable is an extremely flexible function. Given Y_{t-1}, Y_{t-2}, a, b, and σ, this equation indicates the value of Y_t for every period in the future. Given some exogenous disturbance, Y_t can change in a wide variety of patterns over time. The path which Y_t will traverse depends upon the magnitudes of b and σ. Y_t may grow (or decline) slowly or rapidly, it may oscillate or it may trace an oscillating path (about a trend) with increasing or decreasing amplitude over time. Table 5.3 indicates the magnitudes of b and σ which will yield these alternative paths of Y_t over time.

Table 5.3. The Marginal Propensity to Consume, the Capital-Output Ratio, and the Time Path of Output

Structural Requirements	Path of Y_t over Time
(1) $\sigma < (1 - \sqrt{1 - b})^2$	Asymptotically approaches a limit
(2) $(1 - \sqrt{1 - b})^2 < \sigma < 1$	Oscillations with declining amplitudes
(3) $\sigma = 1$	Oscillations with no change in amplitudes
(4) $1 < \sigma < (1 + \sqrt{1 - b})^2$	Oscillations with increasing amplitudes
(5) $(1 + \sqrt{1 - b})^2 < \sigma$	Grows without oscillations at an ever increasing rate

SOURCE: Adapted from R. G. D. Allen, *Mathematical Economics.* Macmillan, 1957, p. 211. Published with permission of the author, Macmillan & Co. Ltd., and St. Martin's Press, Inc.

Table 5.3 indicates that if σ is less than unity, any disturbance will start the economy moving toward a new stable Y_t level. If σ equals unity, then any disturbance will result in fluctuations which will continue with no change in amplitude or duration. Finally, if σ is greater than unity, an initial disturbance will set the economy off on an explosive path unless it is constrained by some exogenous factor such as a ceiling or a floor. Since normally σ will be equal to or greater than unity, if this model is appropriate, we can expect that the interaction of the multiplier and the accelerator will produce movements in the economy which will only be constrained by some external barrier.

Table 5.4. Various Possible Time Paths of a
Lagged Multiplier Accelerator Model

(1) Time Period	(2) $\sigma = .9$	(3) $\sigma = 1$	(4) $\sigma = 1.5$
$t - 2$	100.0	100.0	100.0
$t - 1$	100.0	100.0	100.0
$t = 0$	105.0	105.0	105.0
$t + 1$	112.0	112.5	115.0
$t + 2$	117.3	117.8	127.5
$t + 3$	118.4	119.1	137.5
$t + 4$	115.2	116.0	138.5
$t + 5$	109.3	109.8	125.8
$t + 6$	104.9	103.8	98.8
$t + 7$	103.1	100.9	63.9
$t + 8$	105.0	102.5	34.1
$t + 9$	109.1	107.9	27.4
$t + 10$	113.1	114.4	58.6
$t + 11$	115.4	118.7	131.2
$t + 12$	114.6	118.6	229.5
$t + 13$	111.6	114.3	317.1
$t + 14$	108.1	107.8	345.1
$t + 15$	105.9	102.4	269.4

Three arithmetical examples are presented in Table 5.4. Here, it is assumed that the consumption function in both the $t - 1$ and the $t - 2$ period is $C_t = 50 + 0.5 Y_{t-1}$. Thus, the level of output in each of these periods depends only upon the multiplier, and the intercept of the consumption function. Since the multiplier is 2 and the intercept is \$50.00, income in both periods is \$100.00. It was then assumed that in period t the a intercept of the consumption function increased to $55.00. What will be the resulting time paths of output? Column (2) shows the time path of output if $\sigma = 0.9$. In this case, the path will be one of damped oscillations. When $\sigma = 1$, column (3) indicates the path will be one of regular oscillation. Finally, if $\sigma = 1.5$, then the path, as shown in column (4), will be one of explosive oscillation.

LIMITATIONS OF THE ACCELERATOR AS A THEORY OF INVESTMENT[6]

The accelerator relationship is not an adequate theory of investment. Although the relationship between changes in output and changes in the stock of capital contains elements of truth, actual investment decisions and their timing depend on a number of other factors which severely limit the accelerator explanation of net investment. These factors, which are discussed below, include (1) the problem of distinguishing between net and replacement investment and the possibility of replacement cycles, and (2) the relationship between the degree of utilization of capital and the capital-output ratio, and the fact that the accelerator is based on the assumption that the immediate future will be similar to present circumstances. Although this may be true, capital goods are long-lived and, therefore, expectations about the more distant future are also relevant for investment decisions, but are not accounted for in naive accelerator models.

Replacement versus net investment

The assumptions thus far introduced have avoided but not resolved some difficult aspects of a naive accelerator model. The accelerator has been used to explain changes in net investment, while it is changes in gross investment (i.e., net investment plus replacement investment) which determine changes in total output. Replacement investment expenditures may significantly affect the time path of output. Suppose, for example, the accelerator generated a reduction in net investment,

[6] Much of what follows is based upon A. D. Knox, "The Acceleration Principle and the Theory of Investment: A Survey," *Economica*, 19, 1952, pp. 269–297.

while in the same period, replacement investment expanded to more than offset the fall in net investment. In such circumstances, gross investment and output would rise despite the fall in net investment. Thus it is possible that fluctuations in replacement investment rather than in net investment are the important determinants of the timing of the cycle. The applicability of the acceleration principle, therefore, is severely limited by the fact that it discusses net rather than gross investment.

This problem was avoided in the golden age models by assuming either that replacement investment was zero, or that it was a simple function of the level of output. In the latter case, changes in replacement investment and changes in net investment were related to changes in output. If, however, changes in the level of replacement investment depend upon other factors in addition to changes in total output, then output will not grow at a constant rate. If, for example, replacement investment depends, at least in part, on the age distribution of the stock of capital, and if, as is likely, gross investment was bunched in previous periods, then replacement spending will be bunched in future periods and will tend to generate replacement cycles independent of the accelerator relationship.

Utilization of capital, the capital-output ratio, and the marginal efficiency of capital

If an expected increase in output is to necessitate an increase in the stock of capital, then the existing stock of capital must presently be completely employed. Otherwise, additional output can be produced from the existing unutilized facilities and no net investment will be necessary to expand output, i.e., the accelerator relation will not hold. The usefulness of the accelerator relationship in explaining real world phenomena is limited to situations in which there is no idle capacity. Optimum utilization of capacity can be expected to occur only rarely. If it happens at all, it will probably occur at or near the upper turning point of the business cycle, so that the relevance of the accelerator is limited to brief intervals.

The fact that the accelerator operates only after the capital stock is optimally utilized raises further difficulties. The accelerator relation assumes that expected increases in output will induce net investment. At full capacity, however, total output can not rise at all. Thus we find ourselves in a circular trap in which a prerequisite for the operation of the accelerator is that the economy must be at capacity; but if the economy is at full capacity then there can be no increases in output which is a necessary condition for an increase in net investment. Thus it would appear that the accelerator and the ceiling become relevant at the same time.

One way of breaking out of this trap is to define efficient utilization (capacity) of the capital stock as those instances when business firms produce at the minimum point on their average variable cost curves rather than at the physical limits of output. Thus output can be expanded in the short run, by operating the existing stock of capital more intensively; but because of diminishing returns, the increasing cost of producing additional output from existing facilities will encourage entrepreneurs to enlarge their stocks of capital. Until the minimum point on the average variable cost curve is reached, there is no incentive to increase plant and equipment, while the incentive to expand the stock of capital increases if production occurs at a point beyond the minimum cost level.[7]

Although defining optimum utilization of the capital stock in terms of the minimum average cost position removes the theory from the circular trap indicated above, it reduces its usefulness in that the timing of net investment is now less predictable. The problem facing each entrepreneur now is how far beyond the minimum cost level can he afford to operate before it pays to increase the stock of capital. Also, how long a period can he operate his facilities intensively before adding to capacity? This will depend, in part, upon the entrepreneur's expectations about the durability of the increase in demand; for if the higher level of demand is expected to be short-lived then it will not pay to add to capacity. Once the investment problem has been posed in this manner, it is clear that the entrepreneur must base his investment decision on all factors affecting the future rate of return over the full life of the capital good. In short, he must calculate the marginal efficiency of capital and the accelerator is no substitute for this computation. The accelerator may be a way of introducing the current situation into the investment decision making process, but long-run expectations must also be considered.

---

[7] Of course, even if the incentive to invest is present, entrepreneurs may be unable to acquire the funds necessary to finance new investment.

CHAPTER 6

Simultaneous determination of output

and the rate of interest

The dynamic analysis of Chapter 5 can be extended in a number of directions, but these extensions must be reserved for a text dealing specifically with business cycles or with growth models. For us, there remains at this point the important task of completing the static Keynesian system.

We can summarize what has thus far been said about the Keynesian model with the following set of equations[1]:

The output identity,

$$Y \equiv C + I + G + X, \tag{6.1}$$

where Y is output, C is consumption, I is gross investment, G is government spending, and X is net foreign spending.

The consumption function,

$$C = a_1 + b_1 Y. \tag{6.2}$$

The marginal efficiency of capital schedule,

$$I = a_2 - b_2 r, \tag{6.3}$$

where r is the marginal efficiency of capital, and the a's and b's are

---

[1] Linear equational forms are used merely to simplify the algebra; this does not imply that the actual relationships need be linear.

constants, and the condition that the marginal efficiency of capital equals the rate of interest (i), i.e.,

$$r = i. \tag{6.4}$$

In our simplest case (where $G = X = 0$) we have a linear system of four equations in five unknowns (Y, C, I, r, i), and four statistically determined constants (a_1, b_1, a_2, b_2).

As it stands, the system could not be solved for there would be more unknowns than independent equations. One way out of this is to assume, as in Chapter 4, that the rate of interest is exogenously determined. This would reduce the number of unknowns to four, which is the same as the number of independent equations, and once the magnitudes of the a's and b's were determined a solution would be possible.

The interest rate is, however, a strategic economic variable. It is a determinant of the level of investment and it affects the distribution of income, and consequently, as we shall see in Part III, it indirectly affects the level of employment and prices. Its existence gives rise to a host of financial institutions including the central bank. It continues to be the center of a controversy between Marxist and non-Marxist economists. For these reasons, and many others, it is not satisfactory to treat the rate of interest[2] as exogenously determined. We turn, therefore, to the determinants of the rate of interest by first answering the question, "Why is interest paid?"

To understand the investment decision it was necessary to concentrate attention on those factors which lead some entrepreneurs to choose new investment goods in preference to placements or other secondhand assets. Understanding the process by which the rate of interest is determined turns on a very similar distinction. The key point now is to isolate those factors which lead households and firms to prefer holding some portion of their assets in the form of money rather than in some other form which would generate a future flow of income. (Money is defined as currency plus demand deposits.)

The Keynesian model envisages two separate and distinct decisions that must be made by households and entrepreneurs. The first decision is: what proportion of current income is to be spent? For house-

---

[2] Remember, although we are using the simplification of a single rate of interest, in reality there is a complex structure of interest rates which vary in different degrees from the riskless rate of interest on a perpetual bond.

holds, the decision will be based on their propensities to consume and for entrepreneurs it will depend upon the relationship between the marginal efficiency of capital schedule and the going rate of interest. For that proportion of current income which remains unspent, a second decision must be made: in what form is the unspent income to be kept? Will this unspent margin be kept in the form of money, or will it be converted into some financial asset (placement) from which there is an expected future return? Why would anyone wish to keep his unspent income in the form of money and thereby forego the opportunity to earn a future return? The answer to these questions will explain both the existence and the level of the rate of interest.

LIQUIDITY PREFERENCE: THE MOTIVES FOR HOLDING MONEY

A lusty checking account is obviously an asset calculated to delight households and firms alike. A safe deposit box full of stocks and bonds is also a gratifying possession. Indeed, the safe deposit box is not only gratifying, it is rewarding. Stocks and bonds usually imply that there will be a flow of money payments in the form of dividends and interest. Deposits in a checking account, on the other hand, earn no return. Since every dollar in a checking account, or held as cash, represents a lost earnings opportunity, why would rational income-maximizing households and firms want to hold any money? One possible reason is that cash holdings are temporary—that individuals just cannot unload their money instantaneously. This clearly is not the whole or even a major part of the explanation of cash in pocket and deposits in checking accounts. If it were, then the speed with which money changes hands would be very much more rapid than it is.

In fact, there are excellent reasons for holding money and for foregoing the income which could be earned by giving up money to obtain financial assets. These reasons are conveniently grouped into three categories: the demands for (1) transactions, (2) precautionary, and (3) speculative, cash balances.[3]

---

[3] These three catagories are mainly for analytical convenience, since "money held for each of the three purposes forms, nevertheless, a single pool, which the holder is under no necessity to segregate into three water-tight compartments . . . ." J. M. Keynes, *The General Theory of Employment, Interest and Money*, Harcourt, Brace, 1936, p. 195.

1. Transactions balances

People and firms receive money payments at discrete points in time, but they incur obligations which must be paid more or less continuously. To meet these obligations when they come due, without more than conventional delay, requires having cash balances or money. You can not even buy a bus ride with a coupon from an A. T. & T. bond; you must have cash. Of course, you could try to sell financial assets, as the cash is needed, but managing assets in this way would be costly since brokers' fees must be paid and, in addition, you might pay dearly for having to convert placements into cash if market prices were unfavorable.

The term to remember is *liquidity*. All assets have varying degrees of liquidity, i.e., varying degrees of loss of value involved in converting assets to money, and varying degrees of time lapse before the conversion can be effected. Only demand deposits and currency are perfectly liquid.[4] To minimize the cost of meeting obligations as they come due, it is cheapest to keep some perfectly liquid assets. It is conventional to call the desire to hold money to meet day-to-day obligations the *transaction demand for money*.

The amount of money held for transactions purposes depends primarily on two factors: (1) the length of time between payments periods (e.g., whether wages are paid weekly, bimonthly, or monthly), and (2) the volume of transactions engaged in between payments periods.

The greater the duration of time between payments periods, all other things being equal, the larger the average cash balance the individual must maintain over the period to meet a given level of obligations as they come due. Nevertheless, since payments practices are largely a matter of custom and only change slowly over time,[5] the duration of the payments period is not likely to induce changes

---

[4] Even the liquidity of money is a matter of degree, and sometimes even cash will not do, as anyone who has ever tried to buy a bus ride with a fifty dollar bill will testify.

[5] The growth of the use of the credit card may have a significant effect on transactions balances over time. If everything could be purchased by merely showing a credit card, and if the bill for purchases could be timed to coincide with income receipts, then the individual need hold transactions balances only momentarily before turning them over to his creditors.

in the level of demand for transactions balances in the short run, although it may be significant over a long time span.

The amount of money held as transactions balances depends, therefore, primarily upon the level of expenditures since, as the pace of business activity grows, the larger will be the volume of transactions, in any period, and the larger the amount of cash balances needed for foreseeable expenses. In the forecasting model, however, prices are assumed constant; consequently, only changes in physical output can induce changes in the quantity of money demanded for transactions balances. Assuming that there is desired ratio between the quantity of money held for transactions purposes and the level of output, this relationship can then be expressed as the upward sloping line L_t in Fig. 6.1a. Thus, if the level of output is Y_1, then the quantity of money held for transactions purposes will be m_t^1.

2. Precautionary balances

Liquidity is required not only to match up inflows and outflows of money which are reasonably predictable, but to match up inflows of funds and unexpected demands for cash. The transactions motive is meant to cover the need to meet the normal expenses of running a household or firm. In addition, one can count on the fact that certain transactions will arise from time to time that are totally unexpected. There is no way of knowing when your child will fall into an open manhole, or your wife will mash the car fender, or the chef's best tie will fall into the vichyssoise. You do know, however, that demands will be made upon your money which you do not now foresee. Holding cash to meet these requirements which are unexpected in the specifics, but thoroughly foreseeable in general, is termed the *precautionary demand for money*.

As with transactions balances, the amount of money held as precautionary balances will be directly related to the level of output, since as the pace of economic activity quickens, the volume of contingency expenses tends to increase. In Fig. 6.1b, therefore, the relationship between the quantity of money held for precautionary purposes and the level of output is expressed as the upward sloping line L_p. Thus, if the level of output is Y_1, the quantity of money held for precautionary purposes is m_p^1.

3.   Speculative balances

There is further motive for holding money apart form the mere avoidance of the cost of converting placements to cash.   The rate of return on a placement varies with its price which in turn may vary through time.   Timing in the acquisition of placements, therefore, can affect the rate of return earned from financial assets.   In particular, once money has been converted to a financial asset, the opportunity to buy that asset sometime in the future at a lower price has been foregone.

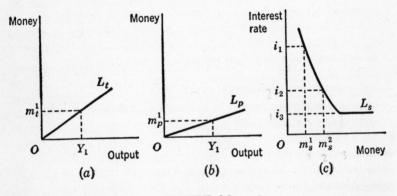

FIGURE 6.1.

For any negotiable bond, there is a direct relationship between its price and the effective interest rate.   For example, a United States Treasury bond which will mature in forty years may have a coupon rate of interest of 3 percent and a face value of $1,000.   Once the coupon rate of interest is printed on the bond it cannot change.   The Treasury will pay the bondholder, whoever he is, $30.00 per year until the bond matures, no matter what price the current bondholder has paid for the bond.   At maturity, the Treasury will redeem the bond from the bondholder at its face value of $1,000.   As long as the bond is outstanding it can be resold in the market at any price that buyers and sellers can agree upon.   It is because the price of the bond can fluctuate, that the effective interest rate to future bondholders can change.

Some bonds have no maturity date.   For example, British Consols are perpetual debt obligations of the British government.   For such bonds it is simple arithmetic to illustrate the relationship between the coupon rate of interest, the effective rate, and the price of the bond. Suppose a previously issued perpetual bond with a $1,000 face value has a coupon rate of interest of 3 percent. If the current rate of interest on newly issued perpetuities is 3 percent, then the previously issued bond would be as desirable as the new bonds. Consequently, holders of the old bonds can sell them for $1,000 each in the market.

If, however, the interest rate rose to 6 percent, then a newly issued bond of $1,000 face value would pay the bond holder $60.00 per year. Holders of the old bond, which still pays $30.00 per year, could induce buyers to purchase them, only if they were willing to sell at a market price of $500 (since $30.00 per annum on $500 is a 6 percent return).[6]

In the liquidity preference theory of interest rate determination, it is usually assumed, for purposes of simplifying the exposition, that perpetual, riskless bonds are the only alternative form of financial assets other than money in which unspent income may be held. (This convention will be adhered to until Chapter 13.) For a potential bond buyer who expects a rise in the rate of interest in the coming year, therefore, holding cash at present may be the most profitable course of action. If the interest earned during the interim between the time the bond is bought and the time the rate of interest is expected to rise is less than the fall in the market price of the asset, it is profitable to postpone purchase of the bond until its price falls. In other words, if an individual expects the rate of interest to rise at an annual rate which is greater than the current rate of interest, then it pays to hold cash in order to buy bonds at a lower price in the future. Holding money in anticipation of a rise in the rate of interest (i.e., an expected drop in future bond prices) is called the *speculative motive for holding money.*

The amount of money held as speculative balances will depend on the relationship between expectations as to the future rate of interest relative to the present rate. When interest rates are high the interest income foregone as a consequence of holding cash will be substantial.

---

[6] The arithmetic is considerably more complicated when the old bond has a maturity date, for then the present value of the bond must take into account not only the value of the future interest payments, but also the redemption payment (properly discounted) at maturity. The market price for this bond can be computed via equation (4.1).

Moreover, when bond yields are high the loss resulting from a possible further decline in bond prices is reduced in two ways. First, the higher the interest income the greater must be the future decline in the bond price in order for the loss in capital value to exceed the earnings. Secondly, and more importantly, if the rate of interest is thought to be high relative to what future rates are expected to be individuals will feel it unlikely that bond prices will fall. In Fig. 6.1c, the relationship between the rate of interest and the quantity of money held for speculative balances is represented by the curve L_s. Our analysis thus far has suggested that if the current rate of interest, say i_1, is high relative to the expected future rate, then the quantity of money held for speculative balances will be small, say m_s^1.

At very low rates of interest, on the other hand, the foregone income from holding cash instead of bonds is very small. Moreover, the potential cost of capital loss from holding a bond is very high. For example, if $1,000 is invested in a perpetual bond paying one percent per annum, then the interest earned is only $10.00 per year. However, if the going interest rate should rise to 1.1 percent the next week, the bond price would decline to $900, implying a capital loss of $100 if the bond must be sold. In addition, if it is believed that interest rates are low, then individuals will believe it is likely that bond prices will fall. Consequently, with any given set of expectations, the lower the rate of interest the more individuals will desire to hold speculative cash balances instead of holding bonds. Thus, if the interest rate is low, say i_2, then the quantity of money demanded for speculative purposes will be m_s^2 (in Fig. 6.1c).

It is usually agreed that at some low, but positive, rate of interest, say i_3, in Fig. 6.1c, the risk of capital loss is so high, while the opportunity cost of holding cash is so low, that demand for cash balances for speculative reasons becomes perfectly elastic, i.e., individuals will be totally unwilling to give up cash to obtain a bond paying such a low rate. When the interest rate is so low that the demand for speculative balances becomes infinite, then the economy is said to be in a *liquidity trap*. The highly suggestive term "trap" is used to connote that the rate of interest cannot be driven any lower, and that further stimuli to investment and employment via reductions in interest, are no longer possible.

In essence, the speculative motive indicates that an individual attempting to manage his assets in the most efficient way is subject to two types of risk: (1) income risk, and (2) capital risk. If an individual holds money he loses income but keeps his wealth intact. If he holds bonds he gains income but risks loss of capital. In an uncertain world both risks are vexatious and an individual will divide his wealth into money and bonds depending upon his disposition at the margin to bear income risks and capital risks. At each rate of interest, an individual will appraise the magnitude of each of these risks differently. Also, as the rate of interest varies, different individuals will appraise the magnitude of each of these risks differently. At each rate of interest, therefore, the public will disagree about the future course of the rate of interest. This disagreement will divide wealth holders into two groups—those who rush to buy bonds (the "bulls") and those who rush to sell bonds (the "bears"). The price of bonds will ultimately equate the demand for bonds by the bulls with the supply of bonds offered by the bears.

The total demand for money will be viewed as the sum of the transactions, precautionary, and speculative demands for money.

THE SUPPLY OF MONEY

For the society as a whole, the amount of money depends primarily upon the actions of the commercial banks and the monetary authority. The monetary authority can manipulate commercial bank reserves. Commercial banks may use their reserves for several purposes. Some portion (the actual fraction depending upon either law or custom) of these reserves will be held to back the banks' liabilities. (These reserves are the banks' equivalent of transactions and precautionary balances.) The remainder, i.e., excess reserves, are used to maximize bank profits. /A bank with excess reserves is faced with the same speculative liquidity decision that confronts individuals. / To hold reserves is to forego possible earnings based on the current rate of interest. As with individuals, if the rate of interest is expected to rise sufficiently in the future, the banks will hold their excess reserves rather than purchase debt securities. Alternatively, if bankers believe interest rates are high, they will want to use these reserves to make loans. Unlike individuals, however, when banks make loans they create additional demand deposits which increase the money supply. Thus, the actions of the monetary authority in creating commercial bank reserves in tandem with the actions of the commercial banks in creating demand deposits determines the supply of money.[7] At any point in time, we will assume that the supply of money has been exogenously determined by the banking system.[8]

THE DETERMINATION OF THE RATE OF INTEREST AND THE LEVEL OF OUTPUT

The banking system determines the supply of money, while the motives for holding cash balances determines the demand for money. The rate of interest brings the demand for money into equality with the supply of money. The interest rate will also affect the level of investment and therefore the level of output which, in turn, will feed back on the demand for transactions and precautionary balances. All these adjustments will be taking place simultaneously in the economy; but for expositional purposes it is necessary to break into this process at some point and to speak as if decisions which are really being made simultaneously occur in some sequence.

Let us start with a given quantity of money which exists in the system due to the decisions of the commercial banks and the monetary autho-

[7] Of course, there are additional factors which may affect the size of bank reserves, e.g., the public's desire to hold its money in the form of currency rather than demand deposits.

[8] The usual procedure of treating the liquidity motives of the nonbank public as the basis for the demand function for money, while treating the liquidity motives of commercial banks as the foundation for the supply function of money, attributes essentially the same motives to demand in the one case and to supply in the other. An alternative formulation would to be include commercial bank liquidity motives in the total demand for balances by including the commercial banks' holdings of excess reserves multiplied by the deposit-expansion coefficient in the speculative demand. For consistency, the supply of money would then have to be defined as the total money potential, i.e., the sum of currency existing plus demand deposits plus the maximum demand-deposits that the banking system could create if it were fully "loaned-up." See S. Weintraub, *An Approach to the Theory of Income Distribution*, Chilton, 1958, p. 163.

rity. Holders of this quantity of money must decide whether or not to keep their cash or acquire bonds. Given the level of output, they determine their transaction and their precautionary needs for cash. Now, what of the remaining quantity of money? Those individuals who hold money in excess of their transactions and precautionary needs and who feel that the rate of interest is sufficient to compensate them for their loss of liquidity, will seek to purchase bonds. Others who presently hold cash and some who hold bonds may expect bond prices to fall and prefer to hold cash. The public will form into two groups—the "bulls" and the "bears." The bulls will wish to buy bonds and the bears will want to sell bonds. If the bulls predominate, then prices of bonds will rise (interest rates will fall). With a fall in the rate of interest, given the marginal efficiency of capital schedule, entrepreneurs will increase real investment. Output will rise by some multiple of the increase in investment which, in turn, will generate an increase in the demand for transactions and precautionary balances. The increased demand for these balances, with a constant money supply, will bring upward pressure to bear on the rate of interest. This process will proceed until the economy eventually reaches a level of output and a rate of interest which will persist as long as the underlying determinants hold fast.

Algebraic solution

The simultaneity of the system is brought out by restating the model algebraically. We have the following system of equations:

The output identity,

$$Y \equiv C + I. \tag{6.5}$$

The consumption function,

$$C = a_1 + b_1 Y. \tag{6.6}$$

The marginal efficiency of capital schedule,

$$I = a_2 - b_2 r. \tag{6.7}$$

The demand for money schedule which is the sum of the demand functions for transactions, precautionary, and speculative balances, which, *outside of the liquidity trap*, may be written as[9]

$$m = \alpha_3 + (\beta_1 + \beta_2)Y - \beta_3 i. \qquad (6.8a)$$

This equation implies that the demand for money is an increasing function of the level of employment and a decreasing function of the rate of interest. In other words, if output rises then the demand for money for transactions and precautionary purposes will increase, while if the rate of interest increases (with a given set of expectations) the demand for speculative balances will decrease. The total demand for money will depend on both of these factors. Equation (6.8a) is applicable at any time except when the economy is in the liquidity trap. When the economy is in the liquidity trap, the demand for speculative balances becomes infinite, so that the demand for money can be expressed algebraically as

$$i = \alpha_2, \qquad (6.8b)$$

where α_2 is a constant.

Equations (6.6) to (6.8) are the behavioral determinants of the system. Several further equations are required to complete the system. Firstly, there is the condition that the rate of interest equals the rate of return of the marginal investment (r):

$$i = r. \qquad (6.9)$$

Secondly, the quantity of money is assumed to be exogenously determined:

$$m = \bar{m}, \qquad (6.10)$$

where $\bar{m}$ is the exogenously determined quantity of money.

Once $\bar{m}$ is set, the system can be solved for all the remaining unknowns (output, consumption, investment, the rate of interest, and the marginal efficiency of capital).

Economists have, however, found their comprehension of the system is improved by reducing the system to two equations in two unknowns.

---

[9] The transactions demand function is $m_t = \beta_1 Y$, the precautionary function is $m_p = \beta_2 Y$, and the speculative function is $m_s = \alpha_3 - \beta_3 i$. Combining these functions we obtain $m_t + m_p + m_s = m = (\beta_1 + \beta_2)Y + \alpha_3 - \beta_3 i$.

Equation (6.11) is formed by combining the output identity, the consumption function and marginal efficiency schedule:

$$Y = \left(\frac{1}{1 - b_1}\right)(a_1 + a_2 - b_2 r).\qquad(6.11)$$

Since from (6.9), $r = i$, therefore

$$Y = \left(\frac{1}{1 - b_1}\right)(a_1 + a_2 - b_2 i).\qquad(6.12)$$

Equation (6.12) traces out all values of output and interest compatible with the investment and consumption functions and summarizes what has been said about real transactions in commodities. Combining (6.10) with (6.8a) and rearranging terms[10] yields (6.13a); combining (6.10) with (6.8b) yields (6.13b). Either of these link the supply and demand for money together:

$$i = a_3 + b_3 Y - c_3 \overline{m};\qquad(6.13a)$$
$$i = \alpha.\qquad(6.13b)$$

Equation (6.13a) may be interpreted as follows: *if the money stock is constant*, then the rate of interest will vary directly with the level of output as the demand for transactions and precautionary balances increases, while, *at any level of gross output*, an increase in the quantity of money will lead to a decrease in the rate of interest as the additional money is absorbed into speculative balances. Equation (6.13b) indicates that at some positive rate of interest the demand for money (for speculative purposes) is infinite. Equation (6.13b) is applicable in the liquidity trap.

While (6.12) summarizes our view of the commodities markets, (6.13a) or (6.13b) summarizes our view of the money market.

The values of Y and i which satisfy both (6.12) and (6.13) (either a or b) reflect the interaction of the commodities and money markets. Output and interest are the determinates of the system, while the money supply, the demand for cash balances, the marginal efficiency of capital schedule, and the consumption function are its determinants.

---

[10] Letting $\dfrac{\beta_1 + \beta_2}{\beta_3} = b_3$, $\dfrac{\alpha_3}{\beta_3} = a_3$, and $\dfrac{1}{\beta_3} = c_3$, and rearranging terms, results in equation 13a.

Graphic solution

Further insight may be gained by a hypothetical example. Let

$$C = 10 + .5Y, \tag{6.6'}$$

$$I = 50 - 5.00r, \tag{6.7'}$$

$$i = .02 + .003Y - .0008\overline{m}, \tag{6.8a'}$$

$$i = .01, \tag{6.8b'}$$

$$\overline{m} = 150. \tag{6.10'}$$

Substituting (6.6') and (6.7') into (6.5) yields

$$Y = 60 + .5Y - 5.00r.$$

Rearranging terms,

$$Y = \left(\frac{1}{1 - .5}\right)(60 - 5.00r), \tag{6.11'}$$

or, making use of (6.9),

$$Y = \left(\frac{1}{1 - .5}\right)(60 - 5.00i). \tag{6.12'}$$

Substituting (6.10') into (6.8a') yields

$$i = -.10 + .003Y. \tag{6.13a'}$$

  In Fig. 6.2, equation (6.12') is plotted and labelled *CI*. Equation
(6.13a') is plotted as the curve L_1M in the same figure. This L_1M function envisages the possibility of the rate of interest falling as low as $-.10$.
In our verbal analysis, however, the point was made that the rate of
interest will not fall below some minimum positive level. Assume that
the minimum rate of interest is about 1 percent. Accordingly, at the
1 percent rate, (6.8b') (where $\alpha = .01$) is relevant. It is for this
reason that the L_1M function is drawn as a dotted line below the 1
percent level. The discontinuous curve L_2M more realistically describes the money market. Given the *CI* curve and the L_2M curve,
the resulting level of output is 55($= Y^*$), while the interest rate is
6.5 percent ($= i^*$).

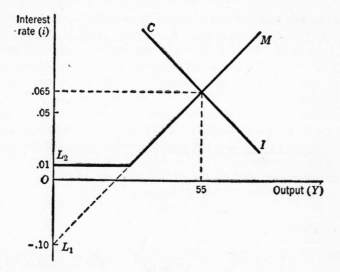

FIGURE 6.2.

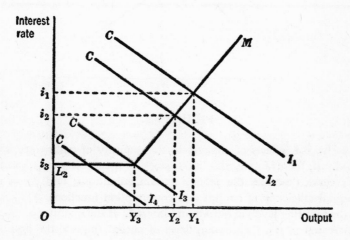

FIGURE 6.3.

Any change in the determinants of the system will yield a new Y^* and i^*. For example, let the CI_1 curve in Fig. 6.3 represent the initial relationship in the commodity markets which when taken with the L_2M schedule results in an output level and interest rate of Y_1 and i_1, respectively. If now we posit a decline in the consumption function, then the CI schedules shift downward to CI_2. As a consequence, output will decline to Y_2 while the rate of interest falls to i_2. If the CI curve were to decline to CI_3, then there would be a further drop in output to Y_3 and the rate of interest to i_3. At this point, however, the economy is on the boundary of the liquidity trap and any further downward shift in the CI function, say to CI_4, will reduce output but will leave the rate of interest unaffected.

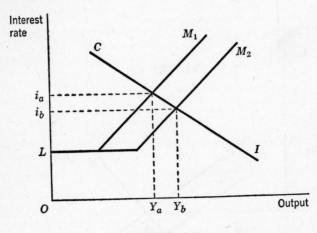

FIGURE 6.4.

In Fig. 6.4, effects of changes in the quantity of money are illustrated. If, for example, the initial stock of money was m_1, then the LM_1 curve describes the money market conditions; and given the marginal efficiency of capital and consumption functions, Y_a and i_a are the resulting levels of output and interest. If the quantity of money is increased to m_2, then at any level of output (outside the liquidity trap), the rate of interest is lower than before. Consequently, the LM curve shifts outward to LM_2, and the level of output rises to Y_b while the rate of interest falls to i_b.

Any change in the underlying determinants will affect the CI and/or the LM schedules. If, for example, the marginal efficiency of capital schedule rises as entrepreneurs become more optimistic, then the CI schedule would shift outward from CI_1 to CI_2 (in Fig. 6.5). At any given rate of interest, such as i_1, the corresponding output level (Y_2) on the CI_2 curve will be greater than the output level *at the same rate of interest* on the CI_1 curve (Y_1). The change in the level of output ($Y_2 - Y_1$) at any given rate of interest is, of course, equal to the change in the level of investment due to the shift in the marginal efficiency of capital schedule multiplied by the simple multiplier.

The actual change in the level of output, however, will be less than $Y_2 - Y_1$. When the marginal efficiency of capital schedule shifts up-

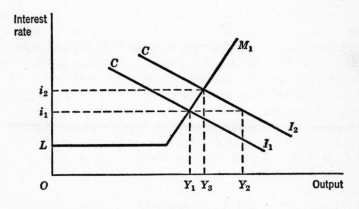

FIGURE 6.5.

ward, output increases and the demand for transactions and precautionary balances will increase. Thus, given the supply of money, there is upward pressure on the rate of interest. As the interest rate rises to i_2, the level of investment actually induced by the shift in the marginal efficiency of capital schedule will be less than if the interest rate remained unchanged. Consequently, the actual change in output (to the Y_3 level) will be less than it would have been had the interest rate remained constant.

Our present analysis indicates, therefore, that an implicit assumption of the simple multiplier analysis of Chapter 3 was that there was

monetary neutrality, that is, that the monetary authority always ad-
justs the supply of money to any changes in demand for cash balances,
so that the rate of interest remains unchanged. Normally, however,
we may expect that changes in spending will partly affect the level of
output and partly affect the rate of interest, so that the simple multiplier overstates the effect on output of a shift in the marginal efficiency
of capital schedule.

In summary, we note that the marginal efficiency of capital schedule
and the consumption function are the basic determinants of the *CI*
schedule, while the demand for cash balances and the supply of
money are the basic determinants of the *LM* curve. Any change in any
of the basic determinants will alter the level of output and the rate of
interest.

Upward shifts in the *CI* schedule may be a result of either an outward shift in the marginal efficiency of capital schedule because of an
improvement in the expected rates of return, or an increase in the consumption function because of a change in consumer tastes. Downward movements in the *CI* schedule will be due to either a decline in
the marginal efficiency of capital schedule or a decline in the consumption function.

The *LM* curve will shift outward if either the supply of money increases or the demand for cash balances declines; while the *LM* function will shift inwards if either the supply of money decreases or the
demand schedule for cash balances increases. Changes in the supply
of money will be the result of action of the monetary authority and the
commercial banks. Changes in the demand schedule for cash balances
will be due to a change in expectations about future rates of interest.

In general, any outward shift of the *CI* schedule will increase output
and the rate of interest, while an outward shift of the *LM* curve will
raise output and *lower* the rate of interest (except in the liquidity trap).

IMPLICATIONS FOR MONETARY POLICY

Monetary policy is that set of decisions and actions taken by the
monetary authority (usually the central bank) to affect aggregate
economic activity. The monetary authority can affect the level of

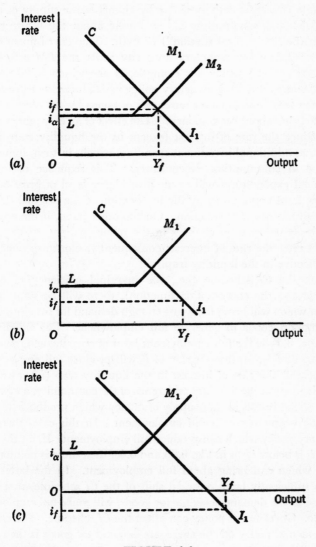

FIGURE 6.6.

aggregate economic activity either by changing the supply of money or by changing expectations of the public about the future rate of interest (i.e., by "moral suasion") or both. The *direct* impact of any policy taken by the monetary authority shifts the *LM* schedule.[11] An "easy money" policy, for example, is one which shifts the *LM* schedule outwards. Any monetary policy which increases the quantity of money (e.g., open market purchases of bonds by the central bank) tends to bring about "easy money." The effect of an easy money policy is to reduce the rate of interest (except in the liquidity trap) which stimulates additional investment spending, which, in turn, induces an increase in consumption expenditures. This sequence of induced additional expenditures will result in a higher level of gross output; the new level being given by the intersection of the original *CI* function with the new *LM* function. On the other hand, if the economy is in the liquidity trap, changes in the money supply, *ceteris paribus*, can not alter the rate of interest; consequently, monetary policy will be ineffective in the liquidity trap.

Given the *CI* schedule (i.e., the marginal efficiency of capital schedule and the consumption function), there will be some rate of interest which will bring forth just enough demand for investment and consumption goods to generate full employment. For example, in Fig. 6.6a, if Y_f is the full employment level of output, then, given the *CI* schedule CI_1, an interest rate of i_f will produce full employment. If i_f exceeds the rate of interest in the liquidity trap (i_α), as in Fig. 6.6a, then, given the liquidity preference of the community, a monetary policy which results in that supply of money which produces the LM_2 schedule would result in full employment. In this case, there is a monetary policy which can produce full employment. If, on the other hand, i_f is below i_α, as in Fig. 6.6b and 6.6c, then there is no monetary policy which can bring about full employment. In the latter case, only a sufficiently large outward shift of the *CI* schedule, that is, an increase in the demand schedule for goods, will make full employment possible. Government policy can affect the *CI* schedule. The effect of governmental policy on the aggregate demand for goods is the subject of the next chapter.

[11] It is conceivable that monetary policy might indirectly affect businessmen's state of confidence and therefore alter profit expectations. Under these circumstances, the *CI* schedule would be altered.

CHAPTER 7

Government and the level of output

FUNCTIONAL FINANCE

The preceding chapters are an abstract view of how an economy comes to produce aggregate private output in some year. Now, it is possible that gross private output, if left to the determinants thus far isolated would not be what the nation wants it to be. Output may be too large, or too small, or composed of the wrong things (where "too large," "too small," and "wrong" refer back to some national consensus about the ideal level and composition of output).

/ If an economy is to satisfy the national consensus by reaching the desired level of output, individuals may be required to take actions which are in conflict with their own self-interest. / A small manufacturer, for example, who plagued by his social conscience raises the salaries of his employees during a recession in order to stimulate spending, will soon find himself out of business and ineligible for unemployment compensation. Since individuals cannot be expected to act against their own self-interest, some goals can be achieved only by a coordinated effort on the part of the whole community; and normally only governments can mobilize such an effort. Broad powers have been given to governments to effectuate such coordination. These powers fall mainly into two categories: monetary powers and fiscal powers. This chapter is concerned only with fiscal policies.

Fiscal policies are governmental decisions taken with respect to receipts and expenditures. These policies involve making decisions concerning expenditures on goods and services, government transfer payments, tax revenues, and the public debt. Our concern in Part II has been with the level of aggregate output, so that this chapter will deal only with how government fiscal decisions affect the size of the gross output; but it is wise to remember that, with rare exceptions, government decisions to affect the size of the pie will have, at least implicitly, implications for what the pie will contain and how its pieces will be distributed.

That part of fiscal theory which is concerned solely with the relationship of government receipts and expenditures to the level of national output is called *functional finance*. The hope of those who favor functional finance is that spending and taxing, borrowing and the repayment of loans will all be undertaken *solely*, "to keep the total rate of spending in the country on goods and services, neither greater nor less than that rate which ... would buy all the goods that it is possible to produce."[1]

GOVERNMENT EXPENDITURES ON GOODS AND SERVICES

Both changes in the level of government purchases and the method of raising government funds will affect gross output. A rise in government purchases is, *ceteris paribus*, an equal increase in gross output. The source of the funds used by the government to purchase goods must also be considered, however, since different sources will have varying effects on the spending decisions of the private sector. In general, the main source of government funds is taxation. Governments, like households and firms, may also borrow. Both taxation and borrowing affect the spending patterns of other participants in the economy. These indirect consequences must also be considered in evaluating the impact of *changes* in government purchases on the level of output.

[1] A. P. Lerner, "Functional Finance and the Federal Debt," *A.E.A. Readings in Fiscal Policy*, A. Smithies and J. K. Butters, eds., Irwin, 1955, p. 469.

THE BALANCED BUDGET THEOREM:
A SIMPLE MODEL

Placing reliance upon functional finance opens many alternative routes to full employment. Three fundamental and alternative fiscal policies may be identified—although, in practice, a government normally will follow a course which will blend all three policies. These three are: (1) a change in tax receipts with government expenditures unchanged, (2) a change in government expenditures with tax receipts unchanged, and (3) simultaneous and equal changes in expenditures and revenues. While any one of these policies, if properly designed, can bring the economy to full employment, each will have a different impact on the size of the public debt, on the one hand, and on the extent to which government directly intervenes in the market as a buyer, on the other.

These thorny interrelationships which make policy matters so difficult can be usefully explored by starting from the following oversimplified algebraic model.

The output identity,

$$Y \equiv C + I + G, \tag{7.1}$$

where Y is gross output (or income), C is consumption spending, I is investment spending, and G is government purchases. The consumption function,

$$C = a + b(Y - T), \tag{7.2}$$

where b is the marginal propensity to consume, T is tax payments (or receipts) and $Y - T$ represents the disposable income of the private sector. If investment is assumed to be exogenously determined, then

$$I = \bar{I}, \tag{7.3}$$

where $\bar{I}$ is some fixed level of investment. Finally, government purchases are also assumed to be exogenously determined, so that

$$G = \bar{G}, \tag{7.4}$$

where $\bar{G}$ is some fixed level of government spending. Initially, it is assumed that T represents a level of tax payments which are fixed in absolute amount, i.e.,

$$T = \overline{T}. \tag{7.5}$$

(Such a tax, one which is independent of the level of economic activity, is not common, but poll taxes, head taxes, and even some property taxes are some possible examples.)

Substituting (7.2) through (7.5) into (7.1) and rearranging terms reduces the system to the single equation:

$$Y = \left(\frac{1}{1-b}\right)(a - b\overline{T} + \overline{I} + \overline{G}). \tag{7.6}$$

If there is an exogenous increase in government spending with no increase in taxes, then the change in output would be given by[2]

$$\Delta Y = \left(\frac{1}{1-b}\right)\Delta G, \tag{7.7}$$

where $\left(\frac{1}{1-b}\right)$ is the simple multiplier. On the other hand, if there is an exogenous increase in taxes with no increase in government purchases of goods and services, then the change in output is given by[3]

$$\Delta Y = \left(\frac{-b}{1-b}\right)\Delta T, \tag{7.8}$$

where $\left(\frac{-b}{1-b}\right)$ is called the tax multiplier since it relates the change

---

[2] With a change in government spending (ΔG), the new level of output $(Y + \Delta Y)$ becomes

$$Y + \Delta Y = \left(\frac{1}{1-b}\right)(a - b\overline{T} + \overline{I} + \overline{G} + \Delta G). \tag{7.6a}$$

Subtracting (7.6) from (7.6a) yields (7.7).

[3] With a change in taxes (ΔT), the new level of output becomes

$$Y + \Delta Y = \left(\frac{1}{1-b}\right)\{a - b(\overline{T} + \Delta T) + \overline{I} + \overline{G}\}. \tag{7.6b}$$

Subtracting (7.6) from (7.6b) yields (7.8).

in output to a given change in taxes. Since $1 > b > 0$, the absolute value of the simple multiplier in (7.7) is larger than the absolute value of the tax multiplier in (7.8).

The economic rationale for the different magnitudes of these multipliers is readily illustrated by a hypothetical example. Suppose, for example, government expenditures are increased by $10 billion. If the marginal propensity to consume is .8 then (7.7) indicates that total output will increase by $50 billion. Ten billion of this increase is due to the initial government purchases, and the additional $40 billion is the result of increased consumption resulting from the increase in disposable income. On the other hand, suppose taxes were reduced by $10 billion. Equation (7.8) indicates that total output will rise by only $40 billion. The initial tax cut of $10 billion does not affect gross output but does increase disposable income which will generate an increase in consumption spending.

If taxes and government expenditures are both simultaneously increased by the same amount, then the resultant increase in output will be equal to the rise in government spending. In other words, adding (7.7) to (7.8) yields

$$\Delta Y = \left(\frac{1}{1-b}\right)\Delta G - \left(\frac{b}{1-b}\right)\Delta T. \qquad (7.9)$$

If $\Delta G = \Delta T$, (7.9) can be rewritten as

$$\Delta Y = \left(\frac{1}{1-b} - \frac{b}{1-b}\right)\Delta G,$$

or

$$\Delta Y = \left(\frac{1-b}{1-b}\right)\Delta G.$$

Therefore,

$$\Delta Y = \Delta G.$$

This result, that an increase in government spending on goods and services when matched by an increase in tax revenues raises output by an amount equal to the rise in government spending, is known as the *balanced budget multiplier*. The balanced budget multiplier, therefore, has a value of unity no matter what the marginal propensity to consume. This surprising result stems from a host of hidden assumptions. These assumptions include: (1) the marginal propensity to consume out of income of the people who pay the tax is the same as the marginal propensity to consume of those who receive the government expenditures as income, (2) as income expands there is no redistribution of income, or if income redistribution occurs, then the marginal propensity to consume of the gaining and losing groups are the same, (3) the tax payment is a fixed absolute amount, (4) there is no foreign trade, (5) there is unemployment, (6) wages and prices are constant, (7) there is no concomitant change in interest rates or investment, and (8) the government expenditures are on new goods and services. The number of assumptions and the extent to which they depart from reality clearly suggest that the balanced budget multiplier ought not be taken literally. However, the balanced budget multiplier highlights some of the considerations inherent in all employment policy decisions.

POLICY IMPLICATIONS OF THE BALANCED BUDGET THEOREM

Unfortunately, the balanced budget multiplier is a name which fails to emphasize those crucial aspects of fiscal policy which it illustrates. While it is true that the balanced budget multiplier demonstrates that the government can bring the economy to any output level without unbalancing its budget, it is more important to learn from the balanced budget multiplier that the impact of a tax is likely to be smaller than the impact of a change in government purchases. Consequently, decisions on the level of taxation, the level of government expenditures, the size of the public debt, and the level of national product are intertwined, and it is impossible to make judgments about one of these facets of the problem without making implicit judgments about the others.

Once government has accepted that its major economic function is to act as the balancing mechanism to assure that total spending in the economy is just sufficient to purchase all the goods that the economy is able to produce, then it is obvious that fiscal policy should be judged by its effects on aggregate demand and not by the resulting balance or imbalance of the budget.

Until further studies provide us with enough evidence to estimate the "true" magnitude of the balanced budget multiplier, however, all we may do is to conclude that changes in taxes, changes in spending, and concomitant changes in taxes and spending are alternative ways of achieving the same objective, although the magnitudes of the effects per dollar of change differ.

Faced with the prospect of unemployment, the government can increase effective demand by increasing government expenditures and taxes by the same amount. Alternatively, the government can leave expenditures alone and run a deficit by cutting taxes, thereby increasing effective demand and the public debt. Or the government can raise expenditures leaving tax receipts constant, thereby increasing output, while running a deficit and increasing the public debt. Because the multiplier on taxes is less than the multiplier on government purchases, for a given desired rise in output, a policy of merely cutting taxes will involve the largest increase in the public debt. An equal increment in taxes and government purchases to produce some given increment in output will involve the largest increases in taxes and expenditures, but will not increase the public debt at all. Increasing government purchases alone will modestly increase government expenditures for any given increase in output and modestly increase the public debt.

For example, suppose the government estimates that in the coming year national output will be $50 billion short of that level which would be required to generate full employment. If the marginal propensity to consume is .8, then it is obvious from (7.7) that a rise in government expenditures (and in the government debt) of $10 billion would carry the economy to full employment. Alternatively, (7.8) says that the government could achieve full employment by reducing taxes (and increasing the public debt) by $12.5 billion. Finally, the economy would reach full employment if government tax receipts and government expenditures were both raised by $50 billion. The choice among these alternatives should rest on the national consensus about the relative merits and demerits of spending, taxing, and the size of the public debt.

Tax receipt as a variable

The model thus far has assumed government tax receipts to be a constant regardless of national output. In most countries, however, tax payments rise and fall with the level of national output. To analyze the effects of a tax system in which receipts vary with the level of output, it is only necessary to substitute (assuming a simple proportional income tax),

$$T = rY, \tag{7.10}$$

where r is the tax rate, for (7.5). Substituting all the functional relationships into the identity, we obtain,

$$Y = a + b(Y - rY) + \bar{I} + \bar{G}.$$

Rearranging terms,

$$Y = \left(\frac{1}{1 - (1 - r)b} \right)(a + \bar{I} + \bar{G}),$$

and

$$\Delta Y = \left(\frac{1}{1 - (1 - r)b} \right) \Delta G.$$

A change in any of the exogenous variables, therefore, will still lead to a multiple change in output; but this multiplier of a change in government spending is smaller than the corresponding multiplier when taxes were fixed in absolute amount, because any rise in gross income when taxes are variable is a smaller rise in disposable income than when taxes are fixed. As a result, increments in consumption spending for a given increment in gross income will be less when taxes depend upon output than when tax receipts are constant.

In addition to a change in any of the exogenous variables, any change in the tax rate will affect the level of output, since the magnitude of the multiplier will be altered. A reduction in r, will increase disposable income out of any level of gross output, and therefore will induce additional consumption expenditures out of each level of gross output. Consequently, a reduction in the tax rate with no change in the level of government expenditures will lead to a rise in gross income (which is taxable). It is conceivable that when all direct and indirect effects are taken into account, gross income will be so large that actual tax receipts may not decline at all, despite the lower tax rate. Actual tax revenues will increase, of course, if the rise in gross income is proportionately larger than the proportional decline in the tax rate. Of course, a reduction in tax rates will normally be accompanied by a reduction in tax receipts. What is important is that the change in actual tax revenues which will result from a tax cut cannot be computed until allowance is made for the stimulating effect that the tax cut will have on the level of economic activity.

With a progressive tax instead of a simple proportional tax, the magnitude of the effects of a tax cut are even more complex; although, in general, the direction of results will be the same, while the increase in gross output is likely to be smaller.

A MORE GENERAL VIEW OF FISCAL POLICY

A model which contained all the economic ramifications of government taxation and expenditures policies would be considerably more complex than any considered thus far. For example, one important additional distinction which must be made concerns the different impact on output of government spending as opposed to government transfer payments. A transfer payment is a payment made without concomitant production of either new goods or services. Suppose, for example, that a state government declares a $100 bonus to all of its citizens who are war veterans. Suppose further that the bonus is to be financed by an increase in the state cigarette tax of two cents per pack. The result is to transfer income from cigarette smokers to veterans, but gross output remains unchanged. (Of course, the largest net transfers will be from cigarette smoking nonveterans to noncigarette smoking veterans.) Since a government transfer payment is merely a negative tax, the multiplier directly associated with the transfer payment is of the same magnitude but has the opposite sign as the tax multiplier. Thus the multiplier effects of the additional cigarette tax and the veterans' bonus offset each other so that there is no change in gross output.

Compare this situation with one in which the government decides to stockpile cough drops, financing these purchases in the same way as the veterans' bonus. Both the government purchases of cough drops and transfer payments to veterans are government expenditures, but the former involves new production and therefore is an addition to national output, while the veterans' bonus does not contribute to output directly. Thus in the cough drop example, the balanced budget multiplier of unity is applicable, while in the veterans' bonus case, there is no resultant multiplier effects.

A second very important complication derives from the fact that changes in government policies may lead to changes in the underlying determinants of the system. A change in receipts or expenditures policy may alter the distribution of income and therefore alter the slope and/or the intercept of the consumption function. Governmental policy may affect profit expectations and therefore have an impact on the marginal efficiency of capital schedule, and it may affect the demand for cash balances, and even the quantity of money.

In general, fiscal policy will affect the shape and position of the consumption function if these policies alter the personal distribution of income. For example, if a fiscal act were to have the effect of transferring income from the rich to the poor, and if the marginal propensity to consume were higher for the low income groups, then the aggregate marginal propensity to consume would rise.

The most important issues, however, relate to the effects of fiscal policy on the level of investment. For example, will accelerated depreciation tax allowances[4] increase the profitability of investment? Do accelerated depreciation allowances reduce the costs of obtaining finance? Will accelerated depreciation allowances improve the psychological relationship between government and business and thereby create a state of confidence on the part of businessmen which will shift the marginal efficiency of capital schedule outwards? These questions are not easily answered. Similar questions can be raised about any other tax proposal or government spending policy, since the ramifications are always widely dispersed and difficult to perceive. This example of a change in depreciation policy merely illustrates the difficulties of appraising the effect of governmental policies on the marginal efficiency of capital schedule.[5]

[4] The Internal Revenue Service determines the rate at which firms depreciate their capital stock for tax purposes. Since depreciation allowances are an expense, an increase in depreciation constitutes a reduction in taxable income.

[5] It has been argued that an increase in government expenditures (with tax receipts unchanged) can serve a "pump-priming" function. The advocates of pump-priming argue that the effect of government spending will be not only to stimulate additional consumption and therefore raise the level of gross output, but also to encourage additional private investment as economic activity increases.

Fiscal policies may also affect the rate of interest. An increase in government expenditures will, *ceteris paribus*, raise output and increase the demand for transactions and precautionary cash balances. If the central bank anticipates and looks with favor upon this expansion in economic activity, it will create enough additional money so as to assure that the rate of interest remains unchanged. If, however, the central bank looks upon this expansion as potentially inflationary and therefore undesirable, it will not accommodate the increase in money demand. The consequences of this clash within the government will be to produce a rise in interest rates which will retard private investment spending. The outcome may be further complicated if increased government activity heightened the fear of socialism within the business community, for this would drive the marginal efficiency of capital schedule downward.

The ultimate effect of changes in spending and taxation will depend, therefore, not only on their direct impact on output, but also on their efficacy in stimulating additional consumption, in altering the state of confidence of the community and, in turn, investment decisions, and in varying the liquidity preference of the community. Accommodating actions on the part of the monetary authority are clearly desirable if there is to be effective fiscal policy.

In general, we may expect that an increase in government spending or a reduction in taxes is likely to encourage additional investment and consumption expenditures, so that the resulting increment in output will exceed the initial change in taxes or spending. Surely in the absence of cataclysmic expectations of social revolution, the ultimate increase in output should be substantial, for the jingling of the cash register, as additional sales are made, will whet entrepreneurial appetites for further profits.

AUTOMATIC VERSUS DISCRETIONARY FISCAL POLICY

So far, the discussion has implied that functional finance decisions are made anew everytime the level of economic activity varies. Government receipts and expenditures will, however, vary as the level of national output changes, even if no new legislative or executive actions are undertaken. For example, if the level of economic activity falls, then receipts from incomes and sales taxes will fall while expenditures on unemployment compensation will rise automatically. That legislation which has the predetermined effect of altering government expenditures and receipts in a way which tends to offset changes in the level of private spending is called an *automatic stabilizer*. The most important automatic stabilizers are the income tax and unemployment compensation. In each of these cases, as national output rises tax receipts will tend to rise while unemployment benefits paid out will fall, so that the ability of the private sector to expand its purchases is partially restrained. If the economy turns down, on the other hand, tax receipts will fall off while benefits paid out will increase, and, as a result, purchasing power in the private sector will fall less than otherwise and therefore private purchases will tend to decline less than otherwise. Although these and other stabilizers impart some stability to the economy, their magnitudes, as presently constituted, are not large enough to guarantee perfect stability at high levels of economic activity.

Advocates of functional finance would prefer automatic stabilizers if it were possible to design a set of such stabilizers which would assure that departures from high levels of activity were brief. Tailoring fiscal policy to the events of the moment (discretionary stabilization policy) has proved difficult to accomplish since, (1) it requires being able to make accurate projections of the future, (2) it requires convincing legislators to act solely on the basis of the priority of stability among alternative economic and social goals, (3) it requires agreement on the part of economists as to what appropriate policy is, and finally (4) it requires convincing the legislature that these policies are the appropriate ones. Up to now, these conditions have not been met, and since at present the automatic stabilizers are not sufficient to assure full employment, there is little justification for believing that functional finance has or will become the guiding principle of free world legislatures. This conjecture, and the many other considerations which ought be treated in a full discussion of public finance are left to books wholly devoted to that most important of subjects.

CHAPTER 8

The level of income and foreign trade

The analysis thus far has assumed a closed economy, i.e., an economy in which its residents do not have any transactions with residents of other nations. Allowance must now be made for the fact that individuals in the home economy will trade with individuals in other nations, and the analysis of changes in the level of domestic output must be modified to take account of these external transactions.

The addition of foreign purchasers of domestically produced goods simply adds another component to the aggregate demand function. The output of the domestic economy depends not only upon the sales of domestically produced goods and services to consumers, businessmen, and domestic governments, but sales to foreigners as well. Foreigners will buy domestically produced goods when they cannot purchase the same goods elsewhere at a lower delivered price. Foreign purchases, therefore, depend upon international price differences. Since we assume, in the forecasting model, that domestic and foreign prices do not vary with changes in output, it can be assumed initially that the total level of foreign purchases in the home country (i.e., exports) are exogenously determined. Exports, in summary, adds to the domestic aggregate demand function.

In Chapters 3, 4, 6, and 7, when total spending by consumers, businessmen, and governments was discussed, no distinction was made between spending on domestically produced goods and spending on goods produced in other countries. In an open economy, however, it is only the spending on domestically produced goods which should enter into the domestic aggregate demand function, since the demand for imports does not lead directly to a demand for the nation's output.

Expenditures on imports must, therefore, be deducted from the total spending behavior of these three domestic spending groups. Consequently, the aggregate demand function is obtained by adding up the total spending functions of consumers, businessmen, and governments, and then deducting the import spending schedules of these groups, and finally adding foreign purchases.

For the moment, exports will be considered to be exogenously determined. Imports, however, must be taken as endogenously determined, even in the absence of any price change, since the volume of imports depends directly upon the level of domestic output. With increases in income, consumption of both domestic and foreign produced goods will increase. Accordingly, for the economy as a whole, there is a propensity to import, and, by analogy with consumption behavior, there is a marginal propensity to import. The *marginal propensity to import*, which measures the change in total imports which accompanies a change in real gross domestic income, will normally be less than unity. For simplicity, the marginal propensity to import is assumed to be constant.

The marginal propensity to import has important implications for both the level of domestic output and the level of output in the rest of the world. Taking the effect on world output first, since the marginal propensity to import exceeds zero, any increase in domestic output will increase imports. If exports are constant, then the country's balance of trade (its exports of goods and services minus its imports) will be altered. (A rise in imports relative to exports is said to cause a deterioration in the balance of trade.) The increase in domestic imports implies that exports by the rest of the world must have risen, so that the output in the rest of the world has increased. The effect on domestic output will require a more extended discussion, to which we now turn.

FOREIGN TRADE AND THE MULTIPLIER ASSUMING EXPORTS ARE CONSTANT

If the marginal propensity to import is greater than zero, it will tend to reduce the magnitude of simple multiplier effects on the domestic output level. In other words, with the opportunity to consume goods from abroad as well as to consume domestically produced goods, it can be anticipated that some of any exogenous increase in income will be spent abroad and the spending multiplier in an open economy will not be as large as it would be in a closed economy.

Suppose the economy is initially at a low level of domestic activity. Assume that for some reason the marginal efficiency of capital schedule shifts outward while the monetary authority takes whatever action is necessary to maintain the domestic rate of interest. As a result, real investment spending will increase. If the additional investment expenditures are spent entirely on domestically produced capital goods, then the level of gross domestic output will rise *pari passu* with the investment spending. This initial rise in domestic income will induce additional consumption expenditures (based on the marginal propensity to consume), but some of this additional consumption will be on imports (as shown by the marginal propensity to import). The upshot of all this is that the second round of domestic income generation is not equal to the additional consumption expenditures; rather, it is equal to additional consumption spending minus additional import purchases. Consequently, the third round of domestic spending will be less than otherwise since all of the second round consumption expenditures did not go into generating domestic income. On each round, additional domestic purchases will, therefore, be less than they would be in a closed economy. In other words, the extent to which an increase in exogenous spending will raise domestic output depends upon the marginal propensity to purchase *domestic* goods. Algebraically, the change in real output (ΔY) resulting from an exogenous change in domestic investment (ΔI) is given by

$$\Delta Y = \left[\frac{1}{1 - (b - p)}\right] \Delta I, \qquad (8.1)$$

where b is the marginal propensity to consume, and p is the marginal propensity to import. The term $b - p$ is the marginal propensity to purchase domestically produced goods.

It is expected that b is equal to or greater than p, i.e., that additional imports are either less than or at most equal to additional consumption. If b equals p, then this multiplier equals one, as all the additional consumption spending is on imports and does not, therefore, generate additional income in the domestic consumer goods industries.[1] If b exceeds p, which will be the normal case, then the multiplier will be greater than unity but less than it would be in a closed economy.

THE MULTIPLIER WHEN EXPORTS ARE A VARIABLE

An increase in domestic output will lead to an increase in imports which will imply an increase in the real income of the rest of the world. Domestic exports will rise as a consequence of a rise in imports, since, as the level of gross income of the rest of the world rises, foreigners will, in all likelihood, increase their purchases of domestically produced products in accordance with *their* marginal propensity to import from the domestic economy. This increase in domestic exports will induce a further increase in the level of domestic activity which, in turn, increases the demand for imports and the level of activity abroad. These repercussions will continue to have further ramifications on both the domestic output level and the output of the rest of the world; but since the marginal propensities involved at home and abroad are less than one, the magnitudes of spending in each succeeding round will diminish until, ultimately, new levels of output are established at home and abroad.

Although it is possible to formulate algebraic statements for the multiplier taking into account foreign repercussions, a host of unrealistic assumptions are necessary and many different situations, each resulting in a different algebraic expression, must be hypothecated, so that there is little point in presenting these alternative algebraic formulations here.[2]

In essence, multiplier analysis of an open economy suggests that any change in output at home or abroad is likely to have an impact on the domestic level of economic activity. The larger the domestic marginal propensity to consume and/or the smaller the domestic

[1] The increase in domestic output is due to the increase in purchases from the domestic investment goods industries. If we had assumed that some of the initial investment expenditures went to buy foreign produced goods, then the domestic income expansion would have to be reduced accordingly.

[2] Those readers who wish to search out many of the possible multiplier relationships should see F. Machlup, *International Trade and the National Income Multiplier*, Blakiston, 1943.

marginal propensity to import, the larger the multiplier effects will be. Moreover, a change in any exogenous variable at home or abroad will have some impact on domestic output. The importance of this impact will vary from country to country depending on the relative importance of the foreign sector in each economy.

In a country such as the United States, where the marginal propensity to import is likely to be low, foreign trade effects will have a small impact on output. In the United Kingdom, on the other hand, the marginal propensity to import is large, and therefore foreign trade has a much greater impact on the level of output. The actual impact of increases in spending on the level of output of any country will depend on the complex interrelationships of the marginal propensities to consume and to import at home and abroad.

LIMITATION OF THIS ANALYSIS

The most serious limitation of the foregoing analysis lies in the assumption of constant domestic and foreign product prices. Since the "raison d'être" for foreign trade is the difference in relative prices among countries, a theory that attempts to analyze the effects of foreign trade is seriously hampered by a constant price assumption. We will again turn our attention to the effect of foreign trade on the multiplier in Chapter 14 after prices have been introduced into the model.

FOREIGN TRADE, FOREIGN EXCHANGE, AND PUBLIC POLICY

With our present analytical tools it is possible to show why domestic and foreign economic policies may conflict.

The cost to the residents of country A of a unit of country B's money, i.e., *the rate of exchange*, depends on the supply and demand for each currency. Foreign currency is required by domestic residents whenever they must pay for imports or whenever they wish to make loans to foreigners, while domestic currency is required by foreigners either to pay for domestic exports or to make loans to domestic residents. Any change in the balance of trade (or any net change in lending between the two economies) will alter the demand relative to the supply of foreign exchange. It has already been noted that an expansion of the level of domestic activity will lead to a deterioration in the balance of trade. As imports grow relative to exports, the demand for foreign exchange will increase relative to the supply, putting pressure on the exchange rate. If the governments concerned do not intervene, then the exchange rate will fall, so that with the same internal prices at home and abroad, foreign goods will become more expensive at home, while domestic goods will become cheaper abroad. As a consequence of this change in the exchange rate, the marginal propensity to import would decline, while exports would increase; as a result, more of the spending repercussions would be kept at home.

Most nations, however, are committed to maintaining a fixed rate of exchange either because (1) they are committed to protecting the international gold standard, or (2) the government desires to avoid undue speculative activity in foreign exchange since such activity may disrupt normal trade patterns. If it is national policy to increase output, then any policy pursued in order to increase the level of domestic spending will have the undesirable side effect of leading to a deterioration in the balance of trade and downward pressure on the exchange rate. The government may therefore be caught between incompatible objectives—the desire to increase the domestic output and the desire to maintain a stable exchange rate.

If the objective is to maintain the exchange rate, then the monetary authority is likely to raise the domestic rate of interest in order to stimulate foreigners to lend domestically and to discourage residents from lending to foreigners. As a result, it is hoped that the demand for domestic currency will increase. With the increase in the domestic rate of interest, however, domestic investment and therefore (via the multiplier) domestic output will decline. This decline in domestic activity will further strengthen the exchange rate by inducing a decline in imports. Thus, exchange rate stability can be maintained by reducing the level of domestic output. If, on the other hand, however, the domestic country pursues a public policy of expansion, it will result in an increase in output of the domestic economy, and via the marginal propensity to import, will lead to an increase in the output of the rest of the world which will have further expansionary ramifications on domestic output. Nevertheless, demand and supply of the domestic and foreign currencies will be altered, and the exchange rate will be affected.

When these two public policies prove to be incompatible, then one must be sacrificed if the other is to be obtained. Which policy is to be sacrificed involves a value judgment on the part of the community.

For example, recently the United States has been faced with the problem that unemployment persists at high levels, and, at the same time, it has been difficult to prevent the quantities demanded from exceeding the quantities supplied of foreign exchange at the existing exchange rates. The international problem has been met, in the main, by the United States selling gold to foreigners in exchange for their excess dollars. In addition, attempts have been made to encourage foreigners to lend their dollars to Americans by maintaining a high domestic rate of interest. But a high domestic rate of interest discourages domestic private investment and exacerbates the unemployment problem. On the other hand, any domestic fiscal policy which stimulates economic activity will, via the marginal propensity to import, cause a deterioration in the balance of trade. Of course, raising import tariffs and/or restricting imports via import quotas would (assuming no retaliatory policies by foreign nations) contribute simultaneously to the solution of both the international and the domestic economic problems faced by the United States. Such a policy would, however, be a severe blow to the efficient allocation of world resources and to free world politics. Under these circumstances, it is clear that the policy choices are difficult and must be resolved in accordance with national priorities.

PART III

AN EQUILIBRIUM MODEL OF EMPLOYMENT,
OUTPUT, AND PRICES

CHAPTER 9

Aggregate supply

In this part of the book an aggregate equilibrium model will be developed. In the forecasting model developed in Part II, supply aspects were suppressed while aggregate demand was emphasized. In Part III both aggregate supply and aggregate demand will be incorporated into an equilibrium model.[1] This model will view the economy as being driven by two innately countervailing forces: (1) short-run profit maximization by entrepreneurs which underlies supply conditions, and (2) utility maximization by consumers and long-run profit maximization by entrepreneurs which form the foundation of aggregate demand. In most circumstances, this interaction of sellers and buyers will tend to create a situation which neither side will act to change, that is, a stable equilibrium results.

In order to develop the equilibrium model, some of the concepts developed in Part II must be redefined, and one new major concept, the aggregate supply function, will be developed. In Chapter 9 the aggregate supply function will be developed. In Chapter 10 the aggregate demand function will be redefined and the equilibrium solution obtained.

THE AGGREGATE SUPPLY FUNCTION

The aggregate supply function relates the number of workers that entrepreneurs would want to hire to each level of expected total

[1] Much of the analysis of Part III rests upon S. Weintraub's, *An Approach to the Theory of Income Distribution*, Chilton, 1958. See also P. Davidson, "More on the Aggregate Supply Function," *Economic Journal*, 72, 1962.

revenue. Entrepreneur's expectations of total revenue will depend upon the market price they expect to receive from selling the output produced by these workers. In short, the aggregate supply function links expected sales revenue to employment. If businessmen expect sales to rise, they will hire more workers. Expectations of sales changes and changes in employment are directly related. In a market economy in which goods are typically produced in anticipation of sales, the aggregate supply function describes a very realistic relationship.

Since all hiring decisions occur at the level of the individual business firm, it is the theory of the firm which provides the foundation for the aggregate supply function. In the following section, the aggregate supply function will be derived from the supply curve of the firm.

DERIVING THE AGGREGATE SUPPLY FUNCTION

Assumptions of the equilibrium model

It is best to list the assumptions underlying the equilibrium model at the outset. These suppositions are common to most short-run equilibrium models, although they are often not explicitly stated. These assumptions are, (1) a purely competitive, closed economy, with profit maximizing entrepreneurs, (2) a constant money-wage rate, (3) a homogeneous labor force as the only variable factor of production, and (4) fully integrated firms which have a given stock of equipment and a given technology. [2] These simplifying assumptions will be relaxed in the final section of this chapter to suggest how alternative assumptions will modify the aggregate supply function.

The supply curve of the firm

Each entrepreneur will hire that quantity of labor which, in combination with his existing plant and equipment, will be most efficient. For any level of output, therefore, the number of hired workers will be the least that technology allows. The relationship between the efficient utilization of workers and the resulting output is the total

---

[2] A fully integrated firm is one which carries on all the production processes from the raw material stage to the retail stage.

product function. This function typically has the shape shown by the curve *TP* in Fig. 9.1a. From the total product curve, a relationship between increments in output and increments in labor, i.e., the marginal physical productivity of labor, which is shown as the curve *M* in Fig. 9.1a, can be derived. The essential characteristic of the marginal productivity curve is that as labor is added to the stock of capital there

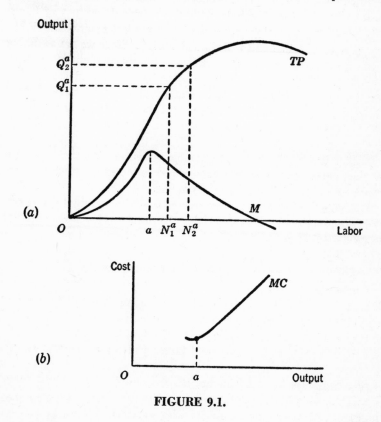

FIGURE 9.1.

is a point (*a* in Fig. 9.1a) beyond which increments in labor yield smaller and smaller increments in output, that is, eventually there are diminishing returns to labor.

The increase in cost associated with an increase in output is called *marginal cost*, and, when labor is the only variable input, is equal to the money-wage rate divided by the marginal product of labor:

$$MC = \frac{w}{M},\tag{9.1}$$

where MC is marginal cost, w is the money-wage rate, and M is the marginal product of labor.   Given a constant money-wage rate, marginal cost varies inversely with the marginal product of labor. When output and employment of the firm exceeds the point of diminishing returns, marginal cost will rise (Fig. 9.1b). Since we are assuming profit maximizing firms which operate in purely competitive markets, each firm will choose to produce at that level of output (and hire a certain quantity of labor) at which market price equals marginal cost.[3] Consequently, the marginal cost curve of the firm is the firm's supply curve. That is, the marginal cost curve of the firm, where it is above the average variable cost curve, indicates the quantity the firm will be willing to sell at each price. Since the marginal cost curve is upward sloping, entrepreneurs will be encouraged to increase output and employment only if they expect prices to rise.

Once the level of output is determined from the marginal cost curve, the entrepreneur can then determine the number of workers required to produce that output by referring to the total product curve.

The industry supply curve and aggregate supply

Given the above assumptions, the industry short-run supply curve is easily determined. It is simply the lateral summation of the marginal cost curve of each firm in the industry. The supply curve for industry A is shown in Fig. 9.2. It represents the alternative collective offerings of output by the entrepreneurs of industry A for alternative market prices.

The variables involved in the industry supply curve are different from those used in the aggregate supply function. The industry supply function relates output quantities with expected market prices; the aggregate supply function, on the other hand, relates expected total revenue (i.e., output multiplied by expected market prices) to employment. The conversion of the industry supply curve to the aggregate

---

[3] In pure competition firms will always operate in the region of increasing marginal costs.

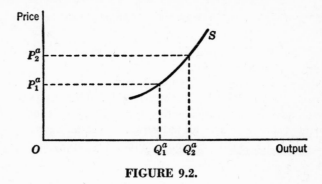

FIGURE 9.2.

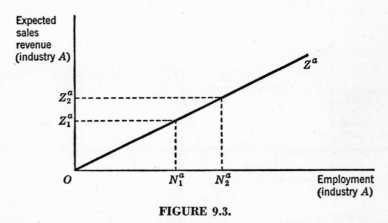

FIGURE 9.3.

supply curve may easily be accomplished with the aid of the total product curve of each industry.

Given industry A's supply curve in Fig. 9.2, if the entrepreneurs of that industry expect a price of P_1^a, they will be willing to produce Q_1^a units of output, and will expect total revenue Z_1^a, which is equal to $P_1^a Q_1^a$. To produce Q_1^a output, a certain number of workers will have to be hired. If the total product curve of industry A is represented by TP in Fig. 9.1a, then to produce Q_1^a output, N_1^a workers will have to be hired. Consequently, if entrepreneurs in industry A expect total revenue of Z_1^a, they will hire N_1^a workers (Fig. 9.3).

Similarly, if businessmen expect the price P_2^a to rule in the market, they will maximize profits by producing Q_2^a output which will necessitate the hiring of N_2^a workers. Anticipated total sales revenue would be Z_2^a which equals $P_2^a Q_2^a$. Thus, an expected revenue-employment curve for industry A can be derived which relates expected total revenue to employment in the industry as in Fig. 9.3.

An expected revenue-employment function may be derived in the same way for each industry in the economy. The aggregate supply function is obtained by aggregating the industry expected revenue-employment functions over all industries. Thus, an aggregate supply function, Fig. 9.4, is derived from the industry supply curves. If the

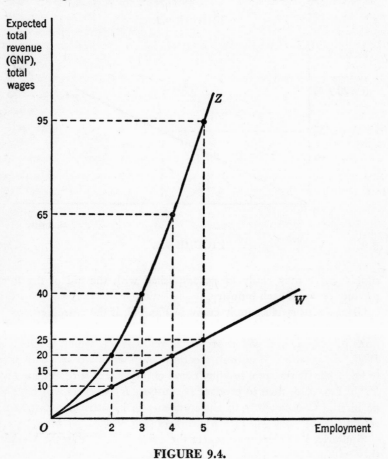

FIGURE 9.4.

industry supply curves are known, and if each aggregate level of expected total revenue corresponds to a unique distribution of this sales revenue among all industries, then a unique aggregate supply function is obtained.

The assumption that all firms are fully integrated implies that aggregate total revenue is equal to the value of gross output, i.e., the gross national product (GNP) of the economy.[4] The value of gross output is also equivalent to the gross money income of the economy. *Thus, the aggregate supply function relates expected levels of GNP to employment.*

A price level is implicit at each point on the aggregate supply function. Since market prices are related to marginal costs, which are rising due to diminishing returns, prices will increase as employment rises, even if the money-wage rate is constant.

A hypothetical example

It may be helpful to use a hypothetical example to indicate how the aggregate supply function should be interpreted. This hypothetical example will also be useful in suggesting several important implications of the aggregate supply function.

Using hypothetical data, the aggregate supply function is illustrated in Table 9.1. Underlying the figures in Table 9.1 is the assumption that the money-wage is $5,000 per year. If entrepreneurs in the

Table 9.1. A Hypothetical Example of Aggregate Supply and the Distribution of Income

(1) Gross National Product Z (billions)	(2) Employment N (millions)	(3) Wage Bill $W = wN$ (billions)	(4) Fixed costs F (billions)	(5) Gross profits $R = Z - F - W$ (billions)
$ 0	0	$ 0	$5	$−5
20	2	10	5	5
40	3	15	5	20
65	4	20	5	40
95	5	25	5	65

[4] Implicit in this statement is the assumption that all production occurs in the private sector.

aggregate were to expect GNP to be zero, they would not hire any workers; consequently, the aggregate supply curve emanates from the origin. If GNP is expected to be $20 billion, then, according to Table 9.1, two million workers would be hired and the total wage bill would be $10 billion (two million multiplied by $5,000). Alternatively, if a GNP of $40 billion were expected, then three million workers would be hired. Thus, by using the data in columns (1) and (2) of Table 9.1, an aggregate supply function (Fig. 9.4) may be plotted. Furthermore, from the data in columns (2) and (3), a total wage bill line (*OW*) can be plotted. The slope of this line is equal to the money-wage rate, *w*, while the line indicates the relationship between total money wage payments and the level of employment.

A DIGRESSION: INCOME DISTRIBUTION AND AGGREGATE SUPPLY

At any level of employment, the position of the aggregate supply curve relative to the wage bill line determines the relative wage share, i.e., the proportion of GNP which is paid to wage-earners. Also, the vertical difference between the aggregate supply curve and the wage bill line at any employment level represents the difference between total revenue and total variable costs for all the firms in the economy. Thus, in Table 9.1, when two million workers are employed, entrepreneurs expect revenue to exceed variable costs (the wage bill) by $10 billion, or alternatively, they expect the wage share to be one-half of GNP. In this hypothetical example, entrepreneurs expect the wage share to decline with increases in employment. The distribution of income and the aggregate supply function are interrelated. A careful examination of the relationship between income distribution and aggregate supply conditions will enable us to draw generalizations about the shape and position of the aggregate supply function.

The distribution of income in the economy reflects the distribution of total revenue at the firm level. To analyze the relationship of employment and distribution, therefore, we must return to the theory of the firm. Under our assumptions of pure competition and profit maximization, each firm, accepting the money-wage rate as a datum, will maximize profits by hiring workers until the additional revenue obtained from the sale of the output of an additional worker (the marginal revenue product) is equal to the money-wage rate. This profit maximizing condition can be expressed as

$$(P)(M) = w,$$

where P is expected market price, M is the marginal product of labor, and w is the money-wage rate. Rearranging terms, we obtain,

$$\frac{w}{P} = M. \tag{9.2}$$

The fraction of total revenue paid to wage-earners is the total wage bill divided by total revenue $\left(\frac{wN}{PQ}\right)$, where N is the level of employment and Q is the quantity of output. Consequently, if both sides of (9.2) are multiplied by the reciprocal of the average product of labor $\left(\frac{N}{Q}\right)$, the result is

$$\frac{wN}{PQ} = \frac{MN}{Q},$$

or

$$\frac{wN}{PQ} = \frac{M}{A}, \tag{9.3}$$

where A is the average product of labor. The important result is that the relative wage share in each firm depends on the firm's M/A-ratio. If all firms are attempting to maximize profits, then the fraction of GNP paid to wage-earners is equal, at any level of employment, to the average M/A-ratio[5] for the economy.

[5] This average may be expressed algebraically as

$$\frac{wN}{Z} = \sum_{i=a}^{m} \left(\frac{Z_i}{Z}\right) \frac{M_i}{A_i},$$

where Z_i is the expected total revenue in industry, i, there are m industries, and other symbols are as they were before.

THE SHAPE OF THE AGGREGATE SUPPLY FUNCTION

Making use of the M/A-ratio and the wage bill line it is possible to specify the shape of the aggregate supply curve. Clearly, the aggregate supply curve is upward sloping since expectations of greater total revenues will induce entrepreneurs to hire more workers. What must still be determined is whether or not the aggregate supply function is linear, is convex, or is concave to the employment axis. That is, which of the shapes in Fig. 9.5a appropriately represents the aggregate supply function?

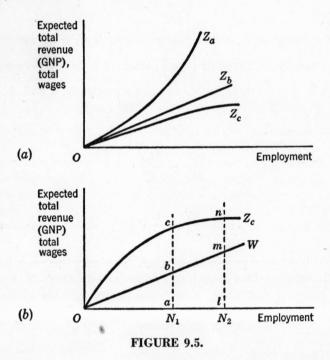

FIGURE 9.5.

At first sight, any of these three shapes may appear reasonable, but in fact, Z_c is not economically sensible. To demonstrate that Z_c cannot describe supply conditions, it is necessary to draw the implications which Z_c holds for productivity relationships. This, in turn, can be demonstrated by use of the wage bill line and the M/A-ratio.

Note that in Fig. 9.5b that as employment expands the wage share eventually increases. For example, at employment level N_1, the wage share is equal to ab/ac. At employment level N_2, the wage share is lm/ln, which is clearly larger than ab/ac. An increasing wage share implies that successively smaller increments in total revenue are required in order to induce entrepreneurs to hire each additional worker.[6]

From (9.3) we know that the wage share will rise only if the M/A-ratio increases. Normally, diminishing returns implies that the M/A-ratio will *not* rise as the quantity of labor employed with a fixed stock of capital grows, since an increasing M/A-ratio implies that as the labor to capital ratio increases, diminishing returns becomes relatively less important.[7] It is not realistic to assume that diminishing returns become less important as employment rises, so that it may be concluded that Z_c cannot describe the shape of the aggregate supply curve.

The same line of reasoning can be used to test the creditability of the Z_a and Z_b curves. The function Z_a implies that the wage share will fall as employment expands, which in turn implies a decreasing M/A-ratio. Production functions (functions which show the relationship between inputs and outputs) which embody this characteristic seem reasonable so that Z_a is a possible shape of the aggregate supply curve. The function Z_b implies a constant wage share at any level of employment, and therefore a constant M/A-ratio. Only if the production function is of a special form will the M/A-ratio be a constant at all levels of employment.

One function exhibiting this characteristic and which has been widely used in empirical research, is the Cobb-Douglas production

[6] More generally, the wage share will increase if the rate of change in the slope of the aggregate supply function is less than the rate of change in the slope of the wage bill line.

[7] If the M/A-ratio is to increase as more labor is hired, then the total product curve must asymptotically approach (from above) either an upward sloping straight line emanating from the origin, or a line parallel to such a ray. In other words, an increasing M/A-ratio implies a situation where, as the proportion of variable to fixed factor increases, diminishing returns rapidly become a relatively unimportant and practically negligible phenomenon. We should expect just the opposite, that is, we expect diminishing returns to grow in importance as output expands, with a fixed stock of capital.

function. This production function is expressed algebraically as

$$Q = jN^\alpha K^{1-\alpha},$$

where Q is output, j and α are empirically determined constants, N is labor, and K is capital. If the production function for each industry is of the Cobb-Douglas type, the M/A-ratio in each industry is a constant,[8] and therefore the average M/A-ratio will almost certainly be constant, the aggregate supply function will be linear, and the wage share will be unchanged as employment varies.[9] In fact, the Cobb-Douglas function has been widely used precisely because it implies a constant wage share. Empirical evidence has suggested that the wage share has been constant in many countries for a long time.

In summary, we expect the aggregate supply function to be upward sloping and either linear or convex to the employment axis.

RELAXING THE INITIAL ASSUMPTIONS

Having derived the aggregate supply function under simplifying assumptions, it will be valuable to suggest how changes in the initial assumptions will modify the aggregate supply function.

Monopoly and the aggregate supply function

First, the assumption of pure competition in the product markets will be relaxed, but the assumption of competition among buyers in labor markets will be maintained. In imperfect competition, each firm recognizing that its actions will affect the market price for its

---

[8] See Appendix B: Note 1.

[9] In a multiproduct, multifirm economy, a smooth linear or upward sloping convex (to the employment axis) aggregate supply function implies that as employment increases, the composition of output does not shift radically from industries with low M/A-ratios to industries with high M/A-ratios. Otherwise, it would be possible because of the changing importance of different industries, for the average M/A-ratio to increase with increasing employment levels, even though the M/A-ratio for each industry was a constant (the Cobb-Douglas case) or was declining. There is no reason to expect radical changes in the *importance of different* industries as employment increases.

products has some degree of monopoly power. The entrepreneur will conceive of this monopoly power as permitting profit maximization to occur at an output level where price exceeds both marginal revenue and marginal costs. In order to maximize profits, the entrepreneur will hire labor until the marginal revenue product equals the money-wage rate. This condition may be expressed algebraically as

$$(MR)(M) = w, \tag{9.4}$$

where MR is marginal revenue. Price exceeds marginal revenue by an amount which depends upon the entrepreneur's expectation of the absolute value of the price elasticity of demand (E_d) for the firm's output, that is, $P(1 - 1/E_d) = MR$.[10] Thus, (9.4) may be rewritten as

$$(P)(1 - 1/E_d)(M) = w. \tag{9.5}$$

Multiplying both sides of (9.5) by the reciprocal of the average product of labor and rearranging terms, we may express the wage share in the total revenue of the firm as

$$\frac{wN}{PQ} = \left(\frac{M}{A}\right)\left(1 - \frac{1}{E_d}\right). \tag{9.6}$$

When profits are being maximized, $1/E_d = P - MC/P$, which is a relative measure of the extent to which prices, set by a firm with monopoly power, deviate from the purely competitive situation of equating marginal costs and price.

Under pure competition the wage share is equal to the M/A-ratio, but once monopoly elements are introduced, the reciprocal of the

[10] Since

$$E_d = \frac{P \, \Delta Q}{Q \, \Delta P},$$

while

$$MR = P \, \Delta Q - Q \, \Delta P, \quad \text{or} \quad Q \, \Delta P = P \, \Delta Q - MR,$$

then, when $\Delta Q = 1$,

$$E_d = \frac{P}{P - MR},$$

therefore,

$$MR = P\left(1 - \frac{1}{E_d}\right).$$

elasticity of demand as well as the M/A-ratio are the determinants of the wage share. Since marginal revenue must be positive at the profit maximizing output position, the elasticity of demand must be greater than unity, and the term $(1 - 1/E_d)$ must be less than unity. The wage share in the monopolistic case, therefore, will always be smaller than the M/A-ratio.

Generalizing from equation (9.6), if each firm is attempting to maximize profits, then the wage share in the gross national product will depend upon the average M/A-ratio and the average degree of monopoly.[11] Using this generalized relationship we may note that at any given level of aggregate employment, given the production functions, the wage share will be lower (or the vertical distance between the aggregate supply curve and the wage bill line will be greater) under monopoly than under competitive pricing. Thus, both the degree of monopoly and the M/A-ratio affect the position and shape of the aggregate supply curve.[12]

What conclusions may we draw about the effect of monopoly on the slope of the aggregate supply function? Given the M/A-ratio at each employment level, in a mixed competitive-monopoly economy, if the degree of monopoly is invariant to employment changes, then conclusions about the slope of the aggregate supply function follow competitive theory, i.e., changes in the M/A-ratio determine the result. On the other hand, if changes in monopoly power are related to changes in the level of employment, then the slope of the aggregate supply function will be affected. If, for example, restrictive business practices are more important in a recession, then the average degree of monopoly may decline with rising employment levels and may, in the most

---

[11] This is expressed algebraically as

$$wN/Z = \sum_{i=a}^{m} \left(\frac{M_i}{A_i}\right) \left(1 - \frac{1}{E_{d_i}}\right) \left(\frac{Z_i}{Z}\right) .$$

[12] It does not follow, however, that the equilibrium wage share in monopoly must be lower than the equilibrium wage share in pure competition. This result is inevitable only if the output of each firm is the same under monopoly and competition. Comparisons under different market structures are difficult. To the extent that monopoly affects the composition of output, the rate of introduction of new products and technological processes, and the distribution of income, monopoly power will have affects on both the aggregate supply and aggregate demand functions.

extreme case, more than offset any declines in the average M/A-ratio so that an aggregate supply function concave to the employment axis is possible. On the other hand, if buyers are less price conscious in prosperous periods, then the average degree of monopoly would tend to rise with employment levels and augment any possible convexity in the aggregate supply function due to productivity phenomena.

In the absence of strong empirical evidence favoring one hypothesis over the other, a tentative assumption that no change occurs in the degree of monopoly appears to be acceptable. It must be recognized, however, that changes in monopoly conditions could alter the slope of the aggregate supply function.

Changes in the money-wage rate and the aggregate supply function

Up to this point the analysis has assumed that the money-wage rate is constant at all levels of employment. Suppose that the money-wage rate tends to vary directly with the level of employment. If this is the case, each increase in the money-wage rate will rotate the wage bill line upwards. Thus, in Fig. 9.6a, OW_1 is the wage bill line when the money-wage rate is w_1; OW_2 implies a higher money-wage rate, w_2, etc. Suppose further that the money-wage rate remains at w_1 until N_1 workers are hired, but when the N_1 plus one worker is employed the wage rate is raised to w_2. The wage rate remains at that level until N_2 workers are hired, and then it increases to w_3, etc. Under these circumstances, the wage bill is described by the discontinuous curve $Oabcde$ in Fig. 9.6a. If, however, we assume that the money-wage rate rises continuously as employment increases, then the wage bill curve will be the smooth function OW, which is derived from a locus of points, where each point is on a different wage bill (straight) line, and each straight line represents a different money-wage rate.

In a similar manner an aggregate supply function based on a changing money-wage rate can be derived. In Fig. 9.6b, Z_1 is the aggregate supply curve when the money-wage rate is w_1. Since the vertical distance between the wage bill line and the aggregate supply function depends only upon the M/A-ratio and the degree of monopoly, which are assumed given for any level of employment, when the money-wage rises, both the wage bill line and the aggregate supply curve will have to shift upwards so that the vertical distance between the two remains unchanged. Z_2 therefore represents the aggregate supply function when w_2 is the money-wage rate. Accordingly, if wages rise discontinuously, the aggregate supply function is represented by the discontinuous curve $Oa'b'c'd'e'$ as employment rises. Alternatively,

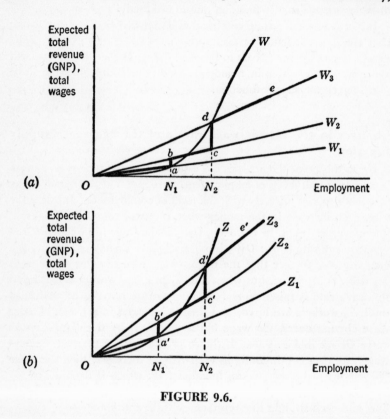

FIGURE 9.6.

the locus OZ in Fig. 9.6b represents the relevant aggregate supply function if the money-wage rate is a continuously increasing function of the level of employment. When both the OW and OZ curves are plotted on the same figure, the vertical distance between the two at any employment level is, as before, dependent on the M/A-ratio and the degree of monopoly.

In summary, increases in the money-wage rate will shift the aggregate supply function upwards. This result will have important implications for our analysis of inflation in Chapter 12.

Changes in capital stock, technology, and the aggregate supply function

Without attempting to catalog all the possible results of changes in the capital stock and/or technology, we may simply note that we would expect these changes to primarily affect the aggregate supply function through their effects on the M/A-ratio.

In the next chapter, the aggregate demand function will be developed, which when used with the aggregate supply function constitutes the equilibrium model.

APPENDIX A. Entrepreneurial Motivation and the Aggregate Supply Function

Some economists believe that entrepreneurs who possess monopoly power do not strive to maximize profits; instead, they seek to maximize total revenue as long as some minimum profit level is maintained. The output and employment decisions of such a firm may be analyzed with the aid of Fig. 9.7, where TR represents the expected total revenue function of the firm, TC represents its total costs, and π is the profit function of the firm. In Fig. 9.7, Q_p is that output level at which profits will be maximized. It will require the hiring of N_p workers. If the minimum profit level which entrepreneurs will accept is OA, then a sales maximizing entrepreneur will produce Q_c output which will require the hiring of N_c workers. Since Q_c exceeds Q_p, N_c must be larger than N_p.

What then would the effect be on the aggregate supply function if it is assumed that all firms are sales maximizers instead of profit maximizers? Figure 9.7 indicates that our hypothetical firm would receive a total revenue of TR_1 at the profit maximizing position. However, if our entrepreneur was a sales maximizer, he would be willing to hire the same N_p workers even if the expected total revenue were only TR_2, since given the total cost curve, total revenue at TR_2 would be just sufficient to yield the requisite minimum profits, OA. Generalizing this result for the economy, for any employment level which yields profits in excess of the minimum required by sales maximizers, expected total revenue would be less for sales maximizers than for profit maximizers.

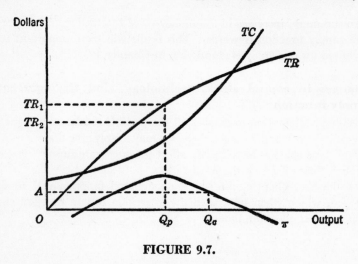

FIGURE 9.7.

Accordingly, when the minimum profit levels are specified, a unique aggregate supply function can be derived under the sales maximizing hypothesis. The vertical distance of the aggregate supply curve from the employment axis at each level of employment will be less with sales maximizers than with profit maximizers.

APPENDIX B.   Mathematical Notes

Note 1

Proposition: To demonstrate what form the production function must have to have a constant ratio of marginal to average product (M/A) at all levels of employment.

Let the M/A-ratio for labor be equal to a constant (α):

$$\frac{dQ/dN}{Q/N} = \alpha,$$

where Q is output and N is labor. Hence,

$$\frac{dQ}{Q} = \alpha \, \frac{dN}{N}.$$

Integrating, we obtain:

$$\log Q = \alpha \log N \dotplus \log a,$$

where *a* is a constant. Thus, the production function will have the following form:

$$Q = aN^\alpha.$$

This function in one variable is mathematically akin to the two-variable Cobb-Douglas function, $Q = jN^\alpha K^{1-\alpha}$, the latter being the production function usually associated with constant relative shares.

Note 2

Proposition: To demonstrate that the M/A-ratio either remains constant or declines with diminishing returns, when the output function is a smooth, continuous, monotonic function within the region of rational factor hire.

Mrs. Robinson has shown[13] that at any given abscissa value, the relation between the points on the marginal and average curves can be expressed as

$$M = A\left(\frac{\epsilon - 1}{\epsilon}\right), \quad \text{or} \quad \frac{M}{A} = \left(1 - \frac{1}{\epsilon}\right),$$

where ϵ is the absolute value of the elasticity of A, at that point.

It follows that the M/A-ratio varies in the same direction as ϵ. It can be shown that if the average curve is a normal, downward-sloping curve, then either ϵ is a constant (and A has the general form $A = (a/N)^{1/b}$, where a and b are constants) or ϵ declines towards unity as employment increases, and M approaches zero.[14] Since M must always be greater than zero in the region of rational factor hire, ϵ can never be equal to or less than unity in this region.[15]

[13] J. Robinson, *The Economics of Imperfect Competition*, Macmillan, 1934, 36.

[14] See S. Carlson, *Pure Theory of Production*, Kelley and Mellman, 1956, pp. 56–8.

[15] For a further discussion of the M/A-ratio, see D. E. Horlacher and E. Smolensky, "Increasing Employment, Diminishing Returns, and Relative Shares," *Canadian Journal of Economic and Political Science*, 26, 1960.

CHAPTER 10

Aggregate demand

Aggregate demand is the sum total of expenditures of all the buyers in the economy. The term demand emphasizes purchases and turns the intellect towards matters of taste, satisfactions, prices, the level of income and its distribution, and expected profits. Except for the previous chapter, it has been the buyers' side of the market which has received most of our attention, and it is to the buyer that we return again in this chapter.

In the equilibrium model, the *aggregate demand function* relates money expenditures of all buyers on domestically produced goods to the level of aggregate employment.[1] It is the schedule which shows the alternative spending totals for alternative levels of employment. Prices, output, income, and perhaps even the money-wage rate will vary as employment varies and, therefore, these factors will have repercussions on the aggregate demand function. Somehow, all these interrelationships must be put into a logical and determinant sequence if spending behavior is to be understood. The aggregate demand function which

[1] In the forecasting model of Part II, on the other hand, the aggregate demand function related real spending by all buyers to the level of real output. The advantages of dealing with Keynesian functions *in money terms* was observed by B. Ohlin to be a considerable improvement over dealing with functions in real terms. Ohlin argued, "A reasoning in monetary terms does not prevent any amount of considerations of the 'real' implications, whenever such considerations may be desirable, e.g., in a discussion of policy. But it has the advantage of permitting a much simpler and less sophisticated explanation of the market phenomena, which are *price* phenomena." (B. Ohlin, "Some Notes on the Stockholm Theory of Savings and Investments II," *Economic Journal*, 47, 1937, p. 230.) Ohlin believed that reasoning in money rather than real terms was one of the two "outstanding characteristics of Keynes' theoretical system." (*Ibid.*, p. 229.)

will be derived, taken together with aggregate supply function which has been derived in Chapter 9, will yield a useful theory of spending behavior. In this chapter, the appropriate aggregate demand function will be developed and then the simplest form of the equilibrium model will be examined.

DERIVING THE AGGREGATE DEMAND FUNCTION

Deriving the aggregate demand function will require a complicated line of reasoning which it is best to summarize briefly at the outset. Four groups of buyers are normally identified in the theory of employment determination—consumers, businesses, governments, and foreign purchasers. Each category consists of buyers who are prompted by a common set of motives but these motives are different for each group. As in the forecasting model, we will initially assume that there are no government and foreign purchases, so that aggregate demand will be the sum of two quantities: (1) the amount spent on consumption, and (2) the amount spent on investment. While this simple dichotomy of spending behavior was adequate for the forecasting model, it will not be sufficient for the equilibrium model where price is a variable, for even though all consumers are similarly motivated, price and money-wage changes will affect the real income of various groups of consumers differently and will lead to diverse behavior patterns among individuals within the consumer category.

The difficult task will be to describe the dependence of aggregate consumption spending (in money terms) on the level of employment. *This aggregate consumption function will be based on the same assumption as in the forecasting model, namely, that real consumption is a function of real income.* [2] Since the price level varies with employment, and since different consumer groups will find that their money income, on the one hand, and that their real income, on the other, are affected differently by wage, price, and employment changes, we will have to

[2] At this stage, we ignore the real balance effect, i.e., we ignore the possibility that changes in the price level will affect the real wealth of the community and as a result may alter the consumption function. This effect will be discussed in Chapter 11. Similarly, we will postpone the discussion of expectations of future price changes on present spending decisions until Chapter 13.

distinguish between groups of consumers. The most useful distinction turns upon the way each group of consumers obtains its income. For each of three consumer groups—wage-earners, rentiers, and profit recipients—the effect of changing employment levels on real income will be deduced. Once the relationship between money income, real income, and employment has been obtained for each group, it will be possible to achieve our first objective which is to describe how consumption expenditures in money terms vary for each group as the level of aggregate employment changes. Adding up these relationships of money consumption to total employment will yield the aggregate consumption function. Finally, real investment spending will be converted to money terms and then added to the aggregate consumption function to obtain the aggregate demand function.

This aggregate demand function, which relates money expenditures to the level of employment, can then be placed on the same axes as the aggregate supply function, which relates expected sales revenue (in money terms) to the level of employment. The intersection of these two functions determines the equilibrium level of spending and employment.

CONSUMPTION BEHAVIOR AND THE LEVEL AND DISTRIBUTION OF INCOME

The consumption function developed in Chapter 3 related real consumption to real income. That real consumption is largely dependent upon real disposable income for each family continues to be fundamental to the analysis. We now introduce the complication that the family must engage in money transactions in order to achieve their real consumption objectives. Since the price level varies with employment, and the real income of individuals will be affected by price level changes, it is necessary to relate the changes in money income, real income, and prices for various consumer groups.

At each level of employment, there will be a flow of money payments from business enterprises to individuals. These payments, which are the personal incomes of individuals, the propensities to consume of these income recipients, and the price level, determine the consumption outlays of the community.

MONEY INCOME AND THE LEVEL OF EMPLOYMENT

It is useful to identify three groups of income recipients: rentiers, wage-earners, and profit recipients. This tripartite division is necessary in order to understand aggregate consumption behavior, since price and employment phenomena will have a different impact on the real income of each of these groups. In this section, variations in money income will be examined and diagrammatically represented in Fig. 10.1. In the next section, money income variations will be related to variations in real income, in order to explain consumption spending of the groups.

Rentiers

At any point of time, most business enterprises will have outstanding debts as a consequence of having borrowed funds in earlier periods. At the time these debts were incurred, these firms entered into contractual agreements to pay the lenders fixed sums of money (interest payments) at specified dates. The current holders of these debt contracts must be paid no matter what the level of economic activity or the profit position of the firms. These payments to the holders of the debt contracts are the fixed costs of the firms. The holders, who are receiving fixed sums of money, are called *rentiers*. Accordingly, the relationship between total rentier income and the level of aggregate employment is represented by the horizontal line *FF'* in Fig. 10.1a.[3]

if prices are const.

Wage-earners

At any given employment level, of course, there will be a flow of money-wage payments to workers to compensate them for their efforts. If the money-wage rate does not vary as employment changes, then total money-wage payments will increase by a constant amount as employment increases. For example, if the wage rate is $5,000 per year, each additional hired worker will raise total wage payments by an additional $5,000. Since, if no workers were to be hired, the wage bill would obviously be zero, the relationship between the aggregate

[3] Besides interest payments, firms may be contractually committed, for short periods of time, to pay salaries and rents. The receivers of these payments may also be considered to be rentiers.

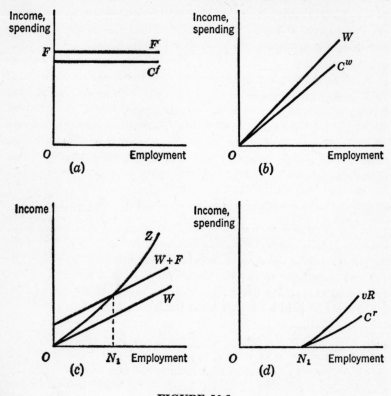

FIGURE 10.1.

wage bill and the level of employment is represented as the straight
line OW beginning at the origin, and having a slope equal to the
money-wage rate (Fig. 10.1b).

Profit recipients

Subtracting total costs from total revenue at each level of employment yields gross profits.[4]   Total costs for fully integrated firms are
simply wage payments plus fixed costs, so that adding the FF' line

---

[4] Gross profits contain many elements which are not often thought of as components of profits, e.g., depreciation and excise taxes.

of Fig. 10.1a to the OW line of Fig. 10.1b, yields the total cost curve $W + F$ in Fig. 10.1c. Total revenue at each level of employment is shown by the aggregate supply curve OZ in Fig. 10.1c.

Since profits equal total revenue less total costs, the difference between the aggregate supply curve (OZ in Fig. 10.1c) and the $W + F$ curve represents aggregate profits. In Fig. 10.1c, at all employment levels below N_1, aggregate profits are negative since the total revenue curve is below the total cost curve. This does not necessarily mean that all firms are making losses; only that total business losses of some firms exceed total profits of the others.[5] At employment levels above N_1, enterprises are, on the average, making profits. For simplicity, it can be assumed that some fraction (v) of total profits (R) is paid out as dividends. Profit recipients begin to receive dividends at N_1, and consequently the curve vR in Fig. 10.1d represents the relationship between dividends and employment.[6]

REAL INCOME AND THE LEVEL OF EMPLOYMENT

Having developed the relationship between money income payments and employment for each income group, the next step is to relate the real income of each group to the level of aggregate employment, and to determine the money consumption expenditures of each group.

In the short run, real income is the basic determinant of real consumption. For simplicity, assume that the real consumption of each income group is a simple proportionate function of the real income of each group. In other words, assume that if the real income of a group of consumers is zero, then their consumption expenditures will also be

[5] Employment levels below N_1 may normally be neglected, for in that range firms will be going bankrupt, so that employment below N_1 will be only temporary. Bankruptcy proceedings will, for the economy as a whole, involve a scaling down of total fixed costs.

[6] Since some firms earn profits even when aggregate profits are negative, and since some corporations pay dividends even with current losses, dividends are likely to appear at employment levels below N_1. The vR function abstracts from this realistic but not very consequential factor, since employment levels below N_1 will involve wholesale bankruptcy proceedings.

zero; and, moreover, that as their real income rises, their marginal propensities to consume remain unchanged.[7]

At this point, it is necessary to explicitly introduce price relationships into the system, so that real consumption behavior can be related to money expenditures. The price level is implicit in every point of the aggregate supply curve. As indicated in Chapter 9, in a competitive economy prices depend on the relationship between the money-wage rate and the marginal productivity of labor. Assuming a constant money-wage rate, as employment increases prices rise due to diminishing returns.

1. Rentier spending on consumption

As employment and therefore prices increase, the real income of rentiers declines, even though their money income remains constant. Since rentiers' real consumption is related to their real income, as the latter declines rentiers' real consumption falls off even though their money outlays on consumption remain unchanged.[8]

The relationship between rentiers' money consumption expenditures and aggregate employment is, therefore, expressed as the horizontal straight line C^f in Fig. 10.1a. The line C^f lies below the line FF', because the marginal propensity to consume of rentiers is less than one. Since rentier consumption behavior is one component of the aggregate consumption function, the C^f line implies that even at zero employment levels, there will be some consumption spending, that is, the aggregate consumption function will have a positive intercept.

---

[7] Although individual families may continue to consume even though their income is zero, they normally can finance these expenditures for any length of time only because other individuals with positive incomes are willing to transfer some of their income to the zero income families. These transfer payments usually take the form of charity payments, unemployment compensation, loans, proceeds from the sale of assets, or gifts. To simplify the algebraic analysis, however, it is expedient to assume that no transfer payments occur; so that the consumption out of zero income for any group can be assumed to be negligible. (The introduction of these transfer payments will not affect the analysis, although the magnitude of some of the parameters may be different.)

[8] If, for example, an increase in employment led to a price rise of 2 percent, then rentiers' real income and their real consumption would decline by 2 percent. In order to buy 2 percent less output at 2 percent higher prices, rentiers would have to spend the same amount of money on consumption as before.

2. Wage-earner spending on consumption

As employment increases, total money-wage payments increase. The newly employed experience a rise in real income and, therefore, increase their real consumption and money consumption expenditures. To the extent that prices increase while the money-wage rate remains constant, those wage-earners who were previously employed are in the same position as rentiers; that is, they find their real income declining in proportion to the price level increase. As with rentiers, these previously employed workers reduce their real consumption while maintaining the same money expenditures on consumption. Thus, total money outlays on consumption by wage-earners is the summation of a constant money outlay by the previously employed and an increase in the money expenditures of the newly employed. Consequently, the relationship between wage-earners' expenditures on consumption and aggregate employment is represented by the upward sloping line C^w, in Fig. 10.1b. The C^w line lies below the OW line because the marginal propensity to consume out of wages is less than one.

3. Profit recipient spending on consumption

As employment rises above N_1, aggregate profits increase. Profit maximizing entrepreneurs are induced to hire more workers only if prices of the goods which they produce rise. This is, in fact, the primary reason for the upward slope of the supply curve of firms and it is the mechanism by which diminishing returns transmits an increase in employment into an increase in prices. Therefore, as employment rises, total real profits as well as money profits must increase. Consequently, if dividends are directly related to profits, then real dividends and real consumption by profit recipients will rise as employment increases. The relationship between money expenditures by profit recipients on consumption goods and aggregate employment is, therefore, represented by the upward sloping C^r line in Fig. 10.1d. The line C^r is below the line vR because the marginal propensity to consume out of profits is clearly less than one since only that part of gross profits distributed as dividends is available for consumption.

THE AGGREGATE CONSUMPTION FUNCTION

The aggregate consumption function is merely the vertical sum of the consumption functions of rentiers, wage-earners and profit recipients and is represented as the upward sloping line D_c in Fig. 10.2. The positive slope of the aggregate consumption function results from the increase in income going to wage-earners and profit recipients and their consequent increase in expenditures as employment rises.

INVESTMENT BEHAVIOR

The forces that determine the level of real investment have been discussed in Chapter 4. For the moment, we will asume that the investment decision is made in real terms at the beginning of the period and then businessmen budget a given sum of money to carry out investment

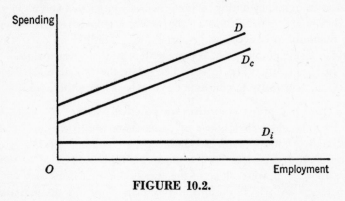

FIGURE 10.2.

during the period. (This assumption will be relaxed in Chapter 13.) Consequently, money investment remains fixed during the period although real investment may depart from the goal set by management at the beginning of the period because of changes in prices. The relationship between expenditures on investment and the level of employment can be depicted as the horizontal straight line (D_i) in Fig. 10.2. The aggregate demand function (D in Fig. 10.2) is obtained by adding D_c to D_i.

EQUILIBRIUM

The aggregate demand and aggregate supply functions have been redrawn in Fig. 10.3. This diagram must be interpreted in the following way. Suppose entrepreneurs expect total revenue to be Z_a.

This will lead them to hire N_a workers. The flow of money payments at the N_a employment level, however, will lead to a D_a level of money expenditures. Since aggregate demand exceeds aggregate supply at the N_a level, entrepreneurs will find that buyers wish to purchase more than sellers wish to sell at going prices and, therefore, entrepreneurs will be induced to expand output. Suppose they now expect Z_b proceeds and hence hire N_b workers. As the stream of payments from

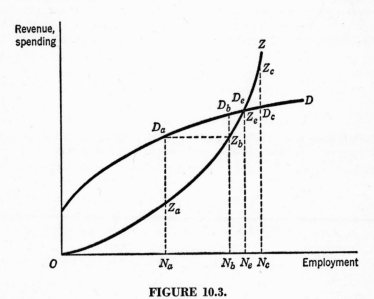

FIGURE 10.3.

firms to wage-earners and profit recipients increase, money consumption outlays will increase raising total spending to D_b. Since D_b is greater than Z_b, entrepreneurs will again find that desired purchases are greater than anticipated and employment will expand again. When entrepreneurial expectations of revenue equal Z_e, they will hire N_e workers, and will discover that the concomitant demand outlays (D_e) are such that their expectations are just fulfilled. At that point, *ceteris paribus*, there will be no inducements to change the employment level.

Similarly, if we start from a level of employment to the right of the intersection of the aggregate demand and supply functions, say N_c, then at that level of employment, entrepreneurs would expect total sales to be Z_c, and they would be disappointed to find that buyers only wished to spend D_c. Thus, actual sales would fall short of sales expectations. This disappointment would induce entrepreneurs to reduce employment as they lowered their sales expectations. As long as entrepreneurs hired more than N_e workers, however, realized sales would continue to be less than expectations. At the N_e employment level, desired purchases equal sales expectations.

The value of total spending as given by the aggregate demand function where it is intersected by the aggregate supply function is called *effective demand*. Effective demand is the point where aggregate spending equals aggregate expectations of sales; it represents an equilibrium level of expenditures, where entrepreneurial expectations are just being realized so that there is no inducement to change hiring policy.

To summarize, given our assumptions, an aggregate supply function reflecting productivity, prices, and wage phenomena can be constructed. From this aggregate supply function a flow of money payments can be derived. Given this income stream, an aggregate consumption function can be obtained. Finally, given investment expenditures, the aggregate demand function can be constructed in such a way as to reflect the same set of prices as are built into the aggregate supply function at corresponding employment positions. So long as the slope of the aggregate demand function is less than the slope of the aggregate supply function, a stable and determinate equilibrium emerges.

EMPLOYMENT AND INCOME MULTIPLIERS AND THE PRICE LEVEL

Our primary objective is to understand the causes of changes in the level of aggregate employment. In other words, we want to understand how the economy moves from one equilibrium position to another, as the exogenous variables change. The starting point in the study of fluctuations in the level of employment is the simple multiplier of Chapter 3. In that chapter, changes in real income were related to exogenous changes in investment or government spending, i.e., to changes in demand conditions (with constant supply prices). In the equilibrium model, an initial change in aggregate demand induces changes in output, employment, and prices. For policy decisions, it is clearly necessary that these resultant effects be separated and the magnitude of each determined.

For expositional purposes, it is useful to summarize in advance all that will be happening in the model. Many things will be occurring simultaneously, but it will be necessary to speak as if things proceed in a simple sequence.

When aggregate spending increases, entrepreneurs will initially hire more workers and (because of diminishing returns) expect higher prices. The relative magnitudes of the price and employment changes will depend on productivity conditions as expressed via the aggregate supply function. As the economy expands, in addition to the increase in aggregate income, there will be a redistribution of income away from fixed income groups as the price level rises. These changes in the level of total income and its distribution will affect aggregate consumption spending and a second round of spending increases will ensue. This process will be repeated until new equilibrium levels of employment, output, and prices are reached.

With this overall view in mind, we can now turn to the derivation of employment and income multipliers which reflect the interaction of demand and supply conditions. First, we will summarize the aggregate supply conditions as discussed in Chapter 9. Then, the related demand conditions will be specified, and the relevant multipliers will be derived.

Supply conditions and the multiplier

As indicated in Chapter 9, the form of the aggregate supply function depends upon three factors: (1) technological relationships between inputs and outputs, i.e., the aggregate production function, since the willingness of employers to hire workers will depend, in part, on the contribution which these workers will make to output, (2) the cost of labor, i.e., the money-wage rate, since workers will be hired only if the contributions they make to total revenue equals or exceeds the cost of hiring the workers, and (3) the degree of monopoly, since the greater the monopoly power, the greater total revenue will be for any level of output, given the money-wage rate and technological conditions.

For simplicity, we will assume pure competition, a constant money-wage rate, and a Cobb-Douglas production function. This production function is written as

$$Q = jN^{\alpha}K^{1-\alpha}, \tag{10.1}$$

where Q is output, N is the level of employment, K is the stock of capital, and j and α are constants. Under these assumptions, the aggregate supply function will be linear,[9] i.e.,

$$Z = kwN, \tag{10.2}$$

where Z is aggregate supply, k is equal to $\dfrac{1}{\alpha}$, and w is the money-wage rate. Thus, the aggregate supply function is plotted as the straight line OZ in Fig. 10.4.

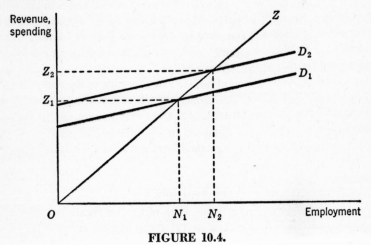

FIGURE 10.4.

The price level (P) is a function of the money-wage rate and the marginal product of labor, i.e.,

$$P = \frac{w}{M}, \tag{10.3}$$

where M is the marginal product of labor. It follows from (10.3)

[9] See Chapter 9.

that changes in the price level will be directly proportionate to changes in the money-wage rate and inversely proportionate to changes in the marginal product of labor. If wages are constant, as it is initially assumed, then the more significant diminishing returns is, the more rapid the price level will rise with expansion.

Equations (10.1) through (10.3) summarize all the interrelated supply conditions in the model.

Demand conditions and the multipliers[10]

The real aggregate demand function is the sum of the real consumption functions of each consumer group and real investment expenditures,

$$D_r = C_r^w + C_r^f + C_r^r + I_r, \tag{10.4}$$

where the subscript r indicates that the variables are expressed in real terms, D is aggregate demand, C^w is the consumption of wage-earners, C^f is the consumption of fixed income recipients, C^r is the consumption of profit recipients, and I is investment expenditures. Assuming the real consumption of each income group is a simple proportional function of the real income of the group, then each consumption function can be expressed as:

wage earners,

$$C_r^w = b\left(\frac{wN}{P}\right); \tag{10.4a}$$

rentiers,

$$C_r^f = f\left(\frac{\overline{F}}{P}\right); \tag{10.4b}$$

profit recipients,

$$C_r^r = r\left(\frac{Z - \overline{F} - wN}{P}\right) = r\left(\frac{(k-1)wN - \overline{F}}{P}\right), \tag{10.4c}$$

where b, f, and r are the marginal propensities to consume out of wages, fixed money income payments, and gross profits, respectively, and $\overline{F}$ is the exogenously determined fixed money payments to rentiers.

[10] The following section is based on P. Davidson, "Income and Employment Multipliers and Price Level," *American Economic Review*, 52, 1962.

In this chapter, it will also be assumed that once the real investment decision has been made, businessmen budget a certain sum of
money to finance these investment expenditures, i.e.,

$$I_r = \frac{\overline{I}}{P},$$ (10.4d)

where $\overline{I}$ is exogenously determined. If prices rise during the period,
monetary investment expenditures will be constant while actual real
investment (contrary to businessmen's plans) will decline. If the period
is relatively short, this supposition may approximate reality.[11]

Since the aggregate supply equation (10.2) is in money terms, the
real aggregate demand function must be converted into money terms
in order that it may be compatible with the supply function. The
aggregate demand function in money terms can be obtained by
substituting (10.4a) through (10.4d) into (10.4) and multiplying
through by the price level to obtain:

$$D = bwN + r(k - 1)wN + (f - r)\overline{F} + \overline{I}.$$ (10.5)

Aggregate demand is, therefore, linearly related to employment and
is drawn as the D_1 line in Fig. 10.4.

In equilibrium, aggregate supply equals aggregate demand, so that
the equilibrium condition can be obtained via (10.2) and (10.5) as

$$Z = D,$$

or

$$kwN = bwN + r(k - 1)wN + (f - r)\overline{F} + \overline{I}.$$ (10.6)

The equilibrium level of aggregate employment is determined by the
intersection of these functions (as N_1 in Fig. 10.4, while the equilibrium level of money income is Z_1). Suppose there is an exogenous
increase in money investment expenditures (ΔI). If the money-wage
rate is constant, then the aggregate supply function will be unchanged,
while the aggregate demand function will shift up to D_2, raising the
level of employment to N_2 and money income to Z_2 (in Fig. 10.4).

_____

[11] This assumption will be relaxed in Chapter 13.

The change in money income due to a change in investment is given by[12]

$$\Delta Z = \left[\frac{1}{1-\beta}\right]\Delta I, \tag{10.7}$$

while the change in employment due to an exogenous change in investment is given by[13]

$$\Delta N = \left[\frac{1}{kw(1-\beta)}\right]\Delta I, \tag{10.8}$$

where β is the weighted average of the marginal propensity to consume out of wages and gross profits. The weighting of these respective marginal propensities will be based on the distribution of income between wages and profits as expressed through the factor k.

Clearly, the money income multiplier in (10.7) is the same as the simple multiplier of the forecasting model. Since prices were assumed constant in the forecasting model, changes in money income could be directly converted into changes in real income.

---

[12]Letting $\left[b\left(\frac{1}{k}\right) + r\left(1 - \frac{1}{k}\right)\right]$ equal β, and substituting $\frac{Z}{kw}$ for N into (10.6), and solving for Z, we obtain

$$Z = \left[\frac{1}{1-\beta}\right][(f-r)\overline{F} + \overline{I}]. \tag{10.6a}$$

Therefore,

$$Z + \Delta Z = \left[\frac{1}{1-\beta}\right][(f-r)\overline{F} + \overline{I} + \Delta I]. \tag{10.6b}$$

Subtracting (10.6a) from (10.6b) yields (10.7).

[13] Solving (10.6) for N,

$$N = \left[\frac{1}{kw(1-\beta)}\right][(f-r)\overline{F} + \overline{I}]. \tag{10.6c}$$

Therefore,

$$N + \Delta N = \left[\frac{1}{kw(1-\beta)}\right][(f-r)\overline{F} + \overline{I} + \Delta I]. \tag{10.6d}$$

Subtracting (10.6c) from (10.6d) yields (10.8).

The employment multiplier in (10.8) is merely the money income multiplier multiplied by a conversion factor $\left(\dfrac{1}{kw}\right)$ which converts the increase in total spending into employment units. The rationale behind this conversion factor is as follows. For every dollar of additional spending, given the production function, the wage bill will increase by $\dfrac{1}{k}$ dollars. To hire an additional worker, the employer will have to pay the going money wage, w. Consequently, dividing the increase in total spending by k, gives the increase in the wage bill, while dividing the wage bill by w indicates the number of additional workers who will be hired for that increase in the money-wage bill.

These multipliers indicate that for any exogenous change in investment expenditures, the resultant change in the money income of the economy will depend on (1) the marginal propensity to consume out of wages and profits, and (2) the distribution of the increment in income between wages and profits. The resultant change in employment will depend on the money-wage rate and the proportion of total spending that goes to wages (as expressed by k) as well as the weighted average of the marginal propensities.

As might be expected, the magnitudes of the multipliers vary directly with the marginal propensities to consume, i.e., the greater the additional real consumption out of a given increment in real income for wage-earners and/or profit recipients, the greater the multiplier repercussions. Moreover, since normally the marginal propensity to consume out of wages will be greater than the marginal propensity to consume out of profits, if there is a redistribution of income, at any level of employment, from wages to profits (i.e., if k increases), then the magnitudes of the multipliers will be reduced as overall spending repercussions decline.[14]

The multipliers when the money-wage rate is a variable

Although a complete analysis of the effects of changes in the money-wage rate must wait until Chapters 11, 12, and 13, we may, at this

---

[14] If the aggregate supply curve is convex rather than linear, then the wage share declines with rising employment levels (i.e., k rises) and, therefore, the magnitudes of the multipliers will decline with expansion.

point, inquire into the affects on the multipliers of having the money-wage rate vary concomitantly with changes in effective demand.

Assume that the money-wage rate is an increasing function of the level of employment, i.e., $w = \phi(N)$. This money-wage rate function is *not* to be interpreted as the supply function of labor. Following Keynes' lead, the supply of labor will, in Chapter 11, be related to the real wage rate. Our analysis in the next chapter will, however, show that a function relating labor offerings to the money-wage rate can be derived from the demand curve for labor and its implicit real wage phenomena. Without delving into the analysis of labor supply and the money-wage rate at this point, however, the reader should recognize that the assumption that the money-wage rate increases as employment rises is a good approximation of the real world.

Substituting $\phi(N)$ for w in (10.6) and solving for ΔZ, we obtain the same money income multiplier as before, i.e.,

$$\Delta Z = \left[\frac{1}{1 - \beta}\right] \Delta I. \qquad (10.7')$$

Similarly, solving for the change in employment due to an exogenous change in investment, when the money-wage rate is a variable, yields,

$$\Delta N = \left[\frac{1}{k(\phi N + N\phi' N)(1 - \beta)}\right] \Delta I. \qquad (10.8')$$

A priori reasoning suggests that the money-wage rate function $\phi(N)$ should have a positive minimum value (m) and should be an increasing function of employment. Hence, for illustrative purposes, we may assume that

$$\phi(N) = m + nN^2. \qquad (10.8'a)$$

Substituting (10.8'a) into (10.8') yields

$$\Delta N = \left[\frac{1}{k(m + 3nN^2)(1 - \beta)}\right] \Delta I. \qquad (10.8'')$$

Thus, the additional employment created by a given increment in money expenditures depends on the distribution of income (k), the average (weighted) marginal propensity to consume (β) and the initial level of employment. The relationship between changes in the magnitude of the employment multiplier and changes in k and β are the same as in the constant money-wage case. When the money-wage rate is a function of the level of employment, however, the higher the initial employment level, the smaller the increment in employment from the multiplier repercussions, as more of the increment in money spending spills over into bidding up money wages and prices and less into increasing real output.

The price variable

If the money-wage rate is constant, (10.3) indicates that the price level varies inversely with the marginal product of labor; while changes in the marginal product of labor are related to changes in the level of employment via the production function. For the Cobb-Douglas function, the proportionate change in the marginal product of labor is $(\alpha - 1)$ times the proportionate change in employment.[15] Thus, for example, if α equals $\frac{1}{2}$ then a 2 percent increase in employment when the money-wage rate is constant, will lead to a 1 percent increase in the price level.

When the money-wage rate is an increasing function of the level of employment, then price level changes will, according to (10.3), vary directly with the money-wage rate and inversely with the marginal product of labor. Because of diminishing returns, the relative price increase for any given increase in employment will be greater than the relative money wage increase; therefore, any exogenous increase in spending must decrease the real-wage rate while increasing the level of employment.

The ratchet effect

Finally, if it is assumed that changes in the money-wage rate produces a ratchet effect, that is, if money-wage rate increases are ir-

---

[15]For the Cobb-Douglas function, $M = \alpha \dfrac{Q}{N}$. Hence,

$$NdM + MdN = \alpha dQ.$$

Dividing both sides of this equation by NM, it can be shown that

$$\frac{dM}{M} = (\alpha - 1) \frac{dN}{N}$$

reversible, then once a given money-wage rate is established in the market place it can not be lowered. In such a situation, the employment multiplier presented in (10.8′) is applicable to an increment in money expenditures, while the employment multiplier of (10.8) is relevant for exogenous decreases in money expenditures. Accordingly, the employment multiplier may be asymmetric, its magnitude being larger in a contraction than in an expansion. Furthermore, given a ratchet effect for the money-wage rate, (10.3) implies that the price variable may be relatively more stable during a contraction than during an expansion. Consequently, it is not surprising that recessions chiefly affect the level of employment while expansions affect both the employment and the price level.

The full implication of the ratchet effect on prices must be postponed until a theory of the money-wage rate determination is developed. This will be our task in Chapter 11. Using the tools developed in that chapter, we will then be able to obtain useful insights into the process of inflation as analyzed in Chapter 12.

APPENDIX A. A Digression on the
Micro-Foundations of Aggregate Demand

The reader may be confused by the fact that the ordinary demand curve for a single product is typically represented as downward sloping, while the aggregate demand function is upward sloping. There is no contradiction between downward sloping individual demand curves and the upward sloping aggregate demand curve. In fact, the aggregate demand function is logically derived from the micro-theory of consumer behavior.

In Fig. 10.5, S_a represents a typical supply curve for industry A based on factor productivity, and factor prices. (Such a supply curve can be constructed simultaneously for all industries.) At the price P_1, entrepreneurs will supply quantity Q_1 and expect total revenue of z_1 ($= P_1Q_1$). However, output Q_1 in industry A implies concomitant prices and outputs of other industries which will generate a level of aggregate income such that the normal micro-demand curve for the products of industry A is D_1. (The micro-demand curve is always based on the assumptions of (1) given tastes, (2) given aggregate income and its distribution, (3) all other prices given, and (4) a given number of consumers.)

Thus, at supply price P_1, consumers would like to buy Q'_1 output and their intended outlay is $d_1(= P_1Q'_1)$. If entrepreneurs in industry A produce Q_1

output, then intended spending will exceed expected total revenue, i.e., $d_1 > z_1$. Similarly, at supply price P_2, entrepreneurs expect total revenue to equal $z_2(= P_2Q_2)$. Since as industry A has increased output and employment (as have other industries at the same time), the level of aggregate income has risen and its distribution changed, D_2 is the relevant micro-demand curve. At the supply price of P_2, consumers intend to spend $d_2 = P_2Q'_2$, so that d_2

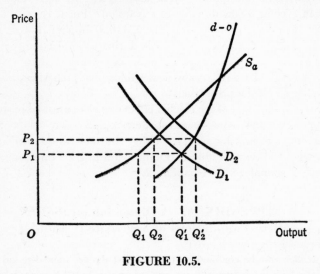

FIGURE 10.5.

exceeds z_2. In this way, a demand-outlay function $(d - o)$ for industry A connecting intended demand outlays at different supply prices which are based on rising outputs in A and other industries, and the attending money income flows throughout the economy, can be derived. This micro-demand outlay curve is the industry analogue of the aggregate demand curve. At any level of aggregate employment, aggregate demand is the summation of intended demand outlays over all industries.

APPENDIX B.   An Estimate of the Income and Employment Multipliers

A.   The Values of the Parameters

1. *The Income Distribution Factor* (k). Statistical evidence indicates that the value of k is approximately 2 for the private sector of the United States economy.

2. *The Marginal Propensity to Consume Out of Wages (b) and Out of the Gross Profit Residual (r).* Although a number of statistical studies on the consumption-savings behavior of various economic groups have been published, none of the marginal (or average) propensity estimates have precise applicability to our theoretical concepts. Nevertheless, by using several studies of consumption propensities by occupational groups, in conjunction with the national income data of the Department of Commerce, crude estimates of b and r can be made.

Estimate of b. The consumption behavior of "all employees" can be used as an approximation for the marginal propensity to consume out of wages. Evidence tends to suggest that b would be in the .75 to .85 range, or approximately .80.

Estimate of r. The marginal consumption out of the gross profit residual is more difficult to estimate. The aforementioned studies suggest that entrepreneurs' marginal propensity to consume out of their disposable income is between 1/2 and 2/3. These estimates, however, are only for entrepreneurs of unincorporated enterprises, self-employed professionals, and farmers, whose total income receipts were only approximately one-third of the total gross

Table 10.2   Gross Profit Residual—1960
(Billions of Dollars)

Business and professional income	$36.2	
Farm income	12.0	
Rental income	11.7	
		$59.9
Capital consumption allowances	$43.1	
Indirect business taxes	45.6	
Corporate profit before taxes	45.1	
		133.8
Gross profit residual		$193.7
Dividends—$14.1		

SOURCE: *Federal Reserve Bulletin,*   September 1961, pp. 1102–1103.

profit residual in 1960 (see Table 10.2). From the other two-thirds of the gross profit residual, a little more than 10 percent was paid out as dividends and was consequently available for consumption by profit recipients. If we assume that the marginal propensity to consume out of profit distributions is approximately the same as the marginal propensity to consume out of wages (i.e., 4/5), then the marginal propensity to consume out of the total gross profit residual can be computed as a weighted average:

$$r = (e)(g) + (d)(h)(1 - g),$$

where e is the marginal propensity to consume out of entrepreneurial income, g is the fraction of the gross profit residual going to entrepreneurs, d is the marginal propensity to consume out of profit distribution, h is the fraction of the corporate gross profit residual that is distributed, and $(1 - g)$ is the fraction of the gross profit residual accruing to corporations. Hence,

$$r = (.50 \text{ to } .67)(.33) + (.80)(.10)(.67) = .220 \text{ to } .275,$$
$$r \approx .25.$$

Thus, the marginal propensity to consume out of the gross profit residual (r) would approximate .25.

3. *The Money-Wage Rate (w).* The money-wage rate may be estimated by dividing total employee compensation in 1960 by total employment in that year (293.7 billion ÷ 66.7 million), i.e., w = \$4.40, or approximately \$4,400 per annum per employee.

4. *The Parameters of the Function for the Money-Wage Rate (m, n).* Our posited money wage function in the second model, $w = m + nN^2$ suggests an *a priori* relationship, where (1) there is a minimum money-wage rate level (m), and (2) as employment increases and the pools of unemployment dry up, the money-wage rate tends to rise at an increasing rate. Crude estimates for m and n can be made as follows.

Given a legal minimum wage rate of \$1.00 per hour in 1960 and a 40-hour work week, the value of m would be \$2.08 (i.e., \$2,080 per annum). If, in 1960, the level of employment was 66.7 million, while the going money-wage rate was \$4.40 and the minimum was \$2.08, then n would be .000521.

B. The Magnitude of the Multipliers

Using the above values for the parameters, the money income multiplier can be estimated from (10.7) to be 2.11. If w is constant, then the employment multiplier in (10.8) is .239; if w is an increasing function of N, then the employment multiplier in (10.8'') is .116. Thus, for example, an increment of \$1 billion in exogenous spending would increase *GNP* by \$2.11 billion, while employment would rise by 239 thousand, if the money-wage rate were constant, or by 116 thousand if the money-wage rate were an increasing function of employment.

With these multiplier values, the output, income, and price effects and consequently the anti-recessionary policy implications of President Kennedy's decision, in July 1961, to increase military expenditures by $3.5 billion (without increasing taxes) can be estimated. If wages increase with employment (as in our second model) then the additional defense expenditures will induce a 1 percent increase in prices and a $7.39 billion increase in money *GNP*. The reduction in unemployment would be only 406 thousand, as much of the increase in total spending will raise the average money-wage rate by almost .7 percent. Consequently, unemployment (which was 5.1 million in July of 1961) would still be significantly large. On the other hand, if the money-wage rate could be constrained (by moral suasion or legislative action) then, for the same initial increase in expenditures, the employment effect would be more than twice as large; 837 thousand new jobs would be created, while the concurrent price rise would be relatively small (approximately .6 percent).

CHAPTER II

The money-wage rate[1]

Until now it has been assumed that the money-wage rate is exogenously determined. This aggregate equilibrium model would not be complete, however, without making the determination of the most important of all prices—the price of labor—endogenous to the system. In this chapter, the aggregate demand and supply functions for labor will be derived, so that the money-wage rate is endogenously determined. Furthermore, the use of these functions will lead to an analysis of the effects of changes in the money-wage rate on the level of employment, prices, and the rate of interest.

THE DEMAND FOR LABOR

What will be the effect of a change in the money-wage rate on the amount of labor that businessmen will want to hire? The answer to this question depends upon the aggregate *demand curve for labor*, which shows the quantity of labor entrepreneurs would want to hire at every conceivable price (i.e., at every conceivable money-wage rate). This aggregate demand curve for labor is derived from a loci of effective demand points, where each point depends on a given money-wage rate. It has already been demonstrated that the level of employment is determined by the intersection of the aggregate supply and aggregate demand functions. This point of intersection is the level of

---

[1] Most of the analysis of this chapter has its origins in S. Weintraub's, *An Approach to the Theory of Income Distribution*, Chilton, 1958, pp. 108–130.

effective demand. Both the aggregate supply and the aggregate demand functions are dependent, in part, on the money-wage rate, and both will shift when the money-wage rate changes.

In Chapter 9, it was shown that aggregate supply was a function of the money-wage rate and the level of employment:

$$Z = f_1(w, N). \tag{11.1}$$

In Chapter 10, it was shown that aggregate demand is also a function of the money-wage rate and the level of employment:

$$D = f_2(w, N). \tag{11.2}$$

In equilibrium, aggregate demand equals aggregate supply, so that once the money-wage is specified, the equilibrium level of employment is determined.

For any specified money-wage rate, there is a unique aggregate supply and a unique aggregate demand function which can be derived. By varying the money-wage rate and observing the resulting shifts in the aggregate supply and demand curves, the resulting effective demand points can be obtained and the new equilibrium levels of employment determined. The effective demand points are used to derive the demand curve for labor.

For example, in Fig. 11.1a, if the money-wage rate is w_1, then the aggregate supply function is Z_1, and the aggregate demand function is D_1. The resulting level of employment is N_1. We have therefore derived one point on the aggregate demand function for labor (Fig. 11.1c), for when the money-wage rate is w_1, the number of workers demanded will be N_1. If the money-wage rate rises from w_1 to w_2, then both the aggregate supply and aggregate demand functions will shift upward to Z_2 and D_2 (Fig. 11.1b), respectively, and the new level of effective demand for labor is N_2. We have now derived a second point on the aggregate demand curve for labor (Fig. 11.1c), for when the money-wage rate is w_2, the level of employment is N_2. Repeating this process for each conceivable money-wage rate will enable us to derive the locus of effective demand points that will make up the demand curve for labor. Figure 11.1c suggests that the demand curve for labor is downward sloping. This implies that when the money-wage rate rises, the quantity of labor demanded will fall, which in turn

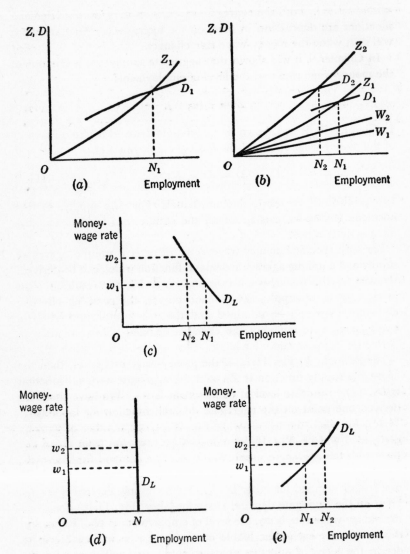

FIGURE 11.1.

implies that as a consequence of the rise in the wage rate the upward shift in the aggregate supply function (in the schedule sense) is greater than the upward shift in the aggregate demand function (in the schedule sense). At first glance, there does not seem to be any reason to expect the shift in the aggregate supply function to exceed the shift in the aggregate demand function and, therefore, it may be that the demand curve for labor is not downward sloping. Indeed, alternative slopes for this function have been suggested. We turn now to an examination of all possibilities.

The classical demand curve for labor

Figure 11.1c depicts what may be called "the classical demand curve for labor," since its downward slope is what most pre-Keynesian economists believed to be the appropriate one.

The Keynesian demand curve for labor

Keynes argued that changes in the money-wage rate were unlikely to change the level of employment. This implies that when the money-wage rate increases, the upward shift of the aggregate demand and supply curves are equal. The resulting aggregate demand curve for labor will be perfectly inelastic as in Fig. 11.1d.

The underconsumptionist demand curve for labor

There have always been a small group of economists who have argued that increase in money wages will lead to a rise in the quantity of labor demanded. In terms of aggregate supply and demand analysis, this result would occur if a rise in the money-wage rate shifted the aggregate demand curve upward by a larger amount than the shift upward induced in the aggregate supply curve. The resulting demand curve for labor would then be upward sloping as in Fig. 11.1e.

Deriving the relevant demand curve for labor

While an absolute statement as to which of these alternatives is, in fact, correct is not possible, it is useful to explore those factors which must be considered if a judgment as to the shape of the demand curve for labor is to be made. The relevant factors are (1) the physical conditions of production, (2) the distribution of income and the spending habits of the different economic groups, (3) inflationary expectations of entrepreneurs and consumers, and (4) the rate of interest.

For the moment assume that production techniques are constant and that whatever the present price level is, individuals believe it will continue into the future. Also assume that the monetary authority takes whatever steps are necessary to maintain a constant rate of interest. Under these assumptions it is only the consumption behavior of the different income groups and investment spending which will affect the demand for labor. If initially the money-wage rate is w_1, then N_1 (Fig. 11.2a) is the level of employment. Suppose the money-wage were to rise to w_2. What would be the effect on the aggregate supply and demand functions?

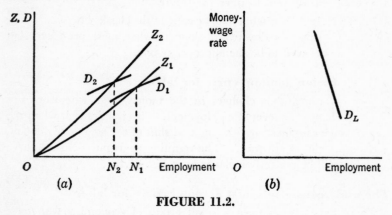

FIGURE 11.2.

A rise in the money-wage rate will increase total money-wage payments at each level of employment, so that, for example, if the money-wage rate were to rise by 5 percent, the wage bill here would be 5 percent higher at each employment level. Since the M/A-ratio at each employment level is unchanged, the aggregate supply curve will also shift upwards by 5 percent so that the wage share, at each level of employment, is unchanged. In other words, a rise in the money-wage rate will lead to a proportionate increase in the aggregate supply function (see Fig. 11.2a).

The effect on the aggregate demand function is more complex for the effects on both the marginal efficiency of capital schedule and the consumption function must be determined. We will take up the effect on each of these behavioral functions in turn.

The marginal efficiency of capital is a relationship between the expected revenue stream, net of future variable costs, and the present cost of capital. Suppose there is a rise in wages of 5 percent. Assuming wage costs to be total variable costs, a 5 percent rise in wages is a 5 percent rise in variable costs. Entrepreneurs, however, will expect prices to rise proportionately *at any given level of employment*, as the marginal cost curves of all firms rise proportionately. Expected net revenue, therefore, will rise by 5 percent. As the marginal cost schedules in the capital goods industries shift upwards, however, the present cost of capital goods will also rise by 5 percent so that the marginal efficiency of capital schedule is unchanged. *Given the rate of interest*, therefore, we can expect real investment to be unaffected by the change in the money-wage rate and consequently employment in the capital-goods industries will be unaltered. If there is to be any change in the total employment, under our assumption that the monetary authority assures a constant rate of interest, it will be due to the impact of a wage change on aggregate consumption.

The major effect of changes in the money-wage rate on consumption results from concomitant changes in the distribution of income. Since money-wages and prices rise proportionately (at each level of employment) real wages, and therefore the real consumption of wage-earners is unchanged at each employment level. The money income of rentiers is unchanged, hence, the consequences of a rise in money-wages is to redistribute real income, at each employment level, from rentier income towards profits. Real consumption by rentiers will decline by an amount as given by their marginal propensity to consume. The transfer of real income to profits is not likely to increase real consumption of profit recipients by the same amount, since some of the increase in profits will remain the property of the firm and will not be distributed as dividends. Since only the dividends are available for consumption spending, profit recipients are not likely to increase their purchases by an amount sufficient to offset the reduction in real consumption of rentiers.

Thus, while real investment is constant, real consumption and therefore total real demand declines at each employment level.[2]

Thus, in Fig. 11.2a, when the money-wage rate rises to w_2, the aggregate demand curve does not shift up sufficiently to intersect Z_2 at the same level of employment (N_1) as before. Instead, since real

---

[2] Since the marginal efficiency of capital schedule is unaffected, the additional retained earnings will not induce additional investment spending.

effective demand has declined, only N_2 workers will be hired. As the money-wage rate rises, the demand for labor (Fig. 11.2b) tends to decline, i.e., the demand curve for labor takes the classical downward sloping shape because of the redistribution of income from rentiers to profits and the fact that marginal propensity to consume out of gross profits is lower than the marginal propensity to consume out of rentier income. However, the larger the marginal propensity to consume out of gross profits, the more inelastic the demand curve for labor will be.

Expectations and the demand for labor

Changes in money-wages may alter peoples' expectations about the future. In particular, if the money-wage rate rises, people may expect wages and prices to continue to rise in the future. This inflationary psychology will have an impact on aggregate demand. If inflation is expected, entrepreneurs will anticipate a larger future net money income stream from each investment. Expectations of future inflation will not affect the present marginal cost curves of the capital goods industries, so that the present cost of capital is unchanged. Consequently, the marginal efficiency of capital schedule will shift outwards and, given the rate of interest, real investment will increase. This increase in real investment demand will tend to offset the decline in real consumption demand resulting from the shift of real income from rentiers to profits at each employment level. Moreover, if consumers expect money-wages and prices to continue to rise in the future, each group of consumers will tend to increase their present real consumption out of their present real income, so that this change in consumption behavior patterns will tend to offset the depressing effects of redistribution on real consumption. Because of these inflation expectations, real demand at each level of employment may not decline. Thus an inflationary psychology on the part of the public will make possible a Keynesian vertical demand curve for labor.

Moreover, if the inflationary psychology was sufficiently strong, the upward sloping underconsumptionist demand curve for labor would become conceptually admissable. This possibility, however, may be rejected as unrealistic on two grounds: (1) the rise in domestic wages and prices would reduce foreign demand for the economy's products and would divert home demand to foreign sources (these foreign effects will be taken up in Chapter 14), and (2) the central bank would take action to raise interest rates if inflationary psychology became that strong.[3]

The real balance effect

It has been suggested that real consumption depends on the real wealth of individuals as well as their real income. If wages and prices were to rise, then the real wealth of those who hold money or interest bearing government debt would decline without any concomitant increase in the real wealth of other individuals in the economy. Holders of money and government bonds would feel poorer, and, it is argued, they would cut real consumption at any level of real income.[4] This effect of changing price levels on real consumption is called *the real balance effect.*

The significance of the real balance effect on aggregate demand depends on the extent of the price rise which is necessary to make creditors feel sufficiently poorer so that their real consumption out of real income would decline. Price changes of this magnitude are likely to wreck confidence in the economy anyway, and it is doubtful therefore that consumers could behave rationally under such circumstances. For less violent, but more realistic price movements, there is little evidence that the real balance effect is significant.[5]

[3] A complete discussion of simultaneous changes in the rate of interest, the money-wage rate, the level of employment, and the price level must be deferred until Chapter 13.

[4] Holders of private debt (creditors) would, of course, feel poorer, and as a consequence might reduce their real consumption, but debtors whose money incomes increase at each level of employment (wage-earners, and profit recipients) would find the burden of debt reduced and might consequently expand their real consumption. The action of the debtors would tend to offset the action of the creditors, so that in the aggregate, the existence of private debt should not give rise to any real balance effect.

[5] Even one of the leading proponents of the real balance effect has suggested that, for all practical purposes, it is not significant. D. Patinkin (*Money, Interest, and Prices,* Harper & Row, 1956), indicated that it would take a major money-wage and price decline to significantly increase the demand for labor and, "it is precisely this necessity for a major price decline which makes this process unacceptable as a primary ingredient of a modern full-employment policy" (*Ibid.,* p. 233). On the other hand, a slow decline in prices and wages will create expectations of further price declines, so that, "the stimulating real-balance effect of a price decline may be more than offset by its depressing expectation effects" (*Ibid.,* p. 235). (We will discuss price expectational effects, which may at times be quite significant, in Chapter 13.) Patinkin argues that it is only in a secular (i.e., long-run) context that it is "almost certain" that the real balance effect will bring about changes in the demand for labor (*Ibid.,* pp. 253–254). Since our model is a short-run policy-oriented model, the real balance effect may safely be ignored.

In summary, a period of moderately rising money-wages will generate some expectations of continuing inflation which, if not frustrated
by monetary policy, is likely to result in a highly inelastic, but not
necessarily perfectly inelastic, demand curve for labor. Thus, modest
changes in the money-wage rate are likely to lead to negligible changes
in employment. With large and rapid changes in money-wages,
monetary policy and perhaps the real balance effect will tend to
mold the extremes of the demand curve for labor into the classical
shape.

THE SUPPLY FUNCTION FOR LABOR

In the relevant range, labor supply is normally taken to be an increasing function of the real wage rate, that is, as the real wage rate
rises, the number of workers who will offer their services on the market
tends to increase. However, since the demand curve for labor relates
the level of labor demanded to the money-wage rate, it is necessary
to convert the typical supply curve of labor from real to money-wage
units.

Deriving the supply function for labor

The real wage is determined by the marginal product of labor.[6]
With diminishing returns, the larger the number of workers hired, the
lower must be the real wage rate. At any given money-wage rate, it is
necessary to determine the number of workers who will be hired, in
order to determine the corresponding real wage rate. With a given
technology, for any money-wage rate, the quantity of labor that will
be demanded is given by the demand for labor curve. Once the quantity of labor that will be hired has been determined, labor's real wage
is equal to the marginal product of the last worker that would be
hired. For every possible money-wage rate, therefore, there will be
a unique real wage rate which will call forth a particular supply of
labor.

In Fig. 11.3, a classical demand curve for labor is drawn (D_L). If
the money-wage rate is w_1, N_1^d workers will be demanded, and the
real wage rate will depend on the marginal product (M_1) of that
amount of labor. At the real wage rate implicit in M_1, a given number
of workers (N_1^s) will offer their services. Since the quantity of labor

[6] Since $P = w/M$, while the real wage rate is equal to w/P, therefore, $w/P = M$.

demanded falls as the money-wage rate increases, if the money-wage rate is w_2 (which is greater than w_1), then only N_2^d workers will be demanded. The marginal productivity of labor (M_2) and the real wage rate, will be higher when less workers are demanded. The real

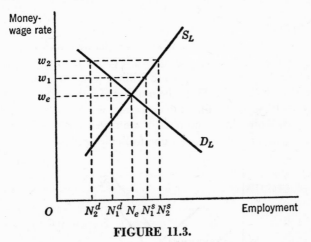

FIGURE 11.3.

wage rate will be higher, therefore, at N_2^d then at N_1^d. At this higher real wage rate, more workers (N_2^s) than before will offer their services.[7] Repeating this procedure for every possible money-wage rate, generates an upward sloping supply curve for labor (S_L).[8] The intersection of the

[7] It is essential to note that what is being analyzed here is the demand and supply schedules for labor and not equilibrium quantities supplied and demanded. It is in this schedule sense, that a rise in the money-wage rate has the same effect as a rise in the real wage rate, that is, in the schedule sense, a rise in the money-wage rate reduces demand and increases the supply of labor.

[8] Alternatively, the supply schedule of labor can be derived directly from effective demand points in the product market. For example, if the money-wage rate is w_1, then the product aggregate supply and aggregate demand functions are Z_1 and D_1 respectively (Fig. 11.2a). At the intersection of the Z_1 and D_1 curves, there is an equilibrium product price level, say P_1 (where $P_1 = w_1/M_1$). If, the money-wage rate is w_2, then Z_2 and D_2 (Fig. 11.2a) are the relevant aggregate supply and demand curves, and the implied equilibrium price level is, say, P_2 (where $P_2 = w_2/M_2$). Since as the money-wage rate rises, the quantity of labor demanded declines ($N_2 < N_1$), therefore, the marginal product rises ($M_2 > M_1$). It follows, therefore, that if the money-wage rate rises from w_1 to w_2, the associated rise in prices (from P_1 to P_2) will be less than proportional to the rise in money wages; consequently, the real wage rate is higher. Accordingly, an increase in the money-wage rate implies a rise in the real wage rate, and hence the supply curve of labor (S_L in Fig. 11.3) will be upward sloping.

demand and supply schedules for labor sets the equilibrium level of employment (N_e) and the equilibrium money wage rate (w_e) in Fig. 11.3. The real wage rate will depend on the marginal product of labor (M_e) at the N_e employment level.

Full employment

This level of employment, where the quantity of labor demanded equals the quantity of labor supplied, is called *full employment*. At full employment, all workers who are willing to work at the going real wage rate can find jobs. Since the number of people who will be willing to work is an increasing function of the real wage rate, full employment does not connote a fixed number of employed workers. It is possible for the economy to move from one full employment level to another.

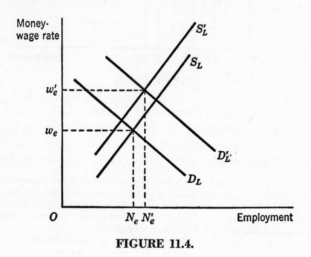

FIGURE 11.4.

Suppose there is an autonomous rise in the government component of aggregate demand, when the economy is already at the N_e full employment level. What are the resulting effects on employment and the money-wage rate? Assuming no change in production functions (and therefore a unique aggregate supply function for any money-wage rate), the increase in effective demand will shift the demand for labor curve to the right to D'_L (Fig. 11.4). A rightward shift in the demand for labor curve, however, involves greater demand for labor at each money-wage rate and therefore a lower marginal product and lower real wage rate at each money-wage rate. Hence the supply for labor curve will shift leftwards to S'_L. The new full employment money-wage rate (w'_e) and employment level (N'_e) is determined by the intersection of the D'_L and S'_L curves. The shift of both curves suggests that an increase in effective demand at full employment is likely to induce a small change in the level of total employment and a large increase in the money-wage rate, since the demand and supply curves for labor shift in opposite directions.

If the new equilibrium level (N'_e) is greater than the original equilibrium level of employment (N_e), then the new equilibrium real wage rate must be greater than the initial real wage rate in order to induce more workers to offer their services. This increase in real wages will occur when the money-wage rate rises more rapidly than consumer good prices which, in the short run, can happen only if the marginal product of labor in the wage-goods (all consumption goods) industries (and therefore the real wage rate) increases. This implies that aggregate real consumption must decline when real investment rises.[9] Since the real income and the real consumption of workers and profit recipients will increase, the money-wage rate and consumer prices must rise sufficiently so that the real consumption of rentiers is reduced by more than the increase in real consumption of workers and profit recipients. Under these circumstances, real aggregate consumption would fall and allow the economy to move from one full employment level to another, as wages and prices rose substantially. If the economy is going to move from one full employment level to a higher full employment level, then consumer prices must rise sufficiently to generate a considerable reduction in the real consumption of rentiers.

Involuntary unemployment

A market economy does not often move from one full employment level to another (except perhaps in times of war). Full employment is a rare phenomena. Most often, the economy is at a level of employment at which some workers are seeking employment at the going real wage rate but cannot find jobs. These workers are *involuntarily un-*

---

[9] Thus the classical position that increases in real investment can occur only at the expense of real consumption (i.e., when people "save" more at any level of employment), is correct, as this analysis shows, only when moving from one full employment level to another.

employed. Involuntary unemployment can exist because the supply curve for labor (in money units) has a perfectly elastic floor which is set by institutional factors. For example, unionized workers cannot take jobs for less than the union scale even if as individuals they would prefer to work at a wage below "scale" rather than be unemployed. Also, no one engaged in interstate commerce can work at an hourly wage lower than that set by the federal minimum wage law.

Figure 11.5 shows how the supply curve for labor is modified by introducing the money-wage floor w_0. Below the money-wage rate w_0, the dotted portion of the S_{L1} curve shows what the supply curve for labor would look like in the absence of the wage floor.

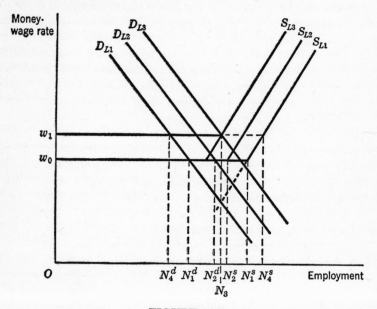

FIGURE 11.5.

Given the demand curve for labor D_{L1} and the concomitant supply curve for labor S_{L1}, the going money-wage rate will be w_0, N_1^d laborers will be demanded while N_1^s workers will be seeking jobs. The difference between N_1^s and N_1^d is the number of involuntarily unemployed workers.

Suppose, despite the existence of involuntary unemployment, profit expectations improve. This leads to an outward shift in the marginal efficiency of capital schedule. What will be the effect on wages and employment? With an increase in the marginal efficiency of capital schedule, entrepreneurs will be willing to hire more workers at each money-wage rate, and therefore, the aggregate demand curve for labor shifts to the right (D_{L2} in Fig. 11.5). Since at each money-wage rate, the demand for workers is greater than before, the real wage at each money-wage rate will be lower. As a consequence, fewer workers will offer their services at each money-wage rate, i.e., the supply curve for labor is shifted to the right (S_{L2} in Fig. 11.5). In equilibrium, w_0 is the money-wage rate, N_2^d workers are hired, and N_2^s workers are willing to work. In this situation involuntary unemployment would decline and is equal to the difference between N_2^s and N_2^d.

If the outward shift of the marginal efficiency schedule is great enough, then the resulting demand for labor curve (D_{L3}) will intersect the relevant labor supply curve (S_{L3}) at a money-wage rate in excess of the money-wage floor. The resulting equilibrium level of money wages will be w_1, and the level of employment will be N_3. In this instance, involuntary unemployment has been eliminated and full employment has been reached.[10]

It has thus far been assumed that the money-wage floor remains fixed. Consequently, the money-wage rate could not increase until full employment was reached. This supposition is unrealistic for several related reasons. As the number of involuntary unemployed decreases and sales increase, unions can become more truculent in their money-wage demands while employers become more willing to grant money-wage increases. As employment expands, prices will rise because of diminishing returns even if the money-wage is unchanged. Those workers who were employed at the outset will find their real wage declining and will seek cost of living increases. Also, as the pools of unemployment dry up, management finds the cost of searching out those who remain unemployed increasing so that it becomes less expensive to bid away workers from other employers than to search out the remaining unemployed. Finally, legislators may now find that the

---

[10] Any further outward shift of the D_L function will intersect the upward sloping portion of the resultant S_L curve. Thus any increase in demand past the initial full employment level will induce an increase in the money-wage rate. The resulting full employment wage-price relationship has already been analyzed in the previous section of this chapter.

legal minimum wage becomes substandard and therefore they may raise the legal minimum. For all these reasons, the perfectly elastic portion of the labor supply curve may move upward before full employment is reached. The rise in the money-wage rate that will result will add impetus to the price rise as employment increases.

Having suggested the inflationary situation which will accompany an increase in effective demand, we may now investigate the effects of a decline in effective demand. Suppose, for example, that "peace breaks out" in the world and as a result, the marginal efficiency of capital schedule shifts towards the origin. Consequently, there will be a leftward shift of the demand for labor curve, say back to D_{L1}, and therefore a rightward shift of the labor supply schedule to S_{L1}. If the money-wage floor has already moved to w_1 before the decline in effective demand occurs, many institutional barriers exist which make it unlikely that the wage floor will fall back to w_0. (These institutional factors and their impact on wages and prices will be discussed in the next chapter.) In other words, there will be a *ratchet effect* on the money-wage rate. As a result, a smaller number of workers will be demanded (N_4^d), while more workers (N_4^s) are willing to offer their services (since the real wage rate is higher) than initially. The labor force has therefore increased in the face of a recession and involuntary unemployment is greater than it was initially.

The interrelationships between the money-wage rate, the price level, and employment as developed in this chapter, will enable us to understand the phenomenon of inflation and to evaluate the policies designed to prevent it. Inflation is the subject of the next chapter.

IMPLICATIONS FOR WAGE POLICY

The money-wage rate is intimately tied to the price level and, therefore, a discussion of the effects of a government policy aimed at controlling money-wages must wait until the phenomenon of inflation has been discussed. Nevertheless, it might be appropriate, at this stage, to indicate the impropriety of attempting to reduce the money-wage rate via public policy in order to increase the level of employment. Assuming a monetary policy which prevents changes in the rate of interest (this assumption will be relaxed in Chapter 13), the analysis of this chapter has suggested that modest changes in the money-wage rate will result in negligible changes in the quantity of labor demanded. A large wage cut would be required to significantly increase the quantity of labor demanded. But large changes in the money-wage rate are, because of legal and other institutional barriers, for all practical purposes, unattainable in a free enterprise society. Moreover, even if such large changes were attainable, the result of a wage policy aimed at altering the level of employment every time aggregate demand changed, would be to concomitantly induce such large fluctuations in prices, that business calculations of expected income streams would become futile.[11]

Accordingly, wage policy should not be oriented towards affecting the level of employment, rather it should be utilized (as will be discussed in Chapter 12) to prevent inflation.

APPENDIX. The Neoclassical Demand for Labor Schedule

Since the demand for labor schedule derived in this chapter departs radically from earlier formulations of the demand for labor schedule, it would appear to be desirable to explain why we, following the lead of Keynes and Weintraub, have rejected the typical formulation.

For many years, economists have attempted to derive an aggregate demand curve for labor based on the supposition that no matter what price was paid for labor services, the demand schedule for any good could be assumed constant.[12] In this typical neoclassical approach, the aggregate demand curve for labor was built up from the firm level in the following manner.

The firm's demand for labor depends upon the marginal revenue productivity of labor. If the firm sells in a purely competitive market, then the firm's labor demand function is obtained by multiplying the marginal physical productivity of labor at each employment level by the product price. The resulting marginal revenue product function shows the addition to total revenue that an additional worker will bring forth at each employment level. An entrepreneur will maximize profits by hiring workers until the money-

[11] The impact of "reasonable" money-wage changes on expectations will be developed in Chapter 13.

[12] See, for example, J. B. Clark, *The Distribution of Wealth*, Macmillan, 1889, pp. 360–361, 365.

wage rate is equal to the marginal revenue product of the last worker hired.

If the product demand curve is assumed unchanged, then if the price of labor falls, all firms in the industry expand output. Given the product demand curve, as the output of the industry expands, the price of the product will decline. If the product price declines, then each firm in the industry will face a new marginal revenue product curve. To obtain the relevant labor demand curve of the firm as the industry's output and product price changes, we must use a cross-cut technique which can best be explained by an example.

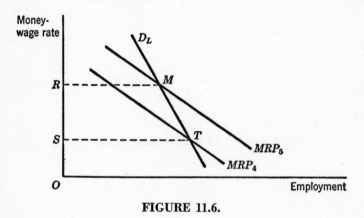

FIGURE 11.6.

In Fig. 11.6, let MRP_5 be the labor demand curve for the firm when the product price is \$5.00. If the price of labor is OR, the firm will hire RM workers. If the price of labor falls to OS for all firms, then the output of the industry will increase so that the product price will fall to say \$4.00. The firm's labor demand curve when the product price is \$4.00 will be MRP_4, and it will hire ST workers. If points such as M and T are connected, we can trace out the labor demand curve of the firm for industry-wide product price changes. The industry's demand curve for labor is then obtained by the lateral summation of the individual firm's demand curve (such as MT). Finally, a summation of all the industry demand curves for labor would, it is usually argued, lead to an aggregate demand curve for labor.

This neoclassical demand curve for labor absolutely requires the assumption of unchanging product demand schedules. The stability of these product demand functions depend on assumptions about (1) the constancy of consumer tastes, (2) the constancy of income and its distribution among consumers, and (3) the constancy of all other prices. These assumptions are obviously inapplicable for any analysis attempting to determine what the effect of changes

in money-wages will have on effective demand. With any change in employment due to a change in the money-wage rate, there must be concomitant
changes in aggregate real income (and its distribution) in the economy. Thus,
at least, assumption (2) underlying the individual product demand curve is
inapplicable. Accordingly, the neoclassical aggregate demand curve for labor
must be rejected as being inapplicable to an analysis which involves changes
in output and employment, and an aggregate demand curve for labor must
be derived which is based on shifting rather than constant product demand
curves.

CHAPTER 12

Inflation

In 1958, the Consumer Price Index rose significantly while the level of employment in the United States declined. The unusual nature of these events is illustrated in Fig. 12.1. As shown in this figure, employment declined in 1949 and in 1954. In 1949, the price index showed a marked decline, while in 1954, a slight decline in prices was observed. The 1958 experience stands out in sharp contrast to these other periods of unemployment.

Until 1958, many economists believed that there was a direct relationship between changes in price and changes in employment (because of diminishing returns). It was widely believed, however, that until full employment was approached, price movements would be insignificant. To simplify the theoretical analysis, therefore, the typical Keynesian approach discussed two distinct cases: (1) the involuntary unemployment case, where prices are assumed constant and output is variable, and (2) the full employment case, where output is constant and prices are variable. Events during the 1958 recession, however, emphasized the need for a theoretical model in which simultaneous changes in prices and employment can be handled. Such a model has been developed in the last few chapters. In this chapter all those parts of the model which bear on price changes will be brought together. An attempt will be made to suggest why prices and employment, which normally increase concomitantly, can, on occasion, move in opposite directions.

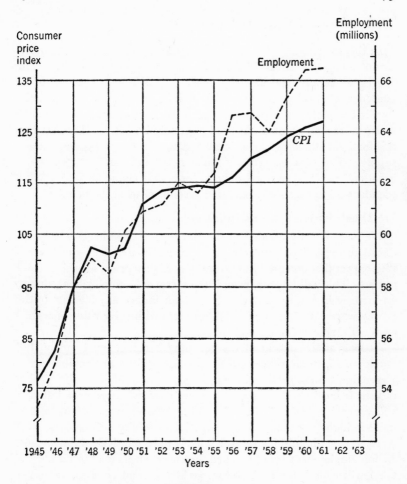

FIGURE 12.1.

Analytically, three basic types of inflation can be identified. Observed price rises will often be due to some combination of these three distinct inflationary processes. If public policy is to stabilize prices with a minimum of undesirable side effects, then it will be demonstrated that it is necessary to design different policies to control each type of inflation.

THE THREE KINDS OF INFLATION[1]

In this section, inflation will be analytically related to either movements along—or shifts in—the aggregate supply function. This aggregate supply classificatory scheme is adopted because of its analytical simplicity and convenience; it in no way implies that inflation is completely a supply determined phenomenon. As Marshall, many years ago, pointed out (and the analysis of Part III is based on this fundamental assertion) prices are determined by both demand *and* supply. The oft-used terms "demand-pull inflation" or "cost-push inflation" can "be excused only so long as it claims to be merely a popular and not a strictly scientific account of what happens."[2]

1. Diminishing returns inflation

We have already alluded to the fact that entrepreneurs will be induced to expand output and employment, in the short run, only if they expect that potential buyers will pay higher prices for this greater output. This will be true, even if the increase in employment, due to an increase in aggregate demand, does not induce any increase in the money-wage rate, because diminishing returns involve rising marginal costs with increases in output.

As long as the output of the economy is rising, but is not at full employment, diminishing returns inflation will be an inevitable and unavoidable consequence of further expansion. Although diminishing returns is inevitable, the significance of diminishing returns inflation will vary with the level of employment. When the rate of unemployment is high (say above 5 percent), idle capacity will exist in most firms, so that diminishing returns is likely to be relatively unimportant. As full employment is approached, however, an increasing number of firms will experience rapid increases in marginal costs as expansion occurs, and, consequently, diminishing returns inflation will become increasingly more important.

In the short run, diminishing returns inflation is an inevitable consequence of an expansion in employment. In the long run, however, diminishing returns inflation can be prevented by improvements in technology and/or increases in real capital per worker.

[1] S. Weintraub, *An Approach to the Theory of Income Distribution*, Chilton, 1958, pp. 162–164.
[2] A. Marshall, *Principles of Economics*, 8th edition, Macmillan, 1938, p. 348.

2. The degree of monopoly: profits inflation

Suppose, for any reason, businessmen come to believe that the demand curves they face have become less elastic at each level of output. Entrepreneurs will then increase the spread between price and marginal costs (i.e., the degree of monopoly power will increase).[3] As a result, at each level of employment, marginal costs are unchanged but prices and therefore profits have increased and the economy experiences a profits inflation.

A recent incident which illustrates the possibility of a profits inflation occurred in the Spring of 1962. After signing a money-wage contract which assured that the marginal cost schedule would remain unchanged during the year, the major steel companies announced an increase in steel prices. This announcement, which implied an increase in the spread between prices and marginal costs, can be interpreted as evidence that profit maximizing entrepreneurs in the steel industry believed that the demand schedule for their output had become less elastic. Since, at each level of aggregate employment, steel prices (and the prices of other products using steel as a raw material) would be higher than before, a profits inflation would result.

Normally, a profits inflation due to a change in monopoly-pricing practices would be combatted via the antitrust laws. In the case of the steel oligopoly, however, it is unlikely that the antitrust laws are applicable. President Kennedy, therefore, used the direct and forceful measures of publicity and an aroused public opinion (as well as government induced dissention by a few firms in the steel industry) to force management to rescind the price increase and prevent the profits inflation temporarily.[4]

---

[3] Since $MR = P\left(1 - \dfrac{1}{E_d}\right)$ while $MR = MC$ at the profit maximizing position, $MC = P\left(1 - \dfrac{1}{E_d}\right)$. Thus if the elasticity of demand (E_d) decreases, at any level of output, the spread between price and marginal cost increases.

[4] By the Spring of 1963, both the steel industry and the President had learned much from their brief but bitter encounter of the previous year. The initial announcement of the price rise by a relatively small steel company rather than by the acknowledged price leader, as well as the selectivity of the products on which prices were increased strengthened the industry's hand. The President's position was weakened by having called "wolf" once already.

3. Wage-price inflation

Every increase in the money-wage rate will, in the short run, shift marginal cost curves upwards, so that entrepreneurs will require higher market prices at any given level of output and employment.[5] Consequently, prices will rise at each level of employment, and a wage-price inflation results. The obvious short-run policy for this type of inflation is the maintenance of a constant money-wage rate.

In the long run, the total product curve can be shifted upwards by either an increase in capital per worker or a change in technology. In either case, if the money-wage rate increases in proportion to the increase in marginal productivity of labor, then the marginal cost curves would be unchanged, and, therefore, in the long run, it is possible for the money wage to rise without producing inflation.

INFLATION AND THE AGGREGATE SUPPLY FUNCTION

The three varieties of inflation can be analytically distinguished by their different effects on the aggregate supply function. Inflationary tendencies may be associated with either movements along the aggregate supply curves or shifts in the aggregate supply curve.

Diminishing returns inflation is associated with a movement along the aggregate supply function induced by an increase in aggregate demand. Movement up an aggregate supply function always implies rising prices if there is diminishing returns. Thus, in Fig. 12.2, a movement from N_1 to N_2 (while the money-wage rate is constant) will involve diminishing returns inflation. Profits inflation will involve an upward shift in the aggregate supply function while the money-wage rate is unchanged; while wage-price inflation is associated with an upward shift in the aggregate supply curve when the money-wage rate increases.

A movement in effective demand along an aggregate supply schedule (diminishing returns inflation), will always increase equilibrium prices. With profits and wage-price inflation, although the price level at each level of employment will be higher, the change in equilibrium prices cannot be specified until changes in the equilibrium level of employment are determined. It is possible, for example, that as a result

[5] See S. Weintraub, *Price Theory*, Pitman, 1949, p. 257.

of an increase in the money-wage rate the equilibrium level of employment declines. Although at any level of employment prices are higher than they would have been before, whether equilibrium prices at the new lower level of employment are higher or lower than the price level that was associated with the original higher equilibrium level of employment is not immediately obvious. In moving from the higher equilibrium employment level to the lower, there are two offsetting factors: prices are being increased because of the upward shift in the

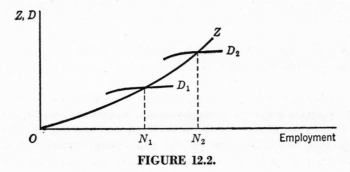

FIGURE 12.2.

aggregate supply schedule, but the downward movement in employment reduces the pressure on prices due to diminishing returns. The movement in equilibrium prices depends upon the net result of these two opposing forces. As indicated in Chapter 11, an increase in the money-wage rate is not likely to substantially reduce employment, so that normally a rise in the money-wage rate can be expected to result in an increase in equilibrium prices.

With profits inflation, on the other hand, the same two offsetting factors must be taken into account in determining the effect on equilibrium prices. In this case, however, the ultimate effect on equilibrium prices cannot be determined *a priori*.

Identifying the "causes" of inflation as diminishing returns, the degree of monopoly, and the money-wage rate, does not imply that any of these factors are necessarily the initiators of any particular inflationary event. For example, an increase in aggregate demand may induce changes in the degree of monopoly and/or the money-wage rate; or, on the other hand, these inflationary forces may be unleashed even in the absence of changes in aggregate demand. Public policies may also affect these inflationary factors directly or indirectly. It is impossible to put these factors into two mutually exclusive compartments marked demand-induced inflation and supply-induced inflation. As the following discussion suggests, our classificatory scheme is oriented towards indicating what policy levers are required to control inflation, rather than towards setting up exclusive, and exhaustive lists of supply factors and demand factors. In the final analysis, inflation is the result of the interplay of demand and supply and is not the exclusive domain of either separately.

CHANGES IN AGGREGATE DEMAND AND TWO KINDS OF INFLATION

Since there is no evidence on the effects of changes in aggregate demand on the degree of monopoly, it will be assumed that monopoly power does not change. Lack of evidence, at this time, should not imply that anti-inflationary policies can ignore monopoly pricing practices. Lack of knowledge does mean, however, that the remainder of this chapter can deal only with diminishing returns and wage-price inflation.

Assume that the labor supply function depends only on the real wage rate implied in the aggregate demand for labor curve. Moreover, assume that the level of the perfectly elastic floor of the labor supply schedule depends, in part, on the number of workers that are hired. What now will be the effects of a change in aggregate demand on wages and equilibrium prices?

Any change in the aggregate demand function implies a change in the demand for labor schedule. Assuming that physical productivity relationships are unchanged at each level of employment, an aggregate supply function can be hypothesized, such as the heavy discontinuous curve in Fig. 12.3a. The reasoning which lies behind this peculiarly shaped aggregate supply function is as follows.

If the initial money-wage rate is w_1, it can be assumed that that rate will continue to prevail as long as employment is less than N_3 (in Fig. 12.3a). If employers desire to hire more than N_3 workers, but less than N_4 workers, however, although there will still be involuntarily unemployed workers, the increase in the demand for labor will induce labor and legislators to raise the wage floor to w_2. Consequently, at the N_3 level, the aggregate supply curve will shift upward to the Z_2 level. Similarly, when the demand for labor exceeds N_4, the wage floor will rise once again so that the new money-wage rate will be w_3. Thus, again at the N_4 level, the aggregate supply curve

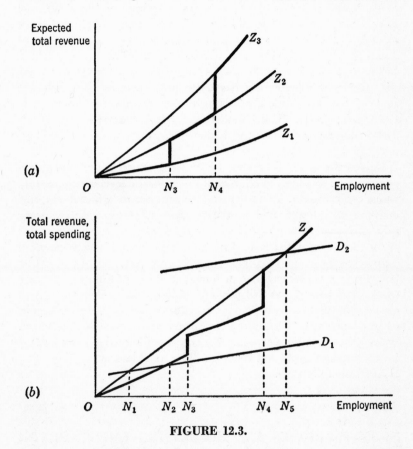

FIGURE 12.3.

will shift upwards to the Z_3 function. Hypothesizing discrete movements in the money-wage rate at critical employment levels results in a discontinuous aggregate supply function.[6]

[6] To make the analysis neater, it could be assumed that beyond the N_3 level, the wage floor rises continuously. The above analysis, however, appears to be more realistic. See J. M. Keynes, *The General Theory of Employment, Interest and Money*, Harcourt, Brace, 1936, p. 301.

The resultant aggregate supply function is redrawn in Fig. 12.3b. If the initial aggregate demand function is D_1, then N_2 is the equilibrium employment level, w_1 is the money-wage rate, and some price level (P_1) exists initially. Suppose now, some foreign nation takes action which precipitates a war scare domestically which induces an increase in government spending so that the aggregate demand curve rises to D_2. The new equilibrium level of employment will now be N_5, while the money wage rate will be w_3. Prices at the N_5 level are higher than they were at the N_2 level for two reasons: on the one hand, the increase in employment has raised prices because of diminishing returns, and, in addition, prices have risen because the money-wage rate has increased. This inflationary rise in equilibrium prices, as is true in most observable rises, is due to a combination of these two forces.

If, after the economy reaches the N_5 level, the crises pass and aggregate demand falls back to D_1, then the equilibrium level of employment would decline to N_1. While demand has returned to its initial schedule, employment is lower and both the money-wage rate and the real wage rate are higher than in the initial situation. The money-wage rate will not return to its initial level, for once the perfectly elastic segment of the labor supply curve has risen, institutional barriers will prevent its fall. Legislators, for example, will not revise the legal minimum wage downwards and unions will not cut "union scale." Consequently, a decrease in the aggregate demand schedule will have a greater impact on employment and less of an impact on prices than the equivalent increase in aggregate demand. Prices will decline when the economy moves from N_5 to N_1 but the fall will be small and attributable only to diminishing returns.

PRICE INCREASES AND DECREASING EMPLOYMENT

The model has, thus far, shown why only small price declines are to be expected in a recession. It is still necessary to explain how it was possible for prices to rise while employment fell in 1958. Two possible theoretical explanations are suggested by the previous analysis.

Since we do not know the relationship between profits inflation and changes in effective demand, it is possible that, during this period, profits inflation occurred simultaneously with the fall in employment.[7] Another possibility is that the strong wage-price inflation of 1955–1957 persisted into the recessionary period. Since the demand for labor was obviously falling during the recession, wage-price inflation could only have occurred if there were semi-autonomous changes in the supply schedule of labor, i.e., if the money-wage floor increased even as employment declined.

Although a perfectly mobile labor force has been assumed, in reality immobilities do exist in the labor market and workers do not move freely from one industry to another. The average real wage rate at any given level of aggregate employment is, of course, set by the marginal product of labor. Thus, at any given level of employment, there is a unique total real wage bill. The struggle for money-wages by different labor groups primarily affects the distribution of total real wages between the different labor groups, but does not affect the average real wage rate at any level of employment.[8] Each group of workers will attempt each year to raise its money-wage in the hope of improving its position vis-a-vis other workers. The amount of increase in the money-wage rate that any group of workers can secure in any given year will depend, in large measure, on their bargaining position, which, in turn, will be related to such diverse factors as the present state of the economy, the profit situation in their own industry, what other workers are getting, and when their wage contract comes up for renewal. In any event, there is continuous pressure on the money-wage floor at all times, although the extent to which the floor can be raised in any year will be partly related to current levels of aggregate economic activity. Thus, with the relatively small decline in employment in the recession of 1958, the money-wage floor may have increased and more than offset the decreasing pressure on prices exerted by diminishing returns, so that the price level crept up while employment declined.

---

[7] See Lerner's analysis of "sellers' inflation," in A. P. Lerner, "On Generalizing the General Theory," *American Economic Review*, 50, 1960, pp. 138–142.

[8] See J. M. Keynes, *op. cit.*, pp. 13–14. This assumes that the distribution of output between consumption and investment is uniquely determined at each level of employment.

THE ROLE OF MONETARY AND FISCAL POLICY IN INFLATION AT LESS THAN FULL EMPLOYMENT

Productivity relations, the degree of monopoly, the money-wage rate, and the level of effective demand are the determinants of the general price level. Since it is often claimed that the price level depends primarily upon the quantity of money, it may seem strange to some that the price level has been made to depend directly upon a large number of variables and only indirectly upon the quantity of money. Our line of reasoning, which was fully anticipated by Keynes, follows from the main body of the theory of the firm; and, after all, it is at the firm level that prices are made. Keynes, expecting doctrinal controversy with followers of the quantity theory of money approach to price level determination, noted that, given the degree of monopoly:

In a single industry its particular price-level depends partly on the rate of remuneration of the factors of production which enter into its marginal costs, and partly on the scale of output. There is no reason to modify this conclusion when we pass to industry as a whole. The general price-level depends partly on the rate of remuneration of the factors of production which enter into marginal cost and partly on the scale of output as a whole, i.e., (taking equipment and technique as given) on the volume of employment.[9]

Given this view of price level determination, what are the policy implications? Monetary and fiscal policy can affect the price level only by altering one or more of the strategic determinants which are:

1. Productivity relations.

2. The average degree of monopoly.

3. The money-wage rate.

4. The level of effective demand (i.e., the level of employment).

It is difficult to see any direct relationship, in the short run, between a monetary or fiscal policy which is likely to be implemented, and productivity, the degree of monopoly, or the money-wage rate.

[9] J. M. Keynes, *op. cit.*, p. 294.

Both fiscal and monetary policy are directed primarily at altering the level of effective demand. Thus, it is through changes in demand, whether induced by public or private spending, and the concomitant changes in employment that such policies can affect the price level. An easy money policy, for example, stimulates demand for investment goods which via the multiplier leads to an increase in employment. Prices will rise because of diminishing returns. Prices may also rise because the increase in demand leads to an increase in the money-wage rate. Alternatively, an increase in government spending will increase effective demand and consequently raise employment and prices. Whether the source of the increase in effective demand is from the public or the private sector, the effect is always to raise prices and employment simultaneously.

If the increase in public spending stimulates different industries than those stimulated by an increment in private spending, then the effect on the price level of an increase in public spending may differ from the effect of an increase in private spending. To the extent that different industries face different rates of diminishing returns, have different degrees of monopoly power, and have different money-wage rates, the resulting increase in prices for an increment in spending will be different. Nevertheless, there is no way of knowing *a priori* whether these possible differential effects are significantly large, or even if they are significant; that is, there is no way of predicting whether an increase in public spending is more, or less, or just as inflationary as an increase in private spending.

A public policy aimed at preventing all price increases before full employment can be successful only if it perpetuates involuntary unemployment. Such a policy which sacrifices employment for price stability has often been recommended and accepted. The reason for the acceptance of such a policy derives from the effects of inflation on the distribution of income. Only the unemployed and the impersonal corporation (and perhaps the entrepreneur of the small unincorporated enterprise) stand to reap unmitigated benefits in real income from a simultaneous increase in employment and prices. Those who are already employed and those who receive fixed money incomes have nothing to gain but much to lose.

THE ROLE OF FISCAL POLICY IN INFLATION AT FULL EMPLOYMENT

Full employment occurs when everyone who is willing to work at the going real wage rate can find a job. Since the number of people who will enter the labor force rises as the real wage rate rises, full employment is a variable and not a fixed number of workers. It is perfectly possible, therefore, for the economy to move from one full employment level to another full employment level, where the latter involves a greater total of employed workers. For this to occur, however, total real consumption must fall as workers' real consumption and aggregate demand rises.

As long as there is involuntary unemployment, the real wage rate can decline as employment rises. Once a full employment level is reached, any further increase in real effective demand requires additional workers to enter the labor force. More workers, however, can be induced to join the labor force only if the real wage rate rises.[10] The real wage rate will rise when the money-wage rate and *prices* rise sufficiently to reduce the real consumption of rentiers by more than the increase in real consumption of workers and profit recipients.[11] In this case, the marginal physical product of labor in the wage-goods industries (all consumption goods) will rise as the number of workers engaged in these industries decline. Since the real wage rate is essentially dependent on the marginal product in the wage goods industries, the real wage rate will rise. Under these circumstances, inflation is likely to be very severe and/or prolonged. In the real world, however, full employment inflations rarely occur, except perhaps in times of war. In wartime, an effort is made to obtain the highest full employment level compatible with other fundamental goals such as freedom of job choice. Governments will normally pursue a policy of price stability at the same time. Relatively successful price stabilization will be achieved if aggregate consumption is restrained while employment is expanding. There are many techniques available to governments to achieve this goal. For example, individuals may be urged to purchase

---

[10] Assuming no change in leisure-income preferences.
[11] This may result in moving individuals from the rentier class into joining the labor force.

war bonds and therefore reduce their consumption. A heavy tax on all consumption expenditures, on the other hand, makes consumption less attractive. Finally, government control of prices combined with rationing can constrain consumption demand and inflation.

INFLATION POLICY: A PROBLEM IN INCOME DISTRIBUTION

The distribution of income is both a cause and a consequence of the inflationary process. As has already been indicated, as employment and prices rise, fixed income groups and already employed workers (including managers) find their real incomes declining while the real income of the previously unemployed, the owners of unincorporated enterprises, and corporations increase. Thus, a consequence of inflation is to increase the well being of some groups in society, while others tend to suffer.

Inflation, on the other hand, may be the result of attempts by some groups to increase their share in the total real income. The aim of these groups is to increase their share of the pie—*no matter what the size of the pie may be*. Profits inflation is clearly such a case. Attempts by unions to raise the money-wage floor is another.

Society has apparently decided that the exercise of increased monopoly power to increase the profit share is socially undesirable. Antitrust laws have indirectly as one of their consequences the prevention of profits inflation. On the other hand, society has, by and large, accepted attempts on the part of labor to raise its share in real income. The primary tool relied upon by labor in attempting to raise the wage share is bargaining for higher money-wages. As is obvious from the model, the attempt to increase the wage share at any level of employment by increasing the money-wage rate will be frustrated by management as it increases prices *pari passu* with the increase in labor costs. Ironically, the upshot of all this is that at any level of employment, it is the gross profit share and not the wage share which rises at the expense of the rentier share, as the money-wage rate increases. Accordingly, if society does in fact wish to redistribute income towards wage-earners, then the appropriate procedure would be a judiciously chosen system of taxes and transfers, rather than by encouraging free wage bargaining.

It is often said that inflation is undesirable because its effects on income distribution are capricious. Nothing is further from the truth. The effects of inflation on redistribution are clear enough. Inflation redistributes real income away from fixed income groups including those who remain unemployed towards corporate profits and, given the progessive income tax, governments. If there are objections to inflation, it is precisely because the effects on redistribution are predictable and the outcome is socially undesirable.

CHAPTER 13

Prices, money-wages, and the simultaneous

determination of the rate of interest and the

level of employment

In Chapter 6, a simple model which demonstrated the simultaneous determination of output and the rate of interest was presented. In that model, price, wage, and productivity effects were suppressed. Making use of the concept of aggregate supply, a more generalized model which takes into account prices, wages, and productivity elements in the simultaneous determination of the level of employment and the rate of interest can be developed. As in Chapter 6, it will be useful to derive one equation that summarizes transactions in goods and services, and another summarizing demand and supply conditions in the money market. Little needs be added in this chapter to the discussion of transactions in goods presented in Chapters 9 and 10, but the treatment of the money market needs to be expanded. In particular, it will be necessary to show that the money-wage rate, as well as the interest rate, links the commodities and money markets.

THE MONEY-WAGE AND THE DEMAND FOR CASH BALANCES

In Chapter 6, the supply of money was determined by the decisions of the monetary authority and the commercial banks. These decisions of the banking system, however, determine the quantity of money in *money* units and not in *real* units. As long as prices were assumed constant, there was no difficulty in reconciling a demand for cash balances in real terms with a supply of money in money units. However, once it is recognized that prices and outputs vary together, then it is necessary to express the demand and supply for money in a common unit. In the following, demand for real cash balances will be converted into a demand in money terms.

The demand for transactions and precautionary balances, in money terms, depends upon the dollar volume of current transactions. It is the size of these monetary sums that matter and the size of these sums depends on (1) the volume of real goods purchased, and (2) the prices of these goods. Prices, therefore, are an important determinant of the demand for cash balances.[1] Since both the demand for goods, and commodity prices tend to increase as employment rises, every increase in economic activity will exert at least a twofold pressure on the demand for cash balances. First, the demand for money will increase to facilitate the exchange of the larger volume of goods. Secondly, demand for cash increases to pay the higher prices resulting from diminishing returns even with a constant money-wage rate. If the money-wage rate were also to increase with expansion, then there would be a third force raising prices and thereby increasing the demand for cash balances. It is inevitable, therefore, that an increase in effective demand will increase the demand for cash balances and, given the supply of money, the rate of interest will increase. To ignore price level movements which occur at less than full employment is to ignore an important factor which tends to create "tight money" during expansion.

One obvious consequence of introducing wage and price phenomena into the system is to highlight the fact that labor unions share responsibility with the monetary authority in affecting the rate of interest. The monetary authorities can either alter the supply of money or induce

[1] For example, from 1940 to 1961, the gross national product of the United States (in constant 1961 dollars) increased from $236.3 billion to $518.7 billion, an increase of 119.5 percent. In current dollars (i.e., unadjusted for price changes) gross national product over the same period increased from $100.6 billion to $518.7 billion, an increase of 415.6 percent. Surely the demand for transactions balances during this period rose more as a consequence of price level changes than in response to increases in real output.

the public to change their expectations about future interest rates while the unions via their wage policy can affect the demand for transactions and precautionary balances. We will live in interesting times when labor unions recognizing their ability to affect the rate of interest advocate across the board wage cuts so as to reduce the rate of interest in order to stimulate new investment.

THE COMPLETE EQUILIBRIUM MODEL

A complete equilibrium model of a purely competitive, fully integrated economy would consist of the following relationships.

First, there is the aggregate supply function which relates entrepreneurs' expectations of sales revenue to any specified level of employment hiring that they would want to offer. For any level of workers employed, entrepreneurs' expectations of total revenue will be related to total wage costs, where the latter is equal to the money-wage rate multiplied by the level of employment. Thus, as indicated in Chapter 9, changes in expected total revenue are related to changes in the wage bill. The aggregate supply function can be generalized, therefore, as

$$Z = f_1(w, N), \tag{13.1}$$

where Z is entrepreneurial expectations of total revenue, w is the money-wage rate, and N is the level of employment.

The price level is implicit in the aggregate supply function since profit-maximizing entrepreneurs will be equating expected price and marginal costs. Since marginal cost is equal to the money-wage rate divided by the marginal productivity of labor, while the latter is related to the level of employment, the price level is a function of the money-wage rate and the level of employment,[2] i.e.,

$$P = f_2(w, N), \tag{13.1a}$$

where P is the price level.

---

[2] Monopoly elements can be introduced into the system via the aggregate supply function but, as indicated in Chapter 9, there is no evidence of significant changes in the degree of monopoly in the short-run, so that the shape of the aggregate supply function tends to follow competitive theory relationships.

Secondly, there is an aggregate consumption function which relates total money consumption spending to the level of employment. This relationship depends upon the real demand for consumption goods by each major category of consumers (wage-earners, rentiers, and profit-recipients) which, in turn, depends upon the level of money income of each group and the price level. Given the fixed money income of rentiers, their real income, which depends upon the price level, is a decreasing function of employment. The money income of wage-earners and profit-recipients varies with the money-wage rate and the level of employment. Consequently, given the propensity to consume out of real income of each group, aggregate consumption spending (D_c) in money terms, depends upon the fixed income payments of rentiers $(\overline{F})$ which is an exogenously determined constant, the money-wage rate, the level of employment, and the price level. Using (13.1a), the aggregate consumption function can be generalized as

$$D_c = f_3(\overline{F}, w, N). \tag{13.2}$$

The demand for real investment goods depends upon the marginal efficiency of capital which in equilibrium must be equal to the rate of interest. Monetary investment expenditures (D_i) are therefore a function of real investment as determined by the rate of interest and the price level. The generalized investment demand function can be written as

$$D_i = f_4(i, w, N). \tag{13.3}$$

The last equation required for describing the commodity side of the economy is the equilibrium condition that aggregate supply must equal aggregate demand, i.e.,

$$Z = D_c + D_i. \tag{13.4}$$

The money market is summarized in the following equations. The demand for transactions and precautionary balances (L_1) depends upon the volume of goods produced and the price level where output is a function of employment, and prices depend upon both the level of employment and the money-wage rate. Therefore,

$$L_1 = f_5(w, N). \tag{13.5}$$

The speculative demand for money (L_2) is a function of the rate of interest (i) and expectations of the future rate of interest. Taking expectations as given,

$$L_2 = f_6(i). \tag{13.6}$$

The quantity of money (m) is exogenously determined by the banking system, so that

$$m = \overline{m}, \tag{13.7}$$

where $\overline{m}$ is a constant.

The final equation, which completes the system, is the equilibrium condition that the total demand for money equals the supply of money, i.e.,

$$L_1 + L_2 = \overline{m} \tag{13.8}$$

Equations (13.1) through (13.4) reduce to one equation in three unknowns (w, N, i). Assuming the money-wage rate is exogenously determined, these equations reduce to a single equation in two unknowns, N and i, which summarize all that has been developed concerning transactions in the commodity markets:

$$N = f_7(i). \tag{13.9}$$

This function is the composite of the consumption, investment, and aggregate supply functions and will be referred to as the *CIZ* function. The *CIZ* function traces out all the values of employment and the rate of interest which, for a given money-wage rate, are compatible with equilibrium between aggregate demand and aggregate supply. The *CIZ* function, a form of which is plotted on Fig. 13.1, is downward-sloping, since as the interest rate declines, real investment will rise and induce a rise in real consumption and a further rise in employment via the multiplier.

Equations (13.5) through (13.8) also reduce to a single equation, and if the money-wage is taken as exogenously determined, then the resulting equation has the same two unknowns, N and i as (13.9), and summarizes what has been said about the money market:

$$i = f_8(N). \tag{13.10}$$

This *LM* function is a composite of the demand and supply for money and it traces out all the values of employment and the rate of interest which, for a given money-wage rate, are compatible with the equilibrium between the demand and supply of money.

A form of the *LM* function is plotted on Fig. 13.1. This function will have a perfectly elastic section at some low level of interest when the economy is in the liquidity trap. Once employment and transac-

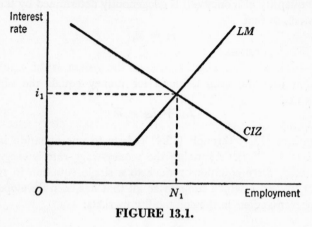

FIGURE 13.1.

tions rise to a level which exceeds the trap, the function slopes upwards, as with a constant money supply and money-wage rate, increasing employment increases the demand for L_1 balances and raises the rate of interest.

Employment and interest are the determinates of the system while the quantity of money, the demand schedule for cash balances, the money-wage rate, and the aggregate demand and supply functions are its determinants. As in Chapter 6, shifts in any of the underlying determinants will shift the *CIZ* or *LM* functions and will change the equilibrium levels of interest and employment.

INTERDEPENDENCE OF THE COMMODITY AND MONEY MARKETS INTRODUCED BY THE MONEY-WAGE RATE

A one-time upward shift in the money-wage rate

In the previous section the money-wage rate was held constant. Now let us examine the effect of changes in the money-wage rate.

We start with the simplest (but most unrealistic) case. What are the implications for the level of employment and the rate of interest when the money-wage rate rises and it is generally expected the wage-rate increase will *not* be repeated in the future? This change will affect both the *LM* and the *CIZ* functions.

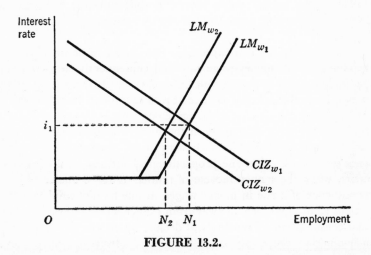

FIGURE 13.2.

The *LM* function will be affected since an increase in money-wages results in an increased demand for L_1 balances at each level of employment. If LM_{w_1} (in Fig. 13.2) is the money market curve when the money-wage rate is w_1, and if the money-wage rate rises to w_2, while the money supply is unchanged, then at every level of employment (except in the liquidity trap), the increased demand for L_1 balances will raise the rate of interest and induce an upward shift in the *LM* function to LM_{w_2} in Fig. 13.2.

The effect of a money-wage rate change on the *CIZ* function is more complex for it is necessary to examine the effects on both the marginal efficiency of capital schedule and the real consumption function.

The effects on the marginal efficiency of capital schedule can be discussed first. The marginal efficiency of capital is a relationship between the expected revenue stream, net of variable costs, and the present cost of capital. Suppose there is a rise in wages of 5 percent. Assuming wage costs to be total variable costs, a 5 percent rise in wages is a 5 percent rise in variable costs. Entrepreneurs, however, will expect prices to rise proportionately at any given level of employment, as the marginal cost curves of all firms rise proportionately. Expected net revenues, therefore, will rise by 5 percent. As the marginal cost curves in the capital goods industries shift upward, however, the present cost of capital goods will also rise by 5 percent so that the marginal efficiency of capital schedule is unchanged. *At any given rate of interest*, therefore, we can expect real investment to be unaffected by the change in the money-wage rate and consequently employment in the capital goods industries will be unaltered. If there is to be any change in total employment at each rate of interest, it will be due to the impact of a wage change on aggregate consumption.

The major effect of changes in the money-wage rate on consumption results from concomitant changes in the distribution of income. Since wages and prices rise proportionately (at any level of employment), while the money income of rentiers remains unchanged, the consequence of a rise in money-wages, at any level of employment, is to redistribute real income away from rentier income towards profits. Real consumption by rentiers will decline by an amount as given by their marginal propensity to consume. The transfer of real income to profits is not likely to increase real consumption by the same amount, since some of the increase in profits will remain the property of the firm and will not be distributed as dividends. Since only the dividends are available for consumption spending, profit recipients are not likely to increase their purchases by an amount sufficient to offset the reduction in real consumption of rentiers. In other words, as a result of the redistribution of income from rentiers to profits and the smaller marginal propensity to consume out of gross profits than out of rentier income, a one-time increase in the money-wage rate will reduce the slope of the aggregate real consumption function. Consequently, the magnitude of the multiplier will decline, which will lead to a lower level of total output and employment for any given level of real investment. The upshot of all this is that at any rate of interest, the level of real investment is unchanged, but total real spending is reduced.[3] A once-over change in the money-wage rate will, therefore,

[3] Since the marginal efficiency of capital schedule is unaffected, the additional retained earnings will not induce additional investment spending, and effective demand will decline at each rate of interest.

shift the CIZ schedule leftward from CIZ_{w_1} to CIZ_{w_2} (Fig. 13.2). At the original money-wage rate, say w_1, the equilibrium level of employment is N_1 and the equilibrium interest rate is i_1. The rise in the money-wage rate to w_2 will lead to a reduction in employment (N_2 in Fig. 13.2), but the effect on the equilibrium interest rate is uncertain. If employment falls off enough, the actual quantity of transactions and precautionary balances demanded may fall and therefore reduce the rate of interest. Alternatively, if total money spending at the new equilibrium level of employment is greater than it was at N_1, the demand for transactions and precautionary balances and, hence, the interest rate, would be greater.

The money-wage rate as a continuous function of the level of employment

Now we turn to the more complex, but more realistic situation in which the money-wage rate rises continuously as employment increases. In Fig. 13.3a, there is a family of LM curves. Each curve represents the money market at a given money-wage rate. As the money-wage rate rises ($w_1 < w_2 < w_3$), the LM function shifts upward from LM_{w_1}, to LM_{w_2}, and to LM_{w_3}, respectively. The reason for this upward shift is, as before, the rise in the demand for L_1 balances at each level of employment. As employment expands and the money-wage rate rises, at each given level of employment, there is a point on one of the curves of this LM family which is relevant for that employment and money-wage rate. The locus of such points is drawn as LM in Fig. 13.3a.

If entrepreneurs expect that each money-wage rate increase will be the last, the effect of any wage rate increase is the same as with a once-over money-wage rise. In Fig. 13.3b, there is a family of CIZ curves where each curve assumes a particular money-wage. If $w_1 < w_2 < w_3$, the CIZ functions shift leftward from CIZ_{w_1} to CIZ_{w_2} to CIZ_{w_3} on Fig. 13.3b. Combining the resultant CIZ and LM curves on Fig. 13.3c. yields the simultaneous solution for interest and employment. The equilibrium money-wage rate which is compatible with this i and N solution is derived as in Chapter 11.

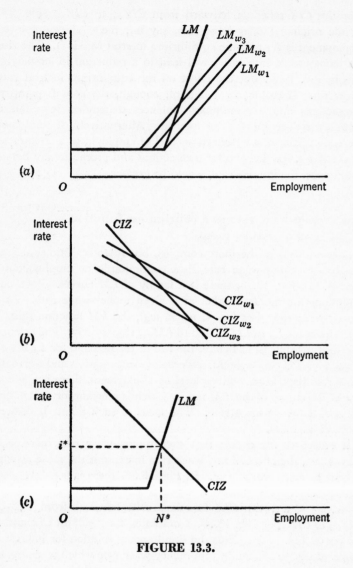

FIGURE 13.3.

EXPECTATIONS OF FUTURE CHANGES IN THE MONEY-WAGE RATE: THE INFLATION PSYCHOLOGY EFFECT

Things are more difficult yet in the most realistic case of them all. When money-wages begin to rise, entrepreneurs may expect wages to rise again in the future. Such expectations will shift the marginal efficiency of capital schedule upward. Expectations of future money-wage increases will not affect the present cost of capital goods, while it will increase the expected net future money income stream of capital goods, therefore raising the marginal efficiency schedule. This outward shift in the marginal efficiency of capital schedule when money-wages rise and are expected to continue to rise in the future will tend to offset the decline in the real consumption function at each employment level due to the redistribution of income. Under these circumstances, when the money-wage rate changes, the upward shift in the marginal efficiency of capital schedule, therefore, will tend to offset the downward shift in the real consumption function due to the change in the distribution of real income. As a result there may be little or no downward shift in the *CIZ* function. Moreover, if consumers expect wages and prices to rise again in the future, they may decide to increase real consumption out of real income now. As a result, the real consumption function will shift upward augmenting the upward shift in the marginal efficiency of capital function, so that the resulting *CIZ* function may shift upward from CIZ_{w_1} to CIZ_{w_2} in Fig. 13.4.

As before, an increase in the money-wage rate increases the demand for transactions and precautionary balances at every employment level. Given the supply of money, these increases in demand for transactions and precautionary balances will, if the speculative demand is unchanged, raise the rate of interest at each level of employment and result in an upward shift in the *LM* function.

Holders of speculative cash balances, however, must also make a judgment. If, as the liquidity preference theory has assumed so far, the speculative choice is between money holdings and a riskless perpetual bond, then as long as an individual expects the future rate of interest to rise at a more rapid per annum rate than he expects the price level to rise, he will desire to hold cash for he expects the price of bonds

to decline at a more rapid rate than the decrease in the purchasing
power of money. A change in the money-wage rate will alter the speculative demand for money, therefore, only if it has a differential impact
on price expectations and interest rate expectations. The total demand
for money will increase at each level of employment if individuals
expect that the rate of increase in prices will be equal to, or less than,

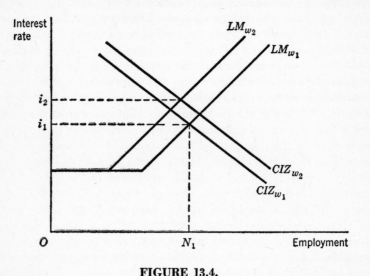

FIGURE 13.4.

the expected rate of change in the rate of interest, for the speculative
demand for money will be at least as large as before but the demand for
transactions and precautionary balances will be greater. Hence, with
a constant money supply, the rate of interest at each employment level
will rise, and therefore the *LM* curve will shift upwards.

Of course, in the real world, perpetual bonds are not the only alternatives to holding money. Another important class of assets are
equities and other second-hand assets. To avoid the complexities of
a complete theory of asset choice at this stage, assume equities to be
the only other alternative. If equity prices are believed to move with
changes in the price level and if the rate of interest on bonds is expected
to move more slowly than the price level, people will prefer, for speculative purposes, equities to bonds. Consequently, the price of equities

will rise while the price of bonds will fall until in equilibrium the rate
of interest has risen sufficiently to compensate bond purchasers for
their expectations of inflation. Moreover, if there is an inflationary
psychosis then we can expect the rise in the rate of interest to be aug-
mented by central bank policy. The central bank will be struggling
to curtail demand in the domestic market. Their tool will be the
quantity of money and their objective will be an increase in interest
rates in order to cut down spending. For all these reasons, then, a rise
in the money-wage rate will shift the *LM* curve upward to LM_{w_2}
in Fig. 13.4, so that the new equilibrium rate of interest will always be
higher than the initial level. The level of employment may or may
not be less than at the outset; it all depends on the relative shifts in
the two functions. Except in the case of expectations of hyper-inflation,
however, it is not unreasonable to expect that an inflationary period
will be ended by labor "pricing itself out of the market."

CHAPTER 14

Foreign trade and the equilibrium model

It was only necessary to redefine the components of the aggregate demand function when the forecasting model was restructured (in Chapter 8) to take account of the fact that individuals in the domestic economy may buy abroad and foreigners may choose to purchase domestic goods and services. It is, however, more complicated to introduce foreign trade into the equilibrium model, since in reality, foreign trade affects aggregate supply as well as aggregate demand. To summarize the rest of this chapter in advance, purchases abroad and purchases by foreigners of domestic goods affects both the level and composition of output and thereby aggregate supply and the price level in all the trading countries, which, in turn, affects the distribution of income and the level and composition of aggregate demand in each country. The task of this chapter is to present an orderly analysis of these diverse interrelationships.

AGGREGATE IMPLICATIONS OF COMPARATIVE ADVANTAGE

A major theorem of the theory of international trade states that, with free trade, the entrepreneurs of each trading nation will find it profitable to specialize and to produce those goods and services which they can make most efficiently and to trade with the entrepreneurs of the other countries for those products which they are least efficient at producing. This proposition has been called the *law of comparative advantage.*

In addition to comparative advantages, difference in the degree of monopoly, tax laws, tastes, and other factors will be reflected in the relative price structure of each trading nation. The exchange rate, that is, the price of one nation's currency in terms of the other's, represents some form of average adjustment of price levels in the two countries. Between the trading nations the relative price structure will be different, and these differences are the signals to which importers and exporters respond.

Foreign trade will modify the equilibrium model in two ways. First, since the domestic economy will specialize in those industries in which it will have a comparative advantage, the composition of output, at each level of domestic employment, will be affected and therefore the shape and position of the aggregate supply function will be different when trade occurs as opposed to a situation in which there is no trade.

Secondly, the aggregate demand function must be defined so that (1) the demand concept involved is only the demand of buyers for domestically produced goods and services, (2) it reflects the internal prices in each trading country which vary with the level of employment in each country, and (3) changes in income abroad, as well as at home, will affect the level of aggregate demand.

Assume constant money-wage rates in the domestic economy and in the rest of the world. Any exogenous increase in domestic expenditures will raise domestic income and induce additional imports. These additional purchases from abroad will raise income and output abroad. As output at home and in the rest of the world increases, prices at home and abroad will rise due to diminishing returns in each country.

If the rate of diminishing returns is not markedly different at home and abroad, domestic prices will rise more than foreign prices since the impact on domestic employment is greater than the induced effect on employment abroad. As a result, foreigners will find import prices rising relative to the prices of their own produced goods,[1] while domestic residents will find foreign products becoming cheaper relative to domestically produced goods. These relative price changes should affect the domestic and foreign marginal propensities to import—the former should rise, while the latter ought to fall.

---

[1] Assuming a fixed rate of exchange.

The upshot of all this is that an exogenous increase in domestic expenditures will tend to raise employment, domestic prices, and imports, while exports are likely to rise only slightly because of the induced expansion abroad. Consequently, there are three implications to be derived from this equilibrium analysis of the effects of an increase in exogenous expenditures on domestic output: (1) in an open economy, a smaller increment in employment will be induced than would be the case in a closed economy since some of the induced spending will be on goods produced abroad, (2) if prices are permitted to rise, then more of the induced spending will spill over into foreign purchases than if prices are held constant at home and abroad, and (3) since imports will increase more than exports, the domestic balance of trade will deteriorate.

Although these conclusions will generally be correct, there is an instance in which an initial increase in expenditures on domestic output will lead to an improvement in the balance of trade. For example, assume two trading countries, A and B. If domestic expenditures in A for A's output are exogenously increased, then A's prices will tend to rise more than B's prices. If B's price elasticity of demand for A's products is inelastic, then B's total expenditures in A will rise. Similarly, if A's price elasticity of demand for B's products is inelastic, A's spending in B will rise but by a smaller amount, since B's prices have increased less than A's. If there were no changes in income levels, there would be a net increase in spending in country A and a decrease in spending in country B. Income levels, however, do change; nevertheless, if price elasticities are low, then income elasticities must be low.[2] Consequently, the shift in spending due to the change in relative prices at home and abroad will more than offset any increase in the domestic demand for imports due to the rise in domestic real income. The upshot of this would be that the domestic expansion would induce a slump in the rest of the world while improving the

---

[2] The price elasticity of demand depends upon the income elasticity and the elasticity of substitution, i.e.,

$$E_p = kE_y + (1 - k)E_s,$$

where E_p is price elasticity, E_y is income elasticity, E_s is elasticity of substitution, and k is the proportion of income spent on the good in question. Since all goods are ultimately substitutes, i.e., $E_s > 0$, then it follows that $E_p > E_y$.

domestic balance of trade and keeping the multiplier repercussions at home.[3]

The necessary conditions for this perverse situation to occur are (1) a low domestic income elasticity for imports, (2) a high rate of domestic diminishing returns so that domestic prices rise substantially as domestic expenditures increase, and (3) the price elasticities of demand for imports in both of the trading countries must be less than unity, so that when foreign products become relatively cheaper, domestic and foreign buyers do not significantly reduce their domestic purchases. The mere statement of these necessary requirements indicates the exceptional nature of this example. In the usual foreign trade situation, not all of these conditions will be met and, therefore, we may expect an increase in domestic expenditures to induce increases in output, prices, and employment at home and abroad. As a result, with an exogenous increase in spending on domestic output, the domestic balance of trade will deteriorate since the domestic demand for the products of the rest of the world will rise more than the foreign demand for domestic exports. Domestic prices will tend to rise more than foreign prices (unless diminishing returns is much more important in the rest of the world than it is domestically). Although the balance of trade will deteriorate, since the increase in domestic prices will be greater than the increase in foreign prices, the real terms of trade will tend to move in favor of the domestic economy, that is, the domestic economy will receive more units of foreign produced goods for every unit of domestically produced goods it sells abroad.

MONEY-WAGE CHANGES AND FOREIGN TRADE

If the money-wage rate at home (abroad) varies directly with the domestic (foreign) level of employment, then the money-wage rate will give added impetus to variations in the price levels of the trading nations. Consequently, the effect of an increase in domestic expenditures on the domestic and foreign levels of economic activity will be reinforced by money-wage rate phenomena. In general, the result will be to raise prices, wages, and employment domestically more than

[3] See J. E. Meade, *The Balance of Payments*, Oxford University Press, 1951, pp. 73–74.

their counterparts abroad and, therefore, to reduce the multiplier ramifications on domestic employment and output. Thus, the magnitude of the multiplier is likely to be smaller in an open economy with flexible wages and prices than in an open economy with constant wages and prices, which in turn will have a smaller multiplier than in a closed economy.

Given stable exchange rates, the international relationship of money prices among the trading nations is clearly a fundamental determinant of world trade, and the role of money-wages must be fully understood when formulating world trade policy. Up to now, this problem has received little theoretical attention. The analysis of this chapter suggests that future developments of international trade theory will have to take into account domestic money-wage changes and variations in the level of employment, as well as the more traditional aspects of international money and commodity markets.

FOREIGN TRADE, THE LEVEL OF EMPLOYMENT, AND THE WAGE SHARE

The multitude of open economy situations which can be analyzed via aggregate supply and demand analysis is too large to be presented in a book that does not deal exclusively with foreign trade. Given the supply conditions and the demand elasticities of prices and incomes, aggregate supply and demand curves can always be derived and the equilibrium solution determined.

One possible situation is presented below, mainly for its pedagogical value, but it does also have some important implications.

Assume there are only two economies (A and B), which produce only two goods (X and Y), using only two factors of production, labor (N) and capital (K). Moreover, assume that initially there is no trade between the two economies and that both commodities are produced in each country by fully integrated firms. In country A, labor is relatively scarce so that capital intensive methods of production are used; while in country B, capital is relatively scarce and therefore labor intensive methods are employed. Under these circumstances, what will be the effect on employment in A if the two nations begin to trade?

The initiation of trade will alter the composition of output at each level of employment as each country tends to specialize in the industry in which it has a comparative advantage. Assuming identity of tastes and identity of production functions (which are assumed to be linear and homogeneous), then in the labor scarce country (A), resources will be shifted from the labor intensive industry (X) into the capital intensive industry (Y). Moreover, as the output of X is reduced, the bundle of resources freed contains a higher proportion of labor to capital than is optimal for industry Y at the prevailing ratio of factor prices, so that labor tends to become cheaper relative to capital at each level of employment. Profit maximizing entrepreneurs will therefore increase the labor to capital ratio in each industry by substituting some of the cheaper factor for the more expensive factor. Finally, assume that because of diminishing returns in each country, neither country completely specializes in the production of only one good, so that the output of industry Y expands, while the output of X is reduced but not eliminated in country A.

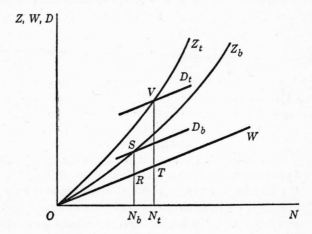

FIG. 14.1. The Effects of Trade on Aggregate Demand and Supply.

In Fig. 14.1, Z_b represents the pre-trade aggregate supply function, while D_b represents the pre-trade aggregate demand function. If the money-wage rate is assumed to be constant (w), then OW is the wage bill line, and in equilibrium, N_b is the level of domestic employment and the wage share is equal to N_bR/N_bS.

For any given ratio of factor prices, the wage share will be greater in the labor intensive industry (X) than in the capital intensive industry (Y). The aggregate wage share at any level of employment is, as indicated in Chapter 9, equal to the weighted average of the M/A-ratios of the individual industries, i.e.,

$$\frac{W}{Z} = \left(\frac{M_x}{A_x}\right)\frac{Z_x}{Z} + \left(\frac{M_y}{A_y}\right)\frac{Z_y}{Z}, \qquad (14.1)$$

where W is the total wage bill, Z is the gross income, Z_x is total income (sales) in industry X, Z_y is total income (sales) in industry Y, M, and A with their respective subscripts representing the marginal and average products of labor in the appropriate industry. The assumption of linear and homogeneous production functions implies that the M/A-ratio in each industry is independent of the output of the industry and will either be a constant (if the production function is of the Cobb-Douglas type) or will decline if the labor/capital ratio increases.[4] With the introduction of trade, therefore, the importance of industry Y increases relative to X, i.e., Z_y/Z increases while Z_x/Z decreases at each level of employment. Thus, even if the M/A-ratio (and therefore the wage share in each industry) is unchanged, (14.1) indicates that the wage share in the gross income of the economy will decline at any level of employment as trade induces a change in the composition of output.

As we have demonstrated in Chapter 9, the wage share depends on the position of the aggregate supply function relative to the wage bill line. The assumption of a constant money-wage rate[5] fixes the position of the OW line in Fig. 14.1, and implies that the aggregate supply function shifts upward to Z_t after trade is established.

Given the income and price elasticities of the various buyers, the aggregate demand curve for home production can be derived. This post-trade demand function would have to be built up through an

[4] See Appendix.

[5] A constant money-wage rate before and after trade is not inconsistent with labor becoming cheaper relative to capital, since the money price of capital can rise. Since the relative wage share depends only on the position of the Z function relative to the wage bill line, a fall in the money-wage rate can also be handled by the analysis. The assumption of a constant money-wage rate, however, simplifies the diagrammatic analysis.

analysis of the propensities to consume and import of the various buying groups in the domestic and foreign economies, and an analysis of the post-trade commodity price ratios. For the present, assume that the post-trade aggregate demand function will be D_t in Fig. 14.1, where D_t includes foreign demand for exports, but excludes domestic demand for imports. After trade, the level of employment will increase[6] to N_t, the money wage bill rises to $N_t T$ and the relative wage share declines to TN_t/VN_t.

The marginal product of labor in each industry is lower (since the labor/capital ratio has increased), and therefore the real wage rate is lower. Since employment has increased, however, one cannot deduce the effect of labor's real absolute income. The possibility exists that labor as a group has improved its real income position, although previously employed workers will find that their real income has fallen.

EPILOGUE TO THE FOREIGN TRADE ANALYSIS

There are many other possible interrelationships between income, employment, prices, wages, and foreign trade which could be elaborated upon.[7] With the growing importance of international trade and the emergence of trading blocs, an understanding of all the possible interrelationships is becoming increasingly important. The detailed analysis, however, must be left to works wholly devoted to these complex international trade problems.

APPENDIX

Proposition: To demonstrate that when a production function is linear and homogeneous, an increase in the labor capital ratio cannot induce an increase in the ratio of the marginal product to the average product of labor.

[6] Whether or not the introduction of trade really increases the real effective demand for home production will, as suggested above, depend on the actual demand elasticities of the various domestic and foreign buyers.

[7] For example, differential growth rates among trading nations may, because of income elasticities of demand for imports, differ among nations. These differences may lead to important complications in the balance of payments and the level of economic activity. See K. Kurihara, "The International Compatibility of Growth and Trade," *Economia Internazionale*, 13, 1960, pp. 3–8.

Assume that in the pretrade position, the labor intensive industry (X) is operating at point R on its isoquant map (Fig. 14.2a). After trade, the output of X is contracted to point S. Erect a line from S, perpendicular to the ordinate axis, which intersects the vector OR at point T. Since the production

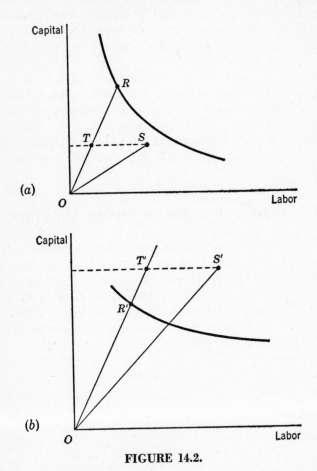

FIGURE 14.2.

function is linear and homogeneous, the M/A-ratio will be a constant along any given straight line emanating from the origin. Thus, the M/A-ratio at R is equal to the M/A-ratio at T. If starting from T, labor inputs are added to reach S (by moving along TS), then the marginal and average products will fall (because of diminishing returns). It can be demonstrated, however, that with diminishing returns, the M/A-ratio will either be a constant (if the function is of the Cobb-Douglas type) or it will decline.[8] Hence the M/A-ratio at point S is equal to, or less than, the M/A-ratio at points T and R. Thus, with an increase in the labor capital-ratio, the M/A-ratio either remains constant or declines in industry X.

In a similar manner, it can be demonstrated that the M/A-ratio in industry Y cannot increase as the labor-capital ratio rises. In Fig. 14.2b, point R' is the pre-trade output position of industry Y, while the post-trade position is represented by S'. By erecting lines similar to Fig. 14.2a, it can be shown that the M/A-ratio at R' is equal to the M/A-ratio at T', which, in turn, is equal to or greater than the M/A-ratio at S'.

[8] See Appendix B, Chapter 9.

PART IV

MEASUREMENT AND ESTIMATION

CHAPTER 15

Social accounts: theory and measurement

Charles L. Leven

SOCIAL ACCOUNTS AND AGGREGATE THEORY

Most of this book has been concerned with an analysis of the functional interdependence of various macroeconomic variables. Moreover, while quantitative materials were introduced from time to time, they served the purpose either of illustrating various relationships or reinforcing deductive conclusions about the nature of the relationships. For example, data on personal consumption expenditures and income were included in Chapter 3, but not primarily because we wanted to know the value of these magnitudes at any particular time. Rather, they were introduced to substantiate certain *a priori* notions important to the theory: (1) that there was a relationship between consumption spending and the level of income and (2) that the consumption function displayed a certain degree of stability over time. In this section of the book we turn again to quantitative materials, but this time with our interest focused on the magnitudes of the variables themselves. This chapter will cover the question of how to measure macroeconomic variables; the following chapter will be concerned with techniques for estimating future values of the variables.

At first glance, the student is likely to feel that the relevant variables have been identified rather obviously and that the data collection problem amounts only to statistical technique and discovery of information sources. This chapter will point out that defining variables for purposes of theoretical exposition and defining them for purposes of empirical measurement are quite different. The former, the abstract theoretical definitions, must precede the presentation of the theory. It is preferable to postpone the precise specifications necessary for actual measurement in the real world until the full theory has been presented.[1] There are two reasons for this somewhat unorthodox departure. First, the issues involved in measurement are, for many purposes, irrelevant to the theoretical formulation and an early detailed treatment tends to disrupt the analysis. More importantly, some of the more subtle issues regarding measurement depend on the *theoretical* relationships between the variables and, thus, require knowledge of the theoretical issues to be fully appreciated.

On the surface the measurement problem might seem rather superficial; little more than observing that one could hardly take measurements of trees until someone had told him what a tree was. But the situation is somewhat more complicated, depending on a rather subtle distinction. Many theories are concerned with explaining changes in various items we see in the world around us. In other words, many theories deal with the functional relationships connecting a set of variables which *are defined prior to and independent of the theory explaining them*. Much social science theory is of this nature. *Economics* is sometimes like this; for example, when it is dealing with individual commodity prices and outputs.

Not all theories are like this, however. Sometimes *a priori* hypotheses lead us to suspect that observable phenomena are explainable not in terms of other phenomena on the same plane of observation, but rather by variables on another plane. For example, modern nuclear physics began with an attempt to explain the behavior of observable particles in terms of the behavior of component particles which at that time were not observable. The concept of an electron existed long before anyone had ever observed one either with his eyes or any other observational device, but electrons did not exist before the formulation of a theory of subatomic physics. Now, of course, we "see" and collect measurements of electrons all the time. But what we are "seeing" is not some kind of object, but only the definitional characteristics of

---

[1] This contrasts with the organization of most macroeconomics textbooks in that the measurement specifications are usually incorporated into an early chapter along with the theoretical definitions.

an object we have invented as an analytical abstraction. Leaving aside rather deep philosophical issues such as the criteria for ultimate existence, it seems fairly clear that whether or not subatomic particles have a conventional existence, like a tree, or a dog, or a ham sandwich, is rather beside the point. As an abstract concept they perform a useful analytical function.

Sometimes, instead of explaining observable phenomena at a sub-observational level, our theorizing leads us to explanations at a superobservational level. A ready example can be found in religious thought. True, for many people, either through faith or revelation, God does have the conventional existence common to any perceived object. But for many others His existence is *inferred* as a (or perhaps the only) plausible explanation of mankind as we perceive it. Moreover, one can certainly have considerable faith in such an inferential concept. It can serve as the basis for moral precepts and personal salvation without the question of the conventional existence of the diety becoming very essential.

And we feel right at home with many other kinds of inferential concepts. We have "ids" and "superegos" living inside of us. We have "nature" and "society" living outside. We theorize as if these were self-conscious, conventionally existing entities acting on us from within and without. Another similar abstraction is "the economy." Thus, when we talk about the economy growing at a particular rate, or about a shift in the willingness of the household sector to spend out of income, or about business investment becoming more sensitive to changes in the rate of interest, we are talking about concepts that cannot be defined independently of the theory itself. At base, then, things like personal consumption expenditure, gross national product, and gross private domestic investment are *not* the names of conventionally existing entities, but the names of analytical concepts which we regard theoretically as the causal agents producing the manifestations we observe.

Clearly, these concepts can have no definition outside of the manifestations assigned to them by the theory. This is another reason why this chapter is located near the end of the book, rather than at the beginning. It would seem cumbersome to teach the student why aggregative economic variables are defined the way they are (or even to make him understand that the definitions are arbitrary) if this material were presented before the theory itself. In short, the sequence of discussion here is meant to convey the impression that the accounts are an empirical implementation of the theory. The opposite course of action would convey the notion that the theory was an explanation of the social accounts magnitudes. This is both logically misleading and contrary to the historical development of macroeconomic thought.

SOCIAL ACCOUNTS AS A TOOL OF ANALYSIS

From the foregoing it should be clear that the problem is not one of measuring conventionally existing items (which would be simply a job of statistical information collection), but rather of accounting for particular abstract phenomena. There are, however, many ways of accounting for phenomena. For example, population can be accounted for as consisting of all humans, or males and females, or adults and children, or people under and people equal to or more than six feet in height. Obviously the question of which way is the "correct" way is meaningless by itself. What we really want is a "useful" way of accounting. But useful for what? The answer is useful for testing a preconceived theory. Thus, we account for a phenomenon in terms of components which are defined as the embodiment of the various sets of forces which the theory suggests as being significant.

There is some ambiguity centering around the word "accounts." Frequently, the body of numbers comprising the national income statistics are referred to as the "national income accounts." Here, however, accounts will be taken to mean the analytical framework within which macroeconomic phenomena can be meaningfully discussed and quantitatively estimated. In short, our discussion will not center primarily on how to obtain numerical estimates of preconceived variables, but on the derivation of good operational definitions of the idealized variables of pure theory. An *operational* definition involves describing a set of specifications which make it possible to obtain quantitative estimates of abstract theoretical variables from the body of statistical information which we do (or could) have at our disposal, in fact. Seen in this light social accounts should be thought of not necessarily as a body of statistics, *per se*, but as a tool of analysis which forms the link between abstract (nonobservational) variables in a formal theory and the body of observable information.[2]

Perhaps it would be easier to see the social accounts as an analytical tool if we look at a particular example which is somewhat less complex than the theory of aggregate supply and demand. For example, suppose that in a large university the provision of parking space for automobiles has been a recurrent problem. Suppose, further, that it is a beneficent university which feels obliged to provide parking space for anyone who wishes to drive there. Also, since we are used to thinking in equilibrium terms, we will assume that a just sufficient number of parking spaces is available currently. However, on the basis of past experience, the university has learned that complacency is unwise. On the one hand, parking lots take considerable time to plan and build, so that if the number of drivers is increasing, a policy of constructing new lots only to accommodate existing excess demand will never enable them to catch up. With growth they would have a perennial parking problem. On the other hand, building lots in anticipation of future need also poses a problem, namely, obtaining accurate estimates of future need at specific future dates; otherwise, the university would run the risk of at least temporary, or maybe permanent, over-building, and even temporary over-building could be a serious problem in the case of something as expensive as parking lots.

Now, how might we face the problem of estimating future parking demand? One possibility would be to keep accurate records of the number of automobiles arriving every day and try to discern an observable trend which could then be projected into the future. We would call this an *extrapolative projection*. Extrapolative projections have at least one important advantage: they are simple and economical. But they also have some very important disadvantages. That they might be wrong is one; however, even the more sophisticated "structural" projections that will be discussed later, mainly in the next chapter, might be wrong. But with a simple extrapolative projection there is nothing in an incorrect forecast which enables us to revise the estimating procedure. Simple extrapolations have another disad-

[2] Also, the discussion here will refer mainly to the question of how to get "real" numerical values *in principle* and not in fact. That is, while the principles underlying the official national income estimates for the U.S. will be covered, we will not discuss the specifics.

vantage, too, namely that they are applicable only to a limited range of possible policies. In this case, for example, suppose the projected increase is very large. If the university is committed to accommodating this increase, no matter how large it is, then the simple extrapolation would be all right so long as it were as accurate as any other prediction. But suppose, as seems more realistic, that the university, while still honoring its commitment to provide space for anyone driving there, might consider inhibiting some people from coming there at all as an alternative to building parking lots without end. An extrapolative projection, *by itself*, does not tell us anything about why people are coming and, therefore, how they might be discouraged. For this we need some kind of insight into the behavioral antecedents of people coming to the university. If we express these insights formally and, usually, symbolically, we call them a *model*. Let us try to construct a model of our university's parking problem.

First of all, we are interested in the total number of automobiles that will arrive at the university on any given day. But, since there is a one-to-one correspondence between the number of cars arriving and the number of people driving cars, we can focus on the latter. We will call these people "drivers" and represent them by the symbol, D. In order to simplify our example we will assume that drivers constitute some known and fixed proportion of the total university population, P. Then,

$$D = D(P). \tag{15.1}$$

The task of the model then is to explain variations in P. If we are to go beyond simple explanation, though, we have to propose some hypotheses about the forces affecting P. If we did not know much about a university, it might seem reasonable to start by observing that different people probably come there for different reasons and then trying to classify people according to these motives. For example, some might be attracted by the football team, some because of high academic salaries or prestige, and some even because of the chance of receiving a good education. If we could classify people in this way, it would help in isolating the critical elements and in evaluating their relative significance. There are two problems with this procedure. First, it might be very hard to derive a mutually exclusive classification scheme since most people would be coming for a variety of reasons.

Second, any given individual's presence is not necessarily independent of the presence of others.

Adjusting for this second difficulty gives us a very powerful theoretical guide. In short, we can write,

$$P = B + A, \tag{15.2}$$

where B are those people whose presence is directly related to the presence of others (call them "come-becauses"), and A are those people whose presence is unrelated to the presence of others (call them "come-anyways"). Thus,

$$B = B(A). \tag{15.3}$$

If, for convenience, we assume a particular form for this function, say

$$B = \alpha A, \tag{15.4}$$

we can solve for P in terms of A:

$$P = \alpha A + A, \tag{15.5}$$

or

$$\Delta P = (1 + \alpha) \Delta A. \tag{15.6}$$

The reader might appropriately wonder what this rather abstract theorizing has contributed to the problem at hand. For one thing, it says that we can confine our attention to those things which affect A as opposed to B. It also says that changes in A will have a multiplied effect on P, and it indicates, although rather vaguely at this point, the nature of the functional relationship which has to be determined in order to estimate the value of the multiplier.

Admittedly, these are not major contributions. We still have to define A and B operationally (in order to generate data for estimating the "come-because" function, equation 15.3), and we have to find some way of making future estimates of A. The problems of estimation and projection remain, but these problems have been simplified by narrowing the problem merely to predicting A, rather than the behavior of the more complex groups, D and P. It is easier to predict A since at the very least we have narrowed the range of variables which might potentially affect the independent variable.

Now to the question of defining A and B operationally. To make any progress on this problem, we have to drop the assumption that we do not know anything about a university. But once we do this, some useful ideas come to mind quite readily. To a considerable extent the administrative staff and faculty of a university are related to the size of the student body. This is not completely true, of course, especially in a large university where research activities may be quite important. Research activities, however, are likely to be related to faculty size. Consequently, while the ratio of faculty to students might vary considerably among universities, it is likely to be fairly stable within a given university, at least over some period of time. The nature of the functional relationship between faculty and students cannot be resolved *a priori*. But that is not the point. Here we are looking only for a hypothesis which seems sufficiently reasonable, deductively, to be worth testing empirically. Thus, we define B as staff plus faculty, who come because there are students at the university, and A as the student body whose presence is virtually independent of the number of A's. It might be noted that this definition of A is not an ideal one. Probably some students come to a university simply because they want to be in a school of a particular size.

At this point, then, we do have conventional definitions for B and A, namely, staff and faculty, and students, respectively. But our observational framework is still not complete. We have to determine who is staff and who are students. Some people at the university may be both; some may be neither. What do we do with them? This is where the functional definitions of the abstract theory help out. Remember "students" are really only a conventionally observable approximation to our idealized concept of "come-anyways," and similarly with staff and faculty as a representation of people whose presence is related to the number of students. Thus, the principle to be followed in assigning people to one sector or the other is the extent to which their attendance is or is not directly related to the size of the institution. In general, any given individual's attendance is partly a function of university size and partly a function of other things. But everybody has to be assigned to one group or the other.[3] This means that specific operational definitions must necessarily be approximations to idealized theoretical concepts and we simply have to rely

---

[3] Otherwise, we have to have a simple extrapolative model, or one which says everything depends on everything else.

on *a priori* judgments of reasonableness in establishing the definitions initially. Later, of course, after sufficient data have been collected, the definitions might be revised in light of the empirical observations. Note, however, that no data can be collected or analyzed until initial definitions have been specified.

In our simple university example some of the sectorial specifications seem rather obvious. All full-time students go into "students" and all full-time staff and all persons of faculty rank go into "staff and faculty." The difficult problems come in the case of people who are both employees and students and those who are neither. Here we just do the best *a priori* guessing we can. For example, we might say that anyone employed by the university is a student if and only if he is taking two or more courses. Business visitors, like telephone repairmen or textbook salesmen, since their number is probably mostly related to the size of the institution, should be designated as "staff and faculty." Visitors to the library are there, however, because of the library itself, so they are defined as "students." These are a few examples of the definitional problems encountered in building a set of social accounts designed to analyze the parking problem of a university.

More important than tracing through these definitional problems to the bitter end is the understanding of the principle involved. Suppose, for example, that the School of Education of the university operated a nursery school where most of the students were children of professors and most of the teachers were candidates for advanced degrees in education. Here the nursery school students would go in sector B, "faculty and staff," for they and their parents come for the same reasons. The nursery school teachers would go in A, "students," for they are in the "come-anyway" category. But this seeming anomaly should not disturb us. We are seeking operational definitions of useful abstractions and it should be clear that the question of who is "really" a student and who is not is as beside the point as the question of whether electrons really exist. There is, of course, an important moral here. When we come to define things like aggregate consumption and aggregate investment we *need not be led astray* by trying to answer such hopeless questions as, "Is a man's overcoat really an item of consumption or is it really an investment?" The relevant issue, of course, is the extent to which a man's decision to purchase an overcoat depends on his current income.

We are almost ready now to build an accounts system for a more complicated (and more interesting) phenomenon, namely, aggregate employment and output. First, however, it might be well to state more formally the generalized nature of a social accounts framework as illustrated by the foregoing example.

Any predictive theory can be written as,

$$T = T(T_1, T_2, \ldots T_j, T_{j+1}, \ldots T_k), \qquad (15.7)$$

where

$$T_i = T_i(T_1, T_2, \ldots T_{i-1}, T_{i+1}, \ldots T_k, T)(i = 1, 2, \ldots j). \quad (15.8)$$

All this says is that any phenomenon, T, can be regarded as functionally dependent on some $(j + k)$ other phenomena, j of which are endogenous variables with respect to the model, while the k other variables are exogenously determined.[4] Moreover, in those cases where T is an abstract concept, the sectoral disaggregation implied by (15.7) becomes an identity or definitional statement. It is the task of theory to propose a meaningful sectorial disaggregation. By a meaningful disaggregation we mean nothing more than a sectorialization which will permit the framing of behavioral hypotheses as indicated in (15.8). It is the task of social accounts analysis to provide the specifications for these variables which are necessary to render them statistically measurable. It is then the job of econometric analysis (which will be discussed in the next chapter) to use these measurements to obtain quantitative estimates of the parameters in the original model. New information and parameter estimates suggest new or revised hypotheses and operational specifications, and new hypotheses call for revised definitions and additional econometric estimation.

ACCOUNTING FOR AGGREGATE SUPPLY AND DEMAND

A Keynesian model of aggregate supply and demand can thus be seen as a particular example of a generalized theoretical form. First,

---

[4] Formally, it would be possible to propose a model which had only endogenous variables, but only in the case of a system which was totally self-determined and unchangeable with respect to outside forces. The possibility of such models arising at an operational level in the social sciences seems rather remote.

we note that many of the variables that interest us, e.g., employment, the interest rate, and the price level, are determined by effective demand. Therefore, we have to account only for effective demand and not the many variables directly dependent upon it. This reduction in focus is analogous to emphasizing the relationship between the driving population, D, and the total population, P, in our university example in (15.1). Thus, we can write,

$$Y \equiv C + I + G + X - M, \qquad (15.9)$$

where

$$C = C(Y), \qquad (15.10)$$

and

$$M = M(Y), \qquad (15.11)$$

where: Y is gross national product, C is consumption expenditures, I is investment expenditures, G is government expenditures, X is exports, and M is imports. Relationship (15.9) is the output identity which is analogous to (15.7), and (15.10) and (15.11) are behavioral equations analogous to (15.8). Equation (15.10) is the consumption function and (15.11), the import function. The social accounting problem is to specify operational definitions for Y, C, I, G, X, and M. Our previous discussion does provide a principle upon which we can make these definitional decisions, namely, the variables are to be defined, *ideally*, to make (15.10) and (15.11) exact relationships. This is how we derived the definitions of "students" and "faculty and staff."

Let us turn first to the specification of Y. It is typically referred to in the national income statistics as output or gross national product (GNP). Here we are seeking a definition of GNP, which will be an index of effective demand and an unambiguous aid in estimating employment, prices, and the other variables whose behavior depend upon its magnitude. As a simple example, suppose an economy had only two activities, the picking of wild blackberries and the making of wild blackberry juice. Further, suppose the berry pickers gathered an amount of berries which they sold to the pressers for $100, all of which were converted into juice which was then sold for $150 to consumers. Given our objective of estimating employment, what is the best index of gross output? The sum of the outputs of all enterprises is $250. This index of gross output, however, could prove to be misleading over time. Suppose, for example, in a subsequent period, the firm producing blackberry juice were to buy the blackberry picking firm. If the level of economic activity were to remain unchanged in the subsequent period, then we would have the undesirable result that our index of output (i.e., the sum of outputs of all enterprises) would fall to $150, while physical output and employment remained unchanged. The customary way of avoiding this problem is to define output as excluding the value of intermediate products. With this adjustment, then, the output of the society is clearly $150, not $250. In other words, we want to define output as excluding the value of intermediate products, i.e., goods consumed in the process of producing other goods. This latter accounting procedure is said to avoid the problem of *double-counting*.

Two alternative definitions of GNP are consistent with the avoidance of double-counting. These are:

The sum of value added in production in all production units, where "value added" is simply the difference between sales and purchased raw materials. (This is the *income* definition of GNP.)

The sum of all purchases for *final* use, where final use is any use except utilization in further production *in the same accounting period*. (This is the *product* definition of GNP.)

These definitions are perfectly consistent. In this simple example, the first definition gives $100 + $50 = $150; the second definition gives simply $150.

Note that since there are two equivalent definitions of GNP they can be written in the form of a double-entry account. This provides two estimating alternatives. On the one hand, if we estimate one of these magnitudes, then the definitional statements embodied in the accounts tells us that the other will have an exactly equal value. On the other hand, if we estimate them independently, any observed difference between the estimates should be relatively small and attributable to "statistical discrepancy." It is very important to note, however, that the statistical discrepancy would not be an estimate of the accuracy of either of the numbers, but only a check on the consistency of the informational sources used to derive them.

The right side of the account is the "product side" and is equal to the sum of final purchases of all buyers.

The left side of the account, aggregate "value added," can be re-written as the sum of income payments to factors of production and other charges against GNP.[5] This is the "income side" of the account. In the simple example here this would be entirely accounted for by a single item, namely, proprietors' income of $150.

In a more complicated situation, the income account would also include wages and salaries, interest, rent, corporate profits, and other charges against GNP. There are a number of complications which have to be taken into account in framing definitions in a real world economy. The most important of these are:

1. The monetary value of both output and sales may understate the actual physical volume because of direct exchanges of goods for services, or production for use directly by the producer, i.e., some transactions may be barter rather than money transactions.
2. Sales may differ from output in any particular period due to the possibility of accumulation or decumulation of inventories.
3. Some intermediate goods may be produced in one period, but used over several periods, i.e., business capital goods like machinery.
4. Production may occur in units other than business enterprises, namely, nonprofit institutions, households, or government, and these products may be valued in ways which do not indicate their contribution to total employment.
5. The price paid by the purchaser may differ from the price received by the seller due to the imposition of excise taxes or because of subsidies paid by the government.
6. Goods and services may be sold to and purchased from abroad.

There are, of course, a variety of ways of adjusting for these ambiguities whose existence renders unadjusted total expenditure an inappropriate index of gross output. Also, as we have seen earlier, there is no "correct" way of making adjustment; only a reasonable way

---

[5] An example of a charge against GNP other than a payment to a factor of production would be a manufacturer's excise tax. If personal consumption expenditures were included at sales price, then the excise tax would have to be added to the left side to make the account balance. Another charge against GNP would be depreciation which is not normally considered part of factor payments or profits.

Table 15.1. National Income and Product Account, 1962 (Billions of Dollars)

	Item			Item	
A1	Wage and salary disbursements	297.1	A16	Personal consumption expenditures	355.4
A2	Excess of wage and salary accruals over disbursements	0.1			
A3	Employer contributions for social insurance	13.7	A17	Gross private domestic investment	78.8
A4	Other labor income	12.1			
A5	Proprietors' income	49.8	A18	Government purchases of goods and services	117.0
A6	Rental income of persons	12.0			
A7	Corporate profits tax	22.2			
A8	Dividends	16.6			
A9	Undistributed profits	8.1	A19	Exports	28.9
A10	Inventory valuation adjustment	0.2			
A11	Net interest	22.0	A20	Less: Imports	−25.1
	NATIONAL INCOME	453.7			
A12	Business transfer payments	2.3			
A13	Indirect business tax and nontax liability	53.0			
A14	Current surplus of government enterprises less subsidies	−1.7			
	NET NATIONAL PRODUCT	507.3			
A15	Capital consumption allowances	49.4			
A21	Statistical discrepancy	−1.8			
	GROSS NATIONAL PRODUCT	554.9		GROSS NATIONAL PRODUCT	554.9

SOURCE: U.S. Dept. of Commerce, *Survey of Current Business*, July, 1963. All other data tables in this chapter are also from this source.

or ways in light of existing theory. In the following paragraphs the conventional definitions employed by the U. S. Department of Commerce and some of the presumptive logic involved in arriving at these definitions will be described. The embodiment of these definitions are the national income and product accounts, of which the summary account is shown in Table 15.1.

Imputations for nonmonetary transactions

The first difficulty arises out of attempting to measure production activity solely by looking at market transactions. There are two kinds of problems here. First of all, transactions can occur without any production, as in the case of exchanges of existing assets. (An example would be the sale of a previously existing painting by one person to another.) No matter what the magnitude of such exchanges, they would not reflect any output during the period in question and, hence, would generate no demand for labor. Consequently, all transactions between households involving the sale of previously existing assets must be disregarded. The sale of an existing asset by a business to a household could similarly be disregarded. For statistical convenience, however, it is simpler to regard them as a positive (personal consumption expenditure) and a negative (decrease in business inventories) purchase of equal value, occurring simultaneously. This treatment will leave the total of GNP unaffected, but will affect the size of "personal consumption expenditures" (Item A16 in Table 15.1) and "gross private domestic investment" (Item A17—which includes increase in business inventories) by equal and opposite amounts. The sale of an existing asset from one business firm to another represents equal and offsetting changes in business inventories (Item A17).

The second difficulty in using market transactions to measure current output is that not all output results in market transactions. For example, a farmer may produce part of his own food supply. Nonmarket transactions, however, are not different from market transactions in their impact on employment. Accordingly, in the accounts, an amount equal to the "imputed value of food and fuel produced and consumed on farms" is added both to "proprietors' income" on the income side (Item A5) and to "personal consumption expenditures" on the product side. Probably the most important of the "imputed" items in the accounts is "imputed rental value of owner-occupied housing." This item is included in both "rental income of persons" on the income side (Item A6) and "personal consumption expenditure" on the product side.

Another instance in which output and employment could be created without giving rise to market transactions is the case of payment of wages in kind, rather than money. An example of this would be the imputed value of clothing provided to military personnel which has been added both to "personal consumption expenditures" on the product side and "wage and salary disbursements" on the income side (Item A1). A complete discussion of all of the imputed items which are actually measured in the accounts can be found in the National Income Supplements published by the Office of Business Economics of the U. S. Department of Commerce.[6]

Accounting for inventory change

Clearly, purchases for final use in any particular time period do not necessarily account for all of the output in that same period. Purchases can exceed output and to the extent that inventories are drawn down, purchases would be a poor correlate of employment. Similarly, if purchases fall short of output in a period, inventories accumulate. One possible way to avoid this problem would be to define consumption as excluding the purchase of goods out of existing inventories. It would be very difficult to measure consumption this way, however. In addition, we want a definition for C that will be most appropriate for testing a relationship, $C = C(Y)$. Therefore, balance in the accounts is maintained by adding the increase in business inventories to the product side (it is part of "gross private domestic investment"). If inventories were to go down this item would be negative.

Because of the earlier assumption that all consumption expenditures are for immediate consumption, only business inventories are counted (i.e., changes in consumer stocks are omitted). But business inventories include changes in all business stocks, *even stocks of intermediate*

---

[6] Of course, not every nonmonetary item of output which could conceivably be allowed actually is included. For example, the value of housewives' services are omitted from the official measure of gross output. Here the problem is mainly one of a method of valuation. In other cases, nonmonetary items may not be imputed simply because we do not really know where to draw the line. For example, is air-conditioning in a business office a productive input or is it wages in kind to the employees?

goods. The rationale for this accounting procedure can be seen rather easily. Clearly, we do not want to count as final output the value of coal used in making steel, as it is already counted in the value of the steel itself. On the other hand, how would we balance the payments to factors of production resulting from the production of coal, which at the end of the year remained in inventory at the mine, or at a wholesalers or even at a steel mill? Thus, if we include the payments arising out of its production on the income side, we have to count it as output on the product side. This method of accounting insures that our gross output measure is a reliable index of employment.

There is one other problem in accounting for inventory change which arises because of changes in the purchasing power of money, namely, the question of the valuation of previously acquired inventory sold during the current period. If prices remain stable from period to period there is no problem. This can be seen rather easily from a simple example. Suppose that there are only two transactions in the economy during a given year and that these are (1) the sale of 100 units of product produced by a firm that year and, (2) the sale of 10 units of product by the same firm out of inventory. If the price of the product was $1.00 in both periods the accounts for each of the individual transactions and for the whole economy would look like the following (for the sake of simplicity we will also assume that the product is one where the value of raw material inputs is negligible, say something like prefabricated sandcastles, so that the only costs are for labor and managerial services and also assume that the wage bill is half of unit cost).

Transaction 1

Wages	$50	Consumption	$100
Profits	50		

Transaction 2

		Consumption	$10
		Increase in inventories	− 10

Income and Product Account

Wages		$50	Consumption	$110
Profits		50	Increase in inventories	− 10
	GNP	$100	GNP	$100

Suppose now that there had been a 100 percent price increase from the previous year (price last year was equal to $0.50). There would still be no problem if the firm valued its inventories for the purpose of computing its profit on a last-in-first-out (LIFO) basis. According to this business accounting convention, items taken out of inventory are valued at the cost of production of the most recently produced unit in the inventory. Here, since sales did exceed production during the year, this would mean that some units produced last year were drawn out of inventory, but only those units produced at the very end of the year. Now if we assume that the price did not go abruptly from $0.50 to $1.00 on December 31, but increased more or less steadily over the whole period (as seems more realistic for the economy as a whole), the LIFO accounting method would give us approximately the same results as shown above.

Suppose, however, that the firm used a first-in-first-out (FIFO) method of valuation. Then Transaction 2 and the Income and Product Account would be as follows (Transaction 1 would be the same):

Transaction 2

		Consumption	$10
Profits	$5	Increase in inventories	−5

Income and Product Account

		Consumption	$110
Wages	$50	Increase in inventories	−5
Profits	55		
GNP	$105	GNP	$105

Even though there is no difference in "real" transactions during the year, GNP would be 5 percent higher due solely to profits earned via windfall capital gains on inventory through price increases. To eliminate windfalls and to put the accounts back into real terms, the change in business inventories is always valued in current prices. However, since the data for the income side is obtained from statistics on reported corporate profits and since some corporations use FIFO, and other valuation techniques not consistent with LIFO, an "inventory valuation adjustment" (Item A10 in Table 15.1) has to be included to preserve consistency in the accounts. This would make the summary account appear as follows.

Income and Product Account

Wages	$50	Consumption	$110
Profits	55	Increase in inventories	−10
Inventory valuation adjustment	−5		
GNP	$100	GNP	$100

For corporations the adjustment is a special computation of the amount of profits earned (lost) on account of price change for those corporations keeping their books on other than a LIFO basis. For unincorporated enterprises the adjustment would be combined with "proprietors' income."

Accumulation of capital goods and depreciation

The problem of the consumption in one year of goods purchased in a different year does require adjustment in the accounts. As was seen above, this presents no special problem (except for the adjustment in valuation due to price change) in the case of many business assets, namely, those assets which unambiguously either are or are not used up in a particular period. We called these assets "business inventories." But there is another category of real business assets which causes a different sort of problem. These are capital goods like machine tools and factory buildings. Such items, which we call "business plant and equipment," are used up over a number of accounting periods. This is in contrast to ordinary business inventories where the utilization of any single unit of inventory can be deferred for any number of periods, but can only be consumed in a single one.

Clearly, the production of capital items does add to employment of labor, and other factors of production in the year in which it is produced, and this production does give rise to wage and salary and other income payments which are included on the income side of the account. It is the counter-balancing item in the account that presents a problem.

A number of alternatives exist for reconciling the accounts to take care of capital goods purchases. First, we could assume that capital goods are completely consumed in the year of their production. To restore balance would then require adjusting the business profits figures by subtracting an amount equal to their total purchases of plant and equipment for that year (except, of course, for any depreciation on *just those items of capital acquired during that year* already charged off against profits). One affect of this treatment would be to make GNP smaller than it is. But this in itself is not such a serious problem. Even though we do use GNP as an index of economic progress, it is only an "index" and not a "measure." There are many items of "real" output which are excluded, such as many of the services we perform for ourselves and, more importantly as noted above, the value of housewives services.[7] But leaving "business plant and equipment expenditures" out of the accounts entirely (i.e., treating them as purely intermediate goods) not only will consistently lower the estimates of GNP, but will also make interpretation of year-to-year changes in GNP difficult whenever the ratio of production of capital to consumption goods shifts. Since this ratio can and does shift substantially from one year to the next, and since from the standpoint of the affect on employment the composition of output is of secondary significance, this treatment is unsatisfactory.

A more suitable method of accounting for capital goods is to add all of the otherwise unaccounted for production of business plant and equipment to the product side of the account. We can think of this addition as being composed of two items. The first is the gross amount of such expenditure. The second would be the depreciation of *these same items* which was already charged off against current sales during that first year of their life. But as soon as we adopt depreciation accounting then we have to add in the current depreciation on assets acquired in earlier periods and still not fully charged off. The current depreciation on newly, as well as previously acquired assets are, of course, lumped together as a single item. Finally, since we want the total of GNP to reflect the demand for factor inputs, it seems more appropriate to move depreciation from a subtraction on the product side to a positive item on the income side. This depreciation is the major component of "capital consumption allowances" (Item A15, Table 15.1). Besides actual depreciation, this figure would also include obsolescence and accidental damage to fixed capital. Combining

---

[7] While the substantive content of GNP may be irrelevant for measuring changes in well-being in a given economy so long as a consistent and unbiased "index" or "proxy" definition is used, the substantive aspects do make a difference in international comparisons or even comparisons for a single nation over long periods of time.

this item with Items A7, A8, and A9, Table 15.1, gives us a measure of gross profits of the corporate sector.

Earlier it was stated that the imputed rental value of owner-occupied housing was added to both "rental income of persons" and "personal consumption expenditure." We have not yet accounted for the production of new housing during the period. All residential construction, whether owner-occupied or business-operated, is accounted for in "gross private domestic investment" and allowances for housing depreciation is accounted for in "capital consumption allowances." In essence a home-buyer is treated as an investor who then provides himself with current services of his house at cost.

Government transactions in the accounts

Up until now, the discussion has proceeded as if governmental units did not exist. This section will discuss the procedures that are required to account for government transactions. The discussion will proceed in terms of "the government," which should be taken to mean the combined activities of federal, state, and local governments.

Government expenditures can be divided into four categories, each of which is handled somewhat differently in the accounts. These four classes, which account for all government outlays are: (1) purchase of goods and services, (2) transfer payments, (3) subsidy payments to private producers, and (4) expenditures of government enterprise.

Clearly, if the factor payments included in the income side of the account are to be inclusive for the whole economy they would include wages and salaries, etc., arising out of the production of goods for government. Accordingly, all "government purchases of goods and services" (Item A18, Table 15.1) must be included in the product side. These items include the purchase of labor services (military and civilian government employees) as well as other services and of newly-produced commodities. Since the government is not regarded as an intermediate producer, "government purchases of goods and services" include all goods and services, whether purchased for immediate use, stockpiling, or further processing. Implicitly, this treatment values government output at its cost of production. For example, the value attributed to the services of the President of the United States is equal to his salary. In the absence of a market valuation via the sale of government services there seems to be no satisfactory alternative to such treatment, but its arbitrary nature should be recognized. The government does not account for its plant and equipment in the same way as the private business sector. The absence of any capital accounting for government, however, does not affect the size of GNP since durable goods purchased by government are included in the accounts. However, during a period of an increasing stock of government assets, for example, there would be an overstatement of the cost of currently provided services by government equal to the amount of the accumulation.

One exception to the inclusion of all goods and service purchased by the government should be noted. Interest on the Federal debt is treated as if it were a transfer payment. Changes in Federal interest payments from year to year reflect primarily monetary and fiscal policy decisions and money market conditions rather than the demand for factors of production. Interest payments by state and local government, however, are included as service purchases in that these governmental units do have to compete with private borrowers in the market for capital funds. In essence, this amounts to treating state and local borrowing in the same way as corporate borrowing. This seems quite appropriate in that the issuance of state and local bonds does add to the demand for funds in the money market and would have the same impact on interest rates and the proportion of income saved, and consequently on the demand for factors of production, including labor, as would private borrowing. The Federal Government, on the other hand, always has the option of monetizing any increase in its debt, and the Federal Reserve System, if it so desires, can neutralize the effects of such debt transactions. True, Federal Government borrowing and debt management policies *may*, and in most instances, probably do affect the money market, and consequently employment. Significantly, such effects are the result of conscious monetary policy and are related only incidentally, if at all, to the magnitude of Federal borrowing. Similarly, the magnitude of current interest payments on the national debt paid to nongovernment recipients is related to the size of the debt only secondarily. Within wide limits the affect of changes in debt outstanding on interest payments can be offset by monetary measures that will directly change the rates, at least on new issues, and by shifting the proportion of monetized to nonmonetized debt.

Transfer payments (e.g., social security benefits, veteran's disability allowances, aid to dependent children, etc.) can simply be excluded from the income and product accounts. By definition they add nothing to output and nothing to the nation's real income. They do, of course, add to personal income and will be considered later in connection with the subsidiary account for the household sector. To avoid any misconception it should be pointed out that even if transfers were paid out of newly created money and spent on goods and services by the recipients they would already be included in the *ex post* personal consumption expenditures and corresponding factor payments for that period.

Subsidy payments pose a different sort of problem. Where a subsidy payment is made by the government to a private producer (e.g., operating subsidies to the merchant marine, soil conservation, and other payments to farmers, etc.) receipts from sale of goods will exceed expenditures on them. While subsidies certainly are part of the total receipts of an enterprise and while an increase in total receipts does increase the capacity of a firm to pay (and *ex post* it actually increases its effective demand) for factors of production, a subsidy payment does so in a peculiar way. The rationale for the subsidy itself is to compensate factors of production which are immobilized in a particular occupation where the market cannot support income payments on a par with the factors' opportunity cost in a perfectly mobile market. The immobilization may be unfortunate, as in the case of farmers trapped by the high transition cost to another occupation, or it may be purposeful national policy, such as the subsidization of a noncompetitive American merchant marine for strategic defense reasons. In either case, however, the effect of the subsidy is to add to the compensation of already utilized factors of production rather than to increase the demand for such factors. Accordingly, output, when it is entered in the product side, is valued at purchase price. This is less than its total cost including "subsidies" so that "subsidies" must be subtracted from the income side in order to preserve balance. In some cases this undervalues output; for example when the output is regarded as more valuable to society than its purchasers are willing to pay for it, primarily because of external benefits to nonusers, e.g., the value to every citizen of having an American merchant marine in the event of war. Where the subsidy is for the purpose of compensating "trapped" factors (i.e., immobile farmers), the current treatment would seem to give a more appropriate valuation.

Government enterprises are units of government which ordinarily receive no appropriation for operating expenses, but instead pay such expenses out of a revolving fund which is replenished by sale of services. Only deficits would be covered by direct appropriation. Examples of government enterprises are the U. S. Post Office, TVA, toll-road authorities, and municipal water companies. Except for the fact that their receipts and expenditures might not be equal, such enterprises are treated like private business. Their sales are recorded in the product side as purchases by consumers, business, or government itself (a U. S. court house may well purchase water from a municipal waterworks). Payments to factors of production are entered in the income side. Purchase of raw materials are ignored as intermediate goods; their value is already included in the sale price of the good or service produced.

Now consider the possibility of such an enterprise running at a deficit, as the U. S. Post Office typically does. Such deficits ordinarily are covered by specific appropriations of general government funds. Essentially, then, so far as the accounts are concerned, the Post Office is treated as if it were a firm in the private sector, but with a subsidy always equal to the difference between production cost (with no allowance for profit) and receipts. Accordingly, deficits of government enterprises should be subtracted from the income side along with subsidies. Alternatively, we could add the surpluses, which in fact is what is done, giving us the item "Current surplus of government enterprises less subsidies" (Item A14, Table 15.1).

The classification problems are somewhat simpler in the case of government receipts than for expenditures. Taxes can be separated into two categories: taxes levied on individuals, including corporations (direct taxes), and taxes levied on activities (indirect taxes). Direct taxes (i.e., income, employment, and estate taxes) simply can be ignored; they have already been accounted for in that the factor payments in the income side are estimated on a before tax basis. Essentially they are no different than government transfer payments, except that they run in the other direction.

Indirect taxes (mostly sales and excise taxes) pose a definitional problem. If expenditures are entered at purchase price on the product side, then the accounts will not balance unless we add in indirect taxes on the income side. Alternatively, we could value expenditures net of excises (here we would have to be careful to take out taxes levied at the manufacturers' level and passed on to the consumer as well as those explicitly paid by the consumer) and leave indirect taxes out of the accounts entirely. Both possibilities have their merits. The former treatment does imply that the governmental activity not only has value in its own right, but also imputes additional value to privately produced goods in the form of free inputs. Valuing output so as to include indirect taxes is really equivalent to regarding the tax component of market price as covering the cost of services provided to producers without direct charge. This will include such things as police and fire protection which do have to be provided and do have to be paid for. Presumably, if they were not provided free by government, private producers could and would obtain them through the private sector and their cost would be reflected in the market price of what they are producing. On the other hand, including indirect taxes does make the level of GNP sensitive to changes in the proportion of total taxes raised by indirect as opposed to direct taxes, even if total tax receipts stay the same. In the national income accounts for the U. S. indirect taxes are included. The nontax liability included in "indirect business tax and nontax liability" (Item A13, Table 15.1) refers to such things as fines, penalties, and receipts from sale of goods and services by government agencies, except government enterprises (i.e., the Bureau of the Census will provide various kinds of special data tabulations for a fee).

Foreign trade

Not all of the final demand for goods produced in the U. S. comes from within the country. Accordingly, "exports of goods and services" (Item A19, Table 15.1) must be entered on the product side to balance income payments generated within the U. S. in their production. Clearly, all exports are included regardless of their use abroad. It would not matter whether they went directly into foreign consumption or were used as intermediate goods for further processing; so far as the U. S. economy is concerned, they are final output.

Imports can be thought of as being of two kinds; imports of goods directly for final use and imports of intermediate goods, i.e., raw materials going into further production. The most difficult problem arises in connection with the imports of goods for intermediate use. Even if purchases shown on the product side of the account are limited to purchases of U. S. produced goods, they will not balance payments to factors of production to the extent that their production involves using imported raw materials (remember the domestically used raw materials will be accounted for by the payments to factors arising out of their production, but for imported raw materials these factor payments would not be paid here). Thus, it would be necessary to add imported raw materials to the income side.

With this kind of adjustment, the accounts would balance and imports going directly to final use by consumers, business, and government simply could be ignored. In that case, however, "personal consumption expenditures," "gross private domestic investment," and "government purchase of goods and services" would have to be regarded as representing only *domestic* purchases of such groups. Clearly, such a convention would be inappropriate for testing the consumption function and other demand relationships. For these purposes it would be desirable to define the final demand components on the product side as comprising the *total* final demand of these groups, including imports. This is what is done in the U. S. National Income Accounts. Thus, to maintain a balance in the accounts it would be necessary to include imports for final demand along with imports for intermediate use, their total being simply total imports.

Finally, since we want the accounts to add up to gross U. S. output, rather than total purchase of goods, "imports" (Item A20, Table 15.1) are moved from the income side, as a positive item, to the product side as a negative item.

One other matter might be noted briefly in connection with the foreign trade aspects of income and product accounts, namely, that the existence of trade between nations makes it possible for income earned by factors of production in a nation to differ from payments to factors of production arising out of production in that nation. An obvious example would be labor commutation across international boundaries or rental payments to foreign owners of domestic property. For a small nation, or a subnational region, especially a metropolitan area, such flows could be significant and the accounts would have to include a reconciliation between income earned by residents of the region and income produced in the same region. For the United States, though, these adjustments would be small so the accounts are forced to equal income accruing to residents (including noncitizens) of continental U. S. by means of certain conventions. For example, wages paid to an American secretary working for a foreign consulate in the United States, are treated as an export of labor service.

Some other adjustments

There are a few remaining items in the U. S. National Income and Product Account shown in Table 15.1 which have not yet been explained. In general, these are balancing items. The first four items on the income side represent compensation of employees. The first item is simply actual cash disbursements during the year. The "excess of accruals over disbursements" (Item A2) is included to convert wages paid into wages earned (these could differ, for example, in the case of weekly employees when the year ended or began in midweek). "Employer contributions for social insurance" (Item A3) are treated essentially as a fringe benefit and thus are added to wages and salaries. "Other labor income" (Item A4) consists mainly of fringe benefits, like business contributions to health and welfare funds and, in addition, a number of minor items like compensation paid to members of boards of directors.

The total of corporate profits (adjusted for inventory valuation) is broken down into four items (A7 through A10). The first three items would be equal to reported corporate profits before tax, while Items A8 and A9 would represent after tax profits.

As noted earlier, "net interest" (Item A11) is "net" of interest on the national debt which is treated as a transfer payment.

"Business transfer payments" (Item A12) constitute charges against final sales which are neither payments to factors of production, nor purchase of intermediate raw materials, nor chargeable to inventory change or depreciation. They would include such items as contest prizes and payments to employees for injuries under Workmen's Compensation laws.

Finally, it should be noted that the income side of the account is arranged so that two frequently used subtotals of GNP can be indicated. *National Income* consists of all payments to factors of production, before payment of direct taxes, including income to corporations as

Table 15.2. Personal Income and Outlay Account, 1962
(Billions of Dollars)

	Item				Item	
A16	Personal consumption expenditures	355.4		A1	Wage and salary disbursements	297.1
				A4	Other labor income	12.1
				A5	Proprietors' income	49.8
				A6	Rental income of persons	12.0
B5	Personal saving	29.1		A8	Dividends	16.0
				A11	Net interest	22.0
	DISPOSABLE PERSONAL INCOME	384.5		B1	Net interest paid by government	8.0
				A12	Business transfer payments	2.3
B4	Personal tax and nontax payments	**57.7**		B2	Government transfer payments to persons	32.5
				−B3	Less: Personal contributions for social insurance	−10.2
	PERSONAL OUTLAY AND SAVING	442.1			PERSONAL INCOME	442.1

well as natural persons. *Net National Product* (NNP) is simply GNP net of capital consumed in the process of producing the current gross output.

SUBSIDIARY ACCOUNTS FOR INDIVIDUAL SECTORS

The summary National Income and Product Account shown in Table 15.1 can be regarded as an aggregation of the purchases of goods for final use (product side definition) or as receipts arising out of production for each of the four sectors of final demand (income side definition). Thus, it would seem possible to list income and product transactions for each of the purchasing sectors (households, government, rest of the world, and business investment) individually. If this were done, however, there would be no necessity for the accounts of each sector to balance. In order to balance the individual sector accounts and, more importantly, to have a more complete record of their income and outgo, the individual sector accounts include all income received (transfers from other sectors plus income received on income and product account) and a complete accounting of its disposition. These sector accounts provide useful data for the study of the behavior of households, governments, business, and the foreign sector.

Table 15.2 shows the Personal Income and Outlay Account. As a start we can enter the income and product transactions involving households from Table 15.1. Each of these items is numbered, with the number being prefixed by the letter "A" to indicate the corresponding item in the National Income and Product Account.[8] The counter-entry to any given item in any one account must be an item of *identically the same amount* either on the *opposite side of another account*, or as a *negative item on the same side of another account*. The ordering (A, B, C, D) of the accounts is arbitrary, we could have started with any one of them and derived (with appropriate supplementation) the others in any order.

---

[8] Every item in the National Income and Product Account must be entered in one of the subsidiary accounts since this is a double-entry bookkeeping system. Those items not included in the Personal Income and Outlay Account will show up in one of the other accounts. Also, any additional items added in the Personal Income and Outlay Account (the "B" items) must also show up as a counter-item in some other account and similarly for items added in other accounts (the "C" and "D" items).

The "A" items on the right side (the income side) of the Personal Income and Outlay Account represent income of households from production activities. To get total income of households we must add transfers from other sectors. All but one of these transfer payments have already been accounted for in the National Income and Product Accounts. Transfers between households and the rest of the world are defined away in the forcing of GNP to equal income accruing to U. S. residents. Essentially, gifts made to and received from abroad by all sectors except government are treated as imports and exports of goods and services, respectively. Also, business transfer payments (Item A12, Table 15.2) have already been defined as a charge against GNP. Thus, all that has to be added is transfer payments from government. These transfers are broken into two items, "net interest paid by government" (Item B1—where the "net" means interest paid less interest received) and "government transfer payments" (Item B2). The latter item is simply all transfer payments to persons, except interest on the national debt.

The only outlays of households not yet accounted for are direct taxes. "Personal contributions for social insurance" (Federal Insurance Contributions Act and related payments), however, are shown not as an outlay, but, rather arbitrarily, as a deduction from income (Item B3 on the right, Table 15.2). Other direct taxes are shown on the left (the outlay side) as "Personal tax and nontax payments" (Item B4). Nontax payments are things like the purchase of books from the Government Printing Office and the payment of traffic fines.

Finally, our theory tells us that Disposable Personal Income less personal consumption expenditures must be equal to personal saving. Accordingly, "personal saving" (Item **B5**) is determined as a residual; in short, it is assigned whatever value is necessary to make the Personal Income and Outlay Account balance.[9] Alternatively, a specific estimate of saving could be made. This would permit the determination of the statistical discrepancy arising out of the Personal Income and Outlay Account. (Something like this is done in supplemental analyses published in the national income statistics, where a reconciliation between the personal saving estimate derived from the accounts and

[9]The item number for personal saving is shown in bold face type to indicate that it is computed as a residual. This convention will be used for all residual items in the accounts.

another estimate made by the Securities and Exchange Commission is presented.)

All government receipts (the right side of Table 15.3) are accounted for by items which have already been discussed. The only government outlay not yet discussed is "transfer payments to foreigners" (Item C1). These transfers consist mainly of foreign assistance payments. Not all foreign assistance payments are included, however. For example, assistance payments for purchase of goods in third countries are not

Table 15.3. Government Receipts and Expenditures Account, 1962
(Billions of Dollars)

Item			Item		
A18	Government purchases of goods and services	117.4	B4	Personal tax and nontax payments	57.7
B2	Government transfer payments to persons	32.5	A7	Corporate profits tax	22.2
C1	Government transfer payments to foreigners	1.6	A13	Indirect business tax and nontax liability	53.0
B1	Net interest paid by government	8.0	A3	Employer contributions for social insurance	13.7
−A14	Subsidies less current surplus of government enterprises	1.7	B3	Personal contributions for social insurance	10.2
C2	Government surplus or deficit (−) on income and product account	−3.9			
	GOVERNMENT EXPENDITURES AND SURPLUS	156.8		GOVERNMENT RECEIPTS	156.8

included and some assistance in kind (surplus food stocks) is netted out of the accounts. "Government surplus or deficit (−) on income and product account" (Item C2) is determined as a residual. A reconciliation between this amount and the "budget surplus or deficit" (as shown on the U. S. Treasury Department books) is included in the supplementary analyses.

The Foreign Transactions Account (Table 15.4) includes only items already discussed, except for the balancing item, "net foreign investment" (Item D1). A brief explanation of why this item is called "investment" seems in order. Perhaps this can be seen most easily by considering how exports could exceed imports in a given year. If this were the case, payments for the excess exports would have to be accounted for. Exporters do have to be paid for goods they ship;

Table 15.4.   Foreign Transactions Accounts, 1962
(Billions of Dollars)

Item		Item	
A19 Exports	28.9	A20 Imports	25.1
		C1 Government transfer	
		payments to foreigners	1.6
		D1 Net foreign investment	2.2
RECEIPTS FROM ABROAD	28.9	PAYMENTS TO ABROAD	28.9

and they have to be paid in dollars. To the extent that we import from abroad foreigners earn dollars. But, to the extent that we have an export surplus, this is likely to be accompanied by a net increase in loans outstanding to foreigners or a net increase in our holdings of shares in foreign corporations or domestic holding of foreign currencies. In short, the export surplus must be financed by some form of increased financial investment by domestic persons and businesses in the rest of the world. Alternatively, government aid could finance the export surplus, but to the extent that this has occurred it will have been accounted for under Government aid (Item C1). Where imports exceed exports, on the other hand, net foreign investment would be negative.

Finally, the Gross Saving and Investment Account contains no new items. It is simply a statement of the identity relationship between saving and investment. It also shows the sectoral distribution of total saving. Item B5, Table 15.4, is saving of households; Items A2, A9, A10, and A15 are business saving; while Item C2 is government saving.

A final word might be added about the nature of the residually computed items in the accounts. Actually, the summary account and the four sector accounts can be viewed as five relationships in 29 unknowns (21 "A" items; 5 "B" items; 2 "C" items; and one "D" item). However, since all of the items in any one account appear in some one of the other accounts, the relationships are not linearly independent. Any four of them are independent, however. Therefore, if we specify 25 items we can solve for the other four in the accounts.

Table 15.5. Gross Savings and Investment Account, 1961
(Billions of Dollars)

Item		Item	
A17 Gross private domestic investment	69.3	**B5** Personal saving	25.6
		A2 Excess of wage and salary accruals over disbursements	0.0
D1 Net foreign investment	2.4	A9 Undistributed profits	8.3
		A10 Inventory valuation adjustment	0.0
		A15 Capital consumption allowances	45.3
		C2 Government surplus or deficit (−) on income and product account	−4.4
		A21 Statistical discrepancy	−3.1
GROSS INVESTMENT	71.7	GROSS SAVING AND STATISTICAL DISCREPANCY	71.7

Here (see Table 15.5), the four residual items are A21, B5, C2, and D1; but the choice of these four is a matter of the relative quality of available information (except for the statistical discrepancy, Item A21, which must be a residual). In principle, any of the variables could be estimated as residuals. If all variables were estimated independently, then a statistical discrepancy could be derived for any four of the accounts individually. One of the accounts would always have to remain as an identity relationship. Conventionally, the Gross Savings and Investment Account is so regarded.

OTHER KINDS OF SOCIAL ACCOUNTS

This book is primarily concerned with the determination of income and product in a national economy. Accordingly, while there has been some discussion in this chapter of the general principles of social accounting, there has been more specific concentration on the application of these principles to the development of an accounting system designed to account for income and product in the U. S. economy. It should be pointed out that systems have been developed for accounting for other kinds of macroeconomic phenomena at the national level and for income and product in subnational economies. The major kinds of social accounting systems that have not been covered here are (1) interindustry accounts, (2) moneyflows accounts, (3) balance of payments accounts, (4) wealth accounts, and (5) regional accounts.

It is often important to determine the effect of any given increase in real final demand on the levels of output in individual industries. This essentially is the purpose of *interindustry accounts*. The effects on particular industries might be especially important in short-run situations where the supply of some productive inputs is fixed. Industry detail is also useful for planning purposes as well. In accounting for gross output by individual industry, however, a serious analytical difficulty is introduced by the fact that the processes of production are very "round about" in a mature industrial society, i.e., interindustry relationships are very complex. For example, suppose that there were an increase in final demand for steel, say for export. It is not sufficient simply to look at the items going into steel production like coal, iron ore, limestone, chemicals, etc. This would represent only a first-round impact on the levels of activity in supplying industries. We would also have to take into account the inputs needed to produce these inputs. In the case of coal we would need power, chemicals, transportation services, mining machinery, etc. And to produce mining machinery we would need steel! What interindustry accounts are designed to do is to trace through these interindustry relationships in a way that will permit the computation of all of these direct and indirect effects simultaneously.

Given the input coefficients (i.e., the amount of each industry's output needed to produce a unit of output of each other industry) and the amount of fixed input, if any, it is possible to solve for the total output of each industry, when the final demands for each industry are specified. Suppose for example we considered an increase in demand for a given product that is less than would absorb present capacity in that industry. Our interindustry accounts would permit us to determine whether the direct *and indirect* requirements for this and all other industry outputs would result in exceeding capacity anywhere in the economy. In large measure, interindustry accounts focus on an area of transactions that have been suppressed in income and product accounts, namely, the sale and purchase of intermediate goods.

Another area of transactions not fully covered in income and product accounts are money payments other than for currently produced goods or currently provided factor services. In fact, one way of regarding an income and product account is to think of it as a system which records all transactions involving the sale and purchase of factor services or the sale and purchase of outputs, except of intermediate outputs. These would certainly not include all monetary transactions (sales of existing assets, for example, are excluded) and, on the other hand, it would include some nonmonetary transactions (food and fuel produced and consumed on farms, for example). That there is not a one-to-one correspondence between the transactions in an income and product account and all monetary transactions has special implications for the Savings and Investment Account. While this account shows the distribution of savings as between households, business, and government, and their disposition as between domestic and foreign investment, it says very little about equilibrium in the money market, nor do changes in this account from year to year explain changes in interest rates to any important extent. This is mainly because there are segments of both the supply of and demand for money in addition to current savings and current investment, namely, supply and demand for money arising out of desires to purchase or sell existing assets and securities.

The Board of Governors of the Federal Reserve System has compiled, in special studies, accounts of all monetary transactions in the economy. Basically, the accounts divide the economy into a number of "transactor" groups and record the payments of each group to every other group. The critical decision in the design of such *moneyflows accounts* is the definition of the transactor sectors. The principle of selection is quite clear, namely, to obtain as much homogeneity as possible within any single transactor group with respect to the nature of the demand for or supply of money on the part of individuals within the group. At one extreme, it is very difficult to generalize about the factors affecting the demand for or supply of money for groups as broad as "households," "business," and "government." On the other hand, disaggregation all the way down to the level of individual decision-making units, besides requiring a very complex and expensive system, would be limited by our limited understanding, at least at present, of the economic behavior of individual units. In short, what seems to be required is a compromise between a sufficient degree of disaggregation to suggest a reasonable degree of behavioral homogeneity and broad enough categories so that *a priori* assumptions of money market behavior can be constructed and so that the data requirements are not too severe. Examples of the kinds of transactor groups included in the Federal Reserve moneyflows studies are corporate business, state and local governments, insurance companies, etc.

Balance of payments accounts are designed to provide useful analytical detail underlying the "net foreign investment" in the income and product accounts. Suppose, for example, that this item were negative (positive). This would indicate that during the current year the country was a net debtor (creditor) to the rest of the world. Does this suggest fundamental disequilibrium in its international trade position? Will adjustments (which could also affect its domestic equilibrium) be called for? Simply knowing whether a country is a debtor or a creditor in a given year and the extent to which it is so is not of much help. Of course, we could look at its net foreign investment situation over a number of years. But even this is not likely to be very helpful. Many countries occupy a persistent debtor or creditor situation for long periods without adjustment being called for. To make any final judgment we would have to determine such things as the extent to which the maintainance of its present position was dependent on short- as opposed to long-run capital movements. This requires a detailed description of the *gross* flows of capital (as opposed simply to the *net* difference between them) between the domestic economy and the rest of the world. This is the substance of the U. S. Balance of Payments Statement.

Another area completely left out of all of the types of social accounts thus far discussed is the stock of assets in the economy. One reason for desiring an estimate of the total value of such assets is to compare the standing of that economy over time and relative to other countries on a basis other than simply by the size of its current real income. Another interest in wealth stems from an interest in the relationship between the size of the stock of wealth and the size of the current flow of output, especially for different producing sectors. In a sense, this could form the basis for evaluating the relative productivity of capital in different activities and, by so doing, provide better estimates of capital-output ratios.

The problems in constructing wealth accounts are severe. In this regard it should be noted that simply aggregating net investment (gross investment less depreciation) as estimated in the national income accounts over time would not be satisfactory. There is no allowance for nonproduced assets, like natural resources, and, in addition, there is no accounting for the accumulation of physical capital by government or consumers. In turning to a straightforward inventorying of all productive assets at a point in time the valuation problems are very great. Besides the statistical problems, they would involve conceptual issues like the choice between valuing assets at depreciated original cost, current market value, or replacement cost. Even more difficult, they would require the estimation of the value of intangibles like a higher level of educational attainment or more effective national defense.

Another development in social accounting has been the attempt to apply social accounting techniques to regional, and in particular urban, economies. Unlike the other kinds of social accounts discussed in this section, regional accounts do not represent a fundamentally different orientation from the income and product accounts, but rather an attempt to apply these and other types of social accounts to a somewhat different kind of economy. To some extent, there have been experiments at the regional level with all types of social accounts, but of most interest here are the attempts to estimate income and product accounts at a subnational level.

Probably the most important methodological distinction between national and regional accounts is the way in which the multiplier

process works itself out.[10]   Suppose, for example, that there is an
autonomous increase in export demand. There would be two kinds of
multiplier effects. First, the income generated would be respent by
its recipients. Second, there would be interindustry effects in that the
increased demand for exports would generate increased demand for
the raw material inputs going into their production. As long as these
inputs were all obtained from within the same economy, these two
kinds of effects would not have to be distinguished; all of the effects
could be traced eventually to increased factor income. In the U. S.
this is approximately the case; imports are a small proportion of total
requirements of industry, at least on the average.   Accordingly, the
multiplier effect of an increase in income can be calculated as a simple
foreign-trade multiplier

$$\frac{1}{1 - (b - p)},$$

where b is the marginal propensity to consume and p is the aggregate
marginal propensity to import.   Essentially, what this says is that
the size of the import leakage is independent of the industrial composition of the change in final demand.   For the United States, this may
be a reasonable assumption, but for an individual region, say a
metropolitan area, it would probably be seriously in error.   Thus, at
least in the more sophisticated regional income and product studies,
an interindustry analysis to account for the effects of the industrial
composition of changes in final demand must be integrated within
the income and product accounts system.

The integration of interindustry relationships into the income and
product accounts structure is only one of the complications which
make the construction of accounts at the regional level more complex
methodologically.   Another problem is caused by the ambiguity of
the local definition of income and product, i.e., income generated by
production within a given area and income accruing to residents of
that same area would not be the same. Regional accounts must recon-
cile these differences. Also, there is the problem of deciding how to
account for the undistributed profits of multi-regional corporations.

---

[10] The special problems of multiplier effects at the regional level would also
apply to some extent to small nations, especially where export demand was a very
large share of total final demand.

Unlike the situation for international corporations, where different currencies are involved, regional allocations cannot ordinarily be made on the basis of records kept by the firms in question. Other problems involve the treatment of income accruing to transients, like military personnel and college students, activities of installations of super-regional (i.e., Federal) Government, accounting for such things as labor commutation and retail sales to visiting nonresidents. Finally, it should be noted that the data problems are much more serious, in general, in working with areas which might have only a vague political identity.

Obviously, this section does not comprise a thorough discussion of social accounts other than income and product accounts, or even of income and product accounts at a regional level.[11] Nevertheless, it seems useful to mention them, even though little more than a general notion of their characteristics can be elucidated here. First of all, it seems appropriate to make the student aware of them simply for his own information. More important, however, even the mere fact of their existence should help to reenforce the central idea of this chapter, namely, that social accounts systems are the operational specifications necessary to bridge the gap between the abstract world of theoretical conception and the observable world of information. Thus, while the bulk of the discussion in this chapter has centered, and appropriately so, on the accounting system related to the theory of aggregate demand and supply, it should be kept in mind that the general principles underlying the specific accounting definitions developed in the U. S. National Income and Product Accounts can and have been employed in meeting the observational requirements of measurement and hypothesis testing in other related areas of economic analysis. Thus, while it is hoped that this chapter has given the student a fuller appreciation of some of the complexities of the U. S. National Income Accounts, it also is hoped that he has developed a deeper understanding of some social accounting principles in general.

[11] For a more complete discussion of other types of social accounts, see, W. Evans and M. Hoffenberg, "The U.S. Inter-industry Study for 1947," *Review of Economics and Statistics*, 34, 1952; Board of Governors of the Federal Reserve System, *Flow of Funds in the U.S., 1939–1953*, Board of Governors of the Federal Reserve System, 1955; R. D. Goldsmith, "Measuring National Wealth in a System of Social Accounts," in National Bureau of Economic Research, *Studies in Income and Wealth*, 12, 1950, W. Hochwald, ed., *Design of Regional Accounts*, Johns Hopkins Press, 1961.

CHAPTER 16

Econometric applications

One advantage of Keynesian theory is that it lends itself readily to quantifiable mathematical formulation. Consequently, Keynesian theory is well suited to econometric analysis. *Econometrics* is a branch of economics characterized by two essential qualities: (1) economic relationships are expressed in mathematical form, and (2) numerical estimates are made making use of techniques based upon the theory of probability.

THE ESSENTIAL REQUIREMENTS OF AN ECONOMETRIC MODEL

Formulating an econometric model requires four steps: specification, estimation, verification, and prediction. *Specification* involves setting down a precise functional interrelationship connecting one or a set of dependent variables to a set of independent variables. Decisions which are made in this specification stage are (1) which are the relevant dependent and which are the relevant independent variables, (2) among the relevant variables, which are to be considered exogenous and which endogenous, and (3) which mathematical forms should be used to relate these variables. Once the variables and the forms of the functions have been chosen, if data describing these variables can be obtained, the numerical interrelationships can probably be estimated. Through *estimation*, some interrelationships among some variables can be quantified by the use of statistical techniques which rest on the theory of probability. In the estimation stage, a judgment is made about the magnitudes of the important characteristics (or parameters) in the model via these statistical techniques. *Verification* involves the use of statistical criteria to determine whether the theory is applicable to the facts, and whether the estimated parameters are good approximations of the true values. Finally, *prediction* involves the use of a verified econometric model to forecast future economic events. Of course, these stages cannot be performed sequentially, but some movement back and forth among them is required if the model is to be an integrated project.

Although all of these processes are important in econometric analysis, the ultimate raison d'etre for econometrics is its usefulness in the prediction and estimation stages. Examples which illustrate the importance of these two stages may be helpful at this point. In formulating the national budget, for example, it is necessary to know something more than the highly important fact that a rise in government purchases will lead to a somewhat larger rise in the national income. For tax, debt, and full-employment policy-making decisions, it is also very important to know the exact magnitudes of each of the relevant multipliers. Obviously, for policy purposes it is necessary to measure the impact of one economic variable upon many others.

For other problems, theory may require knowledge of particular numerical values even if it is the direction of change (as opposed to the magnitude of change) in a dependent variable, for a given change in an independent variable is all that needs to be known. Often, *a priori* notions or casual empiricism may provide sufficiently accurate estimates of crucial coefficients. When this is the case, refined statistical techniques are not required to judge whether one variable will rise or fall when some other variable changes. For example, the value of the marginal propensity to consume is a crucial parameter in the Keynesian system. The most important question to ask about it is a numerical one, i.e., does its numerical value lie between zero and unity? Keynes answered this numerical question accurately enough on the basis of *a priori* reasoning and casual empiricism. Other questions posed by the Keynesian system which are essentially numerical cannot, however, be answered *a priori*. One example of such a question is: are the magnitudes of the multiplier and accelerator, when taken together, such that they generate the business cycles which are observed in all market economies? These two examples are only illustrative of the many problems for which estimation and prediction are important.

EXACT AND STOCHASTIC RELATIONSHIPS

Keynesian theory is an abstract view of market economy based on a set of exact relationships, that is, on a set of functions in which *all* the variations in the dependent variables are strictly and precisely explained by changes in the specified independent variables. Econometric models of the Keynesian system, on the other hand, involve stochastic relationships. A *stochastic relationship* is a relationship in which variations in the dependent variable are not completely and exactly explained by variations in the specified independent variables; rather, some variations in the former are attributed to factors which have not been specified but which in combination affect the relationship in a random or chance way. In an econometric model, observed variations in the independent variables are not expected to explain all the observed variations in the dependent variable.

Econometricians do not expect their relationships to be exact ones for four main reasons:

1. All theories are abstractions, which for purposes of simplicity ignore some relevant but unimportant factors (environmental factors such as the weather, for example). These factors are assumed, under the *ceteris paribus* assumption, to be constant. Nevertheless, in the real world, these relevant but ignored factors may account for some variation in the dependent variable. (This is true even though econometricians specify more variables than is customary among theorists.)

2. The form of the relationship is likely to be imperfectly specified. Most often econometricians use linear (or log-linear) relationships for simplicity even though the true relationship may take some other functional form. For example, the consumption function may be assumed to be linear, even if the econometrician actually believes that a quadratic function would be more accurate. Such simplifications prevent the relationship from being exact.

3. For many relationships, the theory describes the behavior of a single economic unit, such as a household or a firm, while the econom-

etrician may be forced to use aggregate data. Since the theory does not always specify how the behavior of the economic units combine to produce the aggregate result, the data may not portray the exact relationship specified in the theory.

4. Observations are based on samples and are therefore subject to sampling errors. This last is crucial to the theory of econometrics, for it lays the theoretical foundation for the techniques used, and deserves, therefore, somewhat more extended consideration.

To comprehend what is involved, think, for example, of the level of consumption that turns up each year in the national income accounts as a numbered black ball in "nature's urn," much the way a statistician might use numbered black balls in an urn to randomly select light bulbs which are to be examined for quality from an assembly line. That is, think of the values of consumption which are turned up by the economic statisticians of the Commerce Department each quarter as samples randomly drawn from the potentially large number of values which a vast number of causative factors could have produced. Looked at in this way, the econometrician's task is to infer the true marginal propensity to consume of the economy from his sample, just as the quality control engineer's task is to infer the average quality of all the light bulbs coming off an assembly line from a randomly selected sample. The theory of probability and statistics was used long ago to develop a set of tools to deal with the problem of the light bulbs, and therefore by analogy, there is a kit of statistical tools available to econometricians to deal with the estimation of consumption functions and other similar economic relationships.

The notation to express the consumption function as a stochastic relationship may take the following form:

$$C_t = a_1 + b_1 Y_1 + b_2 Y_2 + b_3 Y_3 + \ldots + b_n Y_n + u_t, \quad (16.1)$$

where C_t is consumption (the dependent variable) in year t, $Y_1 \ldots Y_n$ are all those independent variables (which have been specified) which affect consumption in a systematic way, and u_t is a variable which results from the interaction of a very large number of independent factors each of which has a very small effect on the dependent variable. In any time period, some of these factors affecting u_t tend to raise the value of the dependent variable while others tend to reduce it, so that on the average the effects on the dependent variable will tend to cancel out. Consequently, u_t will have a value of zero more often than any other value. The behavior of u_t can even be more fully described. Since u_t represents chance happenings and will usually have a mean value of zero, it follows that u_t will have a value close to zero very often, and a value far from zero on some rare occasions. In short, it is the variable u_t which represents stochastic or chance happenings. The remaining symbols $a, b_1 \ldots b_n$ are constants whose numerical values are to be inferred from a sample of observations. These constants, which are supposed to be truly descriptive of the *universe* from which the sample was drawn, are the *parameters* which it is the objective of the estimation stage to obtain.

Two points should be made immediately about (16.1). Firstly, it has been written as a linear function. Statistical theory does *not* require that the functional relationship be a linear one, but in practice the need to simplify the mathematics on the one hand, and the paucity of reasons for believing that the relationship ought be other than linear on the other, usually leads to the use of this, the most simple of equational forms. Secondly, it should be pointed out that this simple single-equation model contains many variables, but only one unknown (C_t). To be solvable, the number of equations in a model must, usually, be equal to the number of unknowns.

AN EXAMPLE

The best way to present the flavor of the econometric approach is to present an example in detail. The example chosen and discussed for the remainder of this chapter is an actual econometric analysis in which one of the authors participated.[1]

Specification

The first task in the specification stage is to precisely state the problem to be investigated. In many ways, deciding upon precisely what it is that the research to follow should accomplish is the most difficult aspect of any research effort. For the study design to be econometric, the ultimate result should be either an improvement in forecasting ability or the estimation of parameters not otherwise

[1] R. J. Ball and E. Smolensky, "The Structure of Multiplier-Accelerator Models of the United States Economy, 1909–1951," *International Economic Review*, 2, 1961.

determinable with sufficient accuracy. For this example, the problem chosen was: Is it consistent with the statistical record, to attribute the business cycle in the United States to the interaction of the multiplier and the accelerator?

Having posed the key question the next step is to place the problem in its theoretical framework. As indicated in Chapter 5, many theoretical problems remain in the pure theory of Keynesian dynamics. These unresolved theoretical issues limit the econometrician's ability to satisfactorily attack the problem. First, the econometrician must make a difficult and perhaps unsatisfactory choice in choosing his theoretical model. Secondly, his results can not be definitive, since future revisions of the theory will suggest new testable relationships. Recognizing these limitations, there is, of course, the added dividend that the results achieved may very well suggest new theoretical approaches. In short, the model will have to bear close enough resemblance to the theory, as developed, to be considered a reasonable test of the theory, but several modifications will have to be made.

Other problems will arise in moving from the theoretical to the econometric model. The theory, for example, requires expected values while, at least for the present, data on realized values are all that can be utilized. Consequently, it is assumed that realized values will be projected into the future so that realized values can serve as *proxy* variables for expectational ones. In addition, there is the problem that some of the implicit assumptions of the theoretical model will not be met in the real world. For example, theoretical models based on the interaction of the multiplier and the accelerator typically assume an unchanging population. In order to accommodate the facts of the real world, where population is changing, an exogenous population variable will have to be explicitly included in the econometric model.

Once these and other adjustments are made in order to accommodate the facts to the theory, the econometric model begins to take shape. Whatever the specified relationships of the model turn out to be, it is clear that the model will consist of an output identity, a consumption function in which output is one of the determinants of consumption, an investment function relying, in part, on some form of the accelerator relationship, a full employment ceiling, and, perhaps, a floor to output.

The precise variables to be included in the model ultimately constructed cannot be specified until the available data has been searched and appraised.

Estimation

Armed with an array of potential variables far longer in amount than will eventually enter into the model, the search for data begins. In some cases the investigator may get his data from primary sources, e.g., via direct mail questionnaires to consumers and business firms; but, by and large, the data will come from major data collectors such as the Bureau of the Census, the Bureau of Labor Statistics, the National Income Division of the Department of Commerce, or The Survey Research Center of the University of Michigan, and from major data processors such as the National Bureau of Economic Research.

One fundamental issue in data collection must be quickly decided: should cross-sectional or time-series data be used? *Time-series data* refer to observations of the variables over time, while *cross-sectional data* refer to observations of the variables at a single point in time. For example, the relationship between consumption and income can be estimated from annual or quarterly data on aggregate consumption and income for the years 1929 through 1964. Alternatively, the consumption function can be estimated from data on consumption and income gathered from a number of households at a single point in time, say 1962. Cross-sectional data generally allows a large sample of observations, and their use avoids some technical problems of statistical estimation; but, cross-sectional data are only obtained sporadically and may therefore become outdated. Also, such cross-sectional studies cannot deal directly with factors which change significantly through time (e.g., population and price level changes), and they often yield estimates which tend to be different from estimates of the same parameters which are derived from time-series studies. (Investigators still disagree as to the reasons for the differences in estimates from time-series data as opposed to cross-sectional data.)

In a multi-equation model, the data used is most likely to be time-series data although sometimes cross-sectional and time-series estimates are pooled together. The more general use of time-series data is usually due to its availability, although its use raises a variety of collection and estimation problems.

In any time series which is intended to describe quantities over a long period of time, there is always the danger that the collecting agencies have, from time to time, changed their definitions of the variables and/or their collection procedures. Consequently, the problem of the *comparability* of the series over time arises. Also, certain time-series observations will be the result of unusual circumstances so that it may be inferred that these particular observations come from a different statistical "universe" than the rest of the series. Such observations will have to be discarded if the estimates of the parameters are to represent the normal situation. The most common ample of data which are often discarded are observations obtai uring war periods.

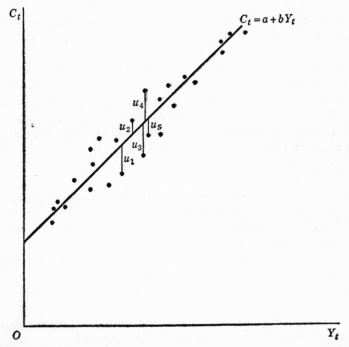

FIG. 16.1. An Illustration of a Least Squares Regression Line.

Once the data have been pieced together and made comparable, and values from outside the universe under study have been eliminated, the investigator can proceed to the estimation of the parameters. The investigator will have to decide upon the statistical procedure that should be employed in the estimation process. Many techniques for estimating the relationship between the independent and dependent variables exist. The most common method is that of *least squares regression*. In Fig. 16.1, the line $C_t = a + bY_t$ is an example of a

regression line fitted by the method of least squares. This line is calculated by formulae which minimize the sum of the squared vertical
distances from each point to the estimated line. There are many
technical difficulties associated with the use of least squares regression
in time-series analysis and in the analysis of simultaneous equations,
most of which are associated with the fact that the error term in such
a regression equation is not truly stochastic. These problems of estimation theory, however, are too complex to be discussed here.[2] Suffice
it to say that while many problems have been solved in the estimation
stage, several others still remain. These remaining estimation problems
have severely blunted the use of econometrics in solving the estimation
problem. Too often the econometrician is forced to conclude that
his results seem "reasonable" when tested against the theory. In the
particular study discussed in this chapter, however, the investigators
were able to sidestep many of the technical estimation problems by
using an estimating procedure only slightly more complicated than the
simple least squares method.[3]

Verification and prediction

In this particular econometric study, a variety of consumption functions (each with somewhat different variables), a variety of investment
functions, and several alternatives of each of the other relationships
were estimated from the collected data. The next step was to select
the "correct" relationship from the various alternatives estimated.
Criteria for selecting among alternative relationships are not perfectly
discriminating and econometric model building is, therefore, a subjective sort of a business. In general, an equation which is simple,
which has an error term which is truly random, which yields a high
degree of correlation, which forecasts accurately outside the period to
which the data apply, and which has "reasonable" coefficients for at
least those variables for which an *a priori* expectation of reasonableness
exists, are among the more important criteria used in the selection
process. In addition, it may be that although one equation is considered
superior by itself, it will be scrapped in favor of another equation which
meets a need of the model taken as a whole. For example, a consump-

---

[2] The problems of estimation are fully and most simply discussed in S. Valavanis,
Econometrics, McGraw-Hill, 1959.

[3] The method employed was the two-rounds least squares method.

tion function which consistently forecasts magnitudes of consumption which are too high when taken by itself (perhaps because of a high intercept value), may be chosen if the model, on the whole, tends to forecast magnitudes which are too low.

After taking all these criteria into account, the following model emerged:

$$C_t = -18.72 + 0.467Y_t + 0.301N_t + 0.224C_{t-1}, \quad (16.2)$$

$$I_t = 7.217 + 0.498I_{t-1} + 0.265\,[(Y + D)_t - 0.498 \\ (Y + D)_{t-1}] - 0.088\,[K_{t-1} - 0.498K_{t-2}], \quad (16.3)$$

$$D_t = -6.28 + 0.0273Y_t + 0.045K_t, \quad (16.4)$$

$$(Y + D)_t = -75.90 + 0.262K_t^* + 0.697(N_{whw})_t + 1.33t, \quad (16.5)$$

$$K_t^* = 75.98 + 0.36K_t + 0.98\,(Y + D)_t, \quad (16.6)$$

$$(N_{fhf})_t = 45.75 + 0.638N_t, \quad (16.7)$$

$$K_t \equiv K_{t-1} + I_t + (I_g)_t - D_t, \quad (16.8)$$

$$(Y + D)_t \equiv C_t + I_t + G_t + F_t, \quad (16.9)$$

where the symbols are: C, consumption; D, depreciation; F, net foreign investment; G, all government purchases; I, investment; Y, net national product; I_g, government investment; K, the stock of capital; K^*, the employed stock of capital; N, population; N_{whw}, manhours worked; N_{fhf}, labor force in man hours; t, time measured in years; and all money terms are in constant 1929 dollars.

Several characteristics of this model should be pointed out. It is a straightforward Keynesian model with a consumption function (16.2), an investment function (16.3) which embodies the accelerator relationship, and the national income identity (16.9). Equation (16.5) represents the economy's aggregate production function, and is to be viewed as the full-employment ceiling. All of the other equations are required only to complete the system, i.e., assure that the number of independent equations is equal to the number of endogenous variables. Equation (16.4) describes depreciation behavior, (16.6) describes the extent of utilization of the stock of capital, (16.7) describes the growth of the labor force through time, and (16.8) defines the capital stock in a period.

The model can be looked upon as being divided into two parts. Until the full-employment ceiling is reached, (16.5) and (16.6) which describe the production function and the employed stock of capital, respectively, are not required for the model, and the rest of the equations describe an extremely simple forecasting model which makes no allowance for monetary or price factors. When the ceiling is reached, on the other hand, output grows along its aggregate production function and the consumption function is, by assumption, dropped from the model. It is assumed that when the total available resources are not sufficient to meet all demands for goods, consumers will be forced to buy less goods than their consumption function indicates that they would want to buy at that income level. Consumption is, in this situation, calculated as a residual via (16.9).

In any investigation of the effect of the multiplier-accelerator interaction inducing business cycles, primary attention must be paid to how the economy behaves at less than full employment and, therefore, the consumption function (16.2) is relevant to our particular task. In this consumption function, the marginal propensity to consume is 0.467, so that the multiplier is approximately 1.9, a value that may seem somewhat smaller than what *a priori* notions might suggest. The output/capital ratio, as shown in (16.3), turns out to be .265. Because of these low values of these strategic parameters, this model will *not* by itself generate cycles. Nor will this model generate a path of economic growth. Thus, if this model and its parameters accurately describe the United States economy, than *all* the sources of the economy's growth and *all* of its cyclical instabilities must be found in factors other than the multiplier-accelerator interaction.

SUGGESTIONS FOR FURTHER ECONOMETRIC RESEARCH ON THE PROBLEM

It is always possible to criticize any econometric study by stating that not all the pertinent variables have been included in the study. In this case, this criticism has perhaps more relevance than usual.

The exclusion of monetary, tax, and price variables may account for the surprising result of this econometric study. There is reason to believe, however, that perhaps the results are truly descriptive of the role of the multiplier-accelerator interaction in the American economy. Models of the American economy which contain many more variables have been built, and these models suggest the same results. The Klein-Goldberger model, for example, has more than thirty endogenous variables. It does not exhibit either cycles or growth due to the multiplier-accelerator interaction, although it will trace out a cyclical path if repeatedly struck by random shocks.[4]

These results suggest that at least for the time being, it would be desirable to divert resources from the econometric testing of the multiplier-accelerator interrelationship to the improving of the multiplier-accelerator theory, on the one hand, and even more importantly, towards developing alternative theories of cycles and growth. The most pressing need is for a new, more operational view of the determinants of the marginal efficiency of capital schedule.

[4] I. and F. L. Adelman, "The Dynamic Properties of the Klein-Goldberger Model," *Econometrica*, 27, 1959, pp. 596–625.

Index